THE SACRED TEXT
of
THE PYRAMID
at
CHICHÉN ITZÁ

ALSO BY MIRIANDRA ROTA

The Divine Mother's Message of Truth

Secrets of the Seven Teachers

Ease of Living

Leave the Insanity Behind

Access Your Clear Guidance, Anytime, Anywhere!

Welcome Home – A Time for Uniting

The Story of the People

Pathways & Parables for a Changing World

Dragon Fire – Secrets of the Last Dragons

The Prophet's Last Breath

THE SACRED TEXT
of
THE PYRAMID
at
CHICHÉN ITZÁ

CHANNELED BY MIRIANDRA ROTA

Published by Visionary Works Publishing

Copyright © 2024 by Miriandra Rota. All rights reserved.
ISBN: 978-1-732374-157

Published by VisionaryWorksPublishing.com

No part of this book may be reproduced or transmitted in any form or by any means whatsoever, including photocopying, recording or by any information storage and retrieval system except for the inclusions of brief quotations in review, without written permission from the author/publisher.

Contact: Visionary Works Publishing, P O Box 81, Troutdale, VA 24378.

FIRST EDITION

Limits of Liability/Disclaimer of Warranty: The author and publisher of this book and the accompanying materials have used their best efforts in preparing this program. The authors and publisher make no representation or warranties with respect to the accuracy, applicability, fitness, or completeness of the contents of the program. They disclaim any warranties (expressed or implied), merchantability, or fitness for any particular purpose. The author and publisher shall in no event be held liable for any loss or other damages, including but not limited to special, incidental, consequential , or other damages. As always, the advice of a competent legal, tax, accounting or other professional should be sought.

This manual contains material protected under International and Federal Copyright Laws and Treaties. Any unauthorized reprint or use of this material is prohibited.

DEDICATED TO THE JOURNEY

CONTENTS

1—*Introduction*
7—*Preface*
25—*Volume One*
    27—*First Layer of the Sacred Text*
        29—*First Transmission*
        37—*Second Transmission*
        47—*Third Transmission*
        59—*Fourth Transmission*
        71—*Fifth Transmission*
        85—*Sixth Transmission*
        99—*Seventh Transmission*
        115—*Eighth Transmission*
    123—*Second Layer of The Sacred Text*
        117—*Ninth Transmission*
        129—*Tenth Transmission*
        139—*Eleventh Transmission*
    161—*Third Layer of the Sacred Text*
        153—*Twelfth Transmission*
        167—*Thirteenth Transmission*
        187—*Fourteenth Transmission*
        205—*Fifteenth Transmission*

225——Sixteenth Transmission
255——Fourth Layer of The Sacred Text
    241——Seventeenth Transmission
    257——Eighteenth Transmission
    269——Nineteenth Transmission

301——Volume Two
    303——Twentieth Transmission
    315——Twenty-First Transmission
    335——Twenty-Second Transmission
    349——Twenty-Third Transmission
    365——Twenty-Fourth Transmission
    375——Twenty-Fifth Transmission

397——Vocabulary

403——Volume Three: Coming Soon

405——Acknowledgments

INTRODUCTION

I wonder if we ever realize that one step in our spiritual journey would lead us to a new phase or a more expanded consciousness or even a new purpose? I certainly didn't recognize anything special when back in February of 2023, in my usual morning meditation, a being appeared before me and introduced herself as Alannah.

She invited me to journey with her. Well, she had just appeared and I'm not one to dive right into a journey with a spirit-being that I didn't know…yet. I told her that I'd have to check with my guide, Teacher. Alannah said that was okay.

I did ask Teacher about Alannah and her invitation and much to my surprise, Teacher said that I needed to ask the Divine Mother about such journeys. Okay. A journey to my Divine Mother resulted in a huge thumbs-up. I reported the positive answer to Teacher and he said, "If the Divine Mother tells you it's okay to journey with Alannah, then it's okay. No further questions need be asked."

My next meditation gave me the opportunity. Alannah appeared and motioned for me to follow her. It was an easy flowing and she led me onto a pathway that was surrounded by green rolling land. My first hint of what this new

INTRODUCTION

experience would be like was when Alannah stopped and pointed to a large picture that was just hanging there in midair beside the path, and casually said, "Go into there."

I flowed into the picture and found myself in a beautiful location of nature and began to check it out. Then she called me to come out, which I did. We journeyed a little further and she pointed to a blue vortex and said, "Go in there." This was beginning to feel like fun and I just jumped right into that vortex. It swirled around me as I flowed downward and I notice that Alannah was following me. We arrived at what appeared to be a cavern in the earth...

This began a series of participations with Alannah. I didn't realize that she was training me for something. I was simply enjoying our traveling as she helped me to refine the way that I journeyed spiritually. For example, I learned that it was absolutely necessary to not allow any other thought to be present. Sounds simple, but when you are journeying through the earth and into separate chambers inside the earth...and then learn that you are actually inside a pyramid, there are thoughts that come! Many thoughts!

Alannah brought me to a new type of discipline. She taught me that if I thought about or worse, interpreted a location, that I was projecting an image upon the journey and then the journey became that projection, which was illusionary. Through many experiences, I finally learned how to not interpret in the slightest bit, while in the midst of a challenging experience. This was one of the experiences.

We had journeyed through a vortex and were inside a chamber within the earth. There was a small round platform on the floor of the chamber and the platform was covered with different symbols. She motioned for me to stand upon the platform and when I did, the symbols activated. What occurred next was beyond what I could imagine, and perhaps that is a good thing, a very good thing.

Somehow a golden essence appeared and flowed into the solar plexus of my being. It filled me with a wonderful feeling of well-being. Next, there appeared seven beings wearing white hooded robes. They stood together and spoke a language that I did not recognize and then came to surround me. I was held within a kind of stasis, an expanded consciousness and could only observe.

One of the beings stepped up to me with a chalice and placed the chalice right in front of that golden essence in my solar plexus! The golden essence flowed forth and into his chalice. The others followed that motion and then when all the chalices were filled, they all stood together in their own circle and drank from their goblets. They began to transform into a great white light, white essence light.

While they transformed, Alannah came to me and pulled my arm, pulled me off of the platform while whispering, "Let's get out of here before they find another purpose for you." We silently moved to the far side of the chamber and entered a portal and flowed down a tunnel into another adventure.

Now this kind of experience only increased and I had the great gift of accompanying Alannah for uncountable journeys, each also developing my expanded consciousness combined with a way of living inside of my spiritual

INTRODUCTION

intuition. I was certain this was the wonderful new phase of my spiritual journey. Little did I know what was waiting for me.

Alannah brought me to Ra's realm. Well. I imagine you are familiar with the large statues in Egypt, the ones with the huge seats and also large kings sitting upon them? I have never had the pleasure of being in Egypt but I did see a picture of a person standing at the base of one of those statues. Yes, the person looked like a small dot. That's how big they are. So, why am I talking about them?

When I first met Ra in his realm…Let's back up a bit.

First, I had to learn how to enter his realm by standing before the portal which is round and covered with symbols. I had to discover how to bring my consciousness to match that portal and its frequencies, and when I did, the symbols began to be alive and the portal opened. Neat.

So, there I was in Ra's realm and Alannah is motioning me toward…two very large seats and there was Ra sitting on one of the seats, large enough to be one of those statues. I was humbled by the high frequencies that flowed forth.

The next learning experience was that if I brought my consciousness as close as I could to the expanded state of what Ra was radiating, I would become nearly as large as was Ra and I could, upon his invitation, sit in the seat beside him. The largeness was my interpretation of the expanded frequencies.

Now my teachings continued with Ra. I learned how to let go of everything and just be in the moment, which usually held expanded frequencies, traveling from one location to

INTRODUCTION

another in the time it takes to say *wow*, and riding on the back of Ra's giant bird. One of those in-the-moments introduced me to an amazing being who I learned was the Holy One. It was not your usual introduction.

While in the second chamber of Ra's realm, Ra held me in his hand. Yes, I was small and he was as large as a huge giant. He placed me into a golden tube, closed the door, and held me in his closed hand as we traveled. I didn't know where or how, but I did realize that we were traveling at a speed beyond time, that I was actually a blur. We arrived at a location and I could see through a little slit in the tube, that a beautiful white-bearded being arrived in white essence. I knew instantly that the being was the Holy One. Ra held out his hand and with me still in the tube and said, "This is the one." Holy One looked and then said, "Huh." Then he turned and flowed away!

Ra returned to that same realm of the Holy One another time and I was again standing in his palm, but not inside of a tube. When he opened his hand, there I stood and there was the Holy One looking at me. He said to Ra, "Are you certain?" Ra nodded yes. "Then it will begin," said the Holy One. That was it.

I had no idea what they were talking about, no idea why I was called the One, and no idea what lay ahead of me. What lay ahead of me came to be a most amazing journey, certainly a new phase in my spiritual development, and a purpose beyond my imagination.

I had been channeling for over forty years and learned how to have an experience and also sit at my computer and

INTRODUCTION

type the words of guidance or a description of the vision or experience. In fact, that came to be the way that I channeled private sessions, a format that beings enjoyed simply because they could read the words of their session's guidance and refer back to any section they were attracted to.

This is the way that all of my further journeys with Ra were recorded, which allowed me to not only receive the Sacred Text but also to place those holy words upon paper, so to speak, *exactly* as they were given.

The journey with the Sacred Texts continues to be wonderful and I am gifted with not only a deeper relationship with Ra and Holy One, but also with an embracing of many Keepers of the Sacred Texts, the Observers, an exceptional being whom I call the Ebony Being, and of course Alannah. They are now my family and perhaps while you receive these transmissions, they will become part of your family.

I am grateful to place these Sacred Texts into your hands and more grateful to be part of this amazing transformation that occurs right now upon our dear earth and within each and every being, you and me and everyone.

I wish your journey with these Sacred Texts to be one of wholeness of being, expanding consciousness and a way to enter into something amazingly deep and meaningful.

With Love and Gratitude for Who We Are Together,
Miriandra

PREFACE

I easily move into an expanded consciousness and am approaching the portal to Ra's realm. I am tempted to just bypass the portal and go directly to him, but this time I will go through the portal. It is golden and when I approach, the symbol is as if the OM symbol. I don't recall that being there before. Previously there were other symbols, many. I approach the portal and bring my consciousness to that frequency.

The portal, the golden disc turns and then opens. I wait a moment out of respect and then enter. Alannah is standing to the left, as she usually is, and she motions for me to go to Ra. I bow to her. It is good to be with her, even if briefly.

I move through the realm slowly. It is white and nothing is formed.

I see Ra in his chair. He is sitting and seemingly not activated. As I approach, everything is white, even Ra and the chair. I stand before the whiteness and wait.

I am being called into the area where Ra and I sit across from each other, and where he speaks to me and from here sometimes we journey together. This has not happened before and I move toward that area. Alannah stands beside

PREFACE

the whiteness of Ra and becomes white, also as if staid or inactivated.

As I move toward that area, I sense that Ra is there…and he is. He is sitting and motions for me to come forth and to sit across from him. Now there are colors, but subdued.

I find that I am slowly moving, but am moving toward my chair. I bow my head to Ra and he is still facing forward and does not respond. I move toward my seat and then I am sitting across from him.

He then nods and I do the same again.

Now we enter into a serious journey, he begins, one that we will have to be focused and you will have to do your best to refuse to interpret. You must stay in the moment and proceed as I direct. This is most important.

I nod yes.

Good, he says.

Now I will speak of this journey, not to describe it because we cannot do that because we are not participating yet. Everything unfolds in the moment. *Yet I wish to tell you that we are entering into a purpose. The purpose is to journey to different locations upon the earth, within and on the surface, and we will together participate with those centers. I will instruct you how to do that as I will participate also.*

Everything will proceed as it will, Ra continued. We will be going forth and I will not speak further of the how or what will occur. I do not wish to pre-program anything. Yet I wish you to know that I am proud of you and am pleased that you have agreed to accompany me during this journey…this purpose.

Do you wish to ask anything?

I look to Ra and he is totally focused on me and I say that I am most willing to do my best and that I am honored that he has asked me to accompany him.

Good, he says. Now let's prepare.

I nod yes.

Ra then waves his right arm outward. He waits to see if I will create something and I nearly did, but stopped myself. I must not think about what occurred in the past but allow myself to be in the moment. Ra says good.

Ra stands and reaches his left hand for me and I stand and take his hand. Now we will proceed, he says.

I feel my consciousness expanding further. Come, he says. And we begin.

Now, Ra says, *we are entering into a way that is ancient, that has been followed by many many ancient beings. They have ceased from participating for reasons that I will not speak of now. We are entering this frequency to activate or to participate as they did long ago. Be prepared to do as I say, as none have entered this frequency for a very long time, though time is non-existent, still this frequency has not had the ancient ones participating as they once did.*

He motions and there appears a type of landscape. He nods to me and still holding my hand, moves into the landscape.

What do you see? he asks.

I look with my eyes and see in a short distance tall rocks, as if a cliff and they are red in color. There is green around in the land, like a country side.

PREFACE

Look with your inner being, says Ra.

I close my eyes and see that there is a very large pyramid in front of the cliff. It is…

Good, he says, do not describe further. That is where we are going.

I nod yes.

Maintain this viewing, he says. Focus on the pyramid.

I nod yes.

He is still holding my hand and we are flowing toward the pyramid. Now as we approach the pyramid, it becomes more solid looking and it is white. It begins to radiate.

Ra says, Now we will align ourselves with this pyramid, with the frequencies. I will assist you, for they will be adjusting to our presence. I nod yes.

Ra lets go of my hand and stands with his feet apart and he holds his arms outward. As he does this, energy or waves of energy flow forth from the pyramid and it causes his hair and robes to move, to flow backward from him. He still stands in this manner. I am unaffected and I am still standing beside him.

He continues in this manner until the flowing, the strong flowing, stops. He nods his head toward the pyramid. Then he steps aside and motions for me to do the same.

I stand before the pyramid, my feet apart and I raise my arms outward. I wait.

From the center of the wall of the pyramid facing me flows forth a slow swirling energy. Beautiful. Tones flow with the swirling and it continues to come toward me. It is a soft frequency as it approaches me.

It envelopes me and then swirls around me, as a vortex. Ra nods that I must not interpret anything. I nod yes.

The swirling is gentle. White, golden and blue. I am still. My arms are now at my sides and I am being still. I hear Ra in my consciousness and he is saying Good.

Now I am being transported within the swirling which has changed to a whiteness. I am being lifted up and I am being moved toward the portal that opened in the side of the pyramid halfway up. I have the sense that Ra is following me and he says, Good. I am flowing into the pyramid.

I am, or my essence is in a location of the pyramid. There are no walls. Whiteness. Ra comes beside me and he nods good. I cannot respond, but am grateful for his acknowledgement that I am doing "good".

The whiteness begins to dissipate. Ra reminds me to not interpret or to assume anything. I nod yes.

There is much gold. There is a gold seat, similar to Ra's seat but not as large. There are objects that are gold…Urns, pieces of golden objects. Ra motions for me to look to the left. I do. There is blue essence. He motions for us to move to that location.

We are now in front of the blue essence. Ra moves his right arm and there appears a portal. He motions for…I check with him that I am not creating this. He says that I am doing good, to go forward into the portal.

I flow into the portal and Ra is with me. My consciousness is expanding further.

Here there is another pyramid, but I am seeing a very white capstone and the rest is but a slight forming. Ra nods good.

He points to the capstone. That, he says, is where we are going. I nod yes.

Then he takes my hand and as he does my consciousness expands further.

We are now inside the capstone. It is a frequency. We are within the frequency which forms as a capstone. But it is a frequency. Ra nods yes.

We reside here and I force myself not to seek anything to appear or to interpret. Ra nods good.

From the top of the capstone comes a strong beam of light. It flows downward and into the capstone. The beam comes between Ra and me but still Ra holds my hand.

Now, he says, we will begin. He begins to walk around the beam of light that has anchored itself into the base of the capstone. He is still holding my hand but he is moving slowly and then faster. I am as if still holding his hand but my arm is outstretched as is his. We are moving around the beam of light, white beam of light. Powerful. Ra nods yes.

We move around so fast that we are but a blur. We are releasing or forming and becoming essence. We are still connected. We spin around the circle, Ra's robes making a red essence and my essence is blue. Ra nods for me to stop trying to see a description. I nod yes, even as I am essence only.

My consciousness is what responds.

Ra puts out his arm and we are slowing and then he is standing again and I am standing also, we are still holding hands. He has not let me go. Ra nods yes.

Ra says, Now you will stand in the beam. It will be forceful…I wait to see if I am creating this. Ra says good. I wish you to stand in the beam of white. It will be forceful but you will be able to easily stand there. You will receive words. Allow them to come, do not make them to be. I nod yes. Then he motions for me to stand in the strong beam of white light.

I stand before it and look at it. Then I move toward it and am entering the white light. There is not a force, but I am dissolving and taking form in the moment.

I am in the white light, it is a force. I wait. And be. The frequency is adjusting my being. There is a swirling about me as if clearing my essence. Ra reminds me to not interpret. I agree.

There is a slight sound. Very faint. I force myself not to strain to hear it. I still wait.

A darker beam inside the white comes forth to enter my being, into the top of what would be my head. It is a bluish-grey. It seems to be like a drill. Ra says, Yes. Do not be concerned. I agree.

The very large drill enters my being. When it does, I am transported to a chamber where there are several beings. They are in robes that are also bluish-grey. I am in the center of a circle, as the drill transports me there. I stop to be sure I am not creating this. Ra says to continue. I agree.

PREFACE

I say, Ra help me to be true to this. He says not to be concerned, but to continue. I agree.

My essence flows outward to each of the beings in robes, as if beams of light from my being to them, each of them. They begin to make a low sound together. They begin to sway as they continue to stand in a circle around me. My consciousness expands further.

All that I am flows to them. Yet I am not depleted. I am standing inside a stone circle, made of different stones. It comes to my knees in height. Ra nods yes.

The bottom of the circle where I am standing dissolves and I am flowing downward. My hands and arms are straight upward and I am flowing downward. I no longer hear the beings' low tone.

I am entering light, white light. Ra steps forth to greet me. I am glad that you have come, he says. *I am the Ra of long ago* and I am the Ra who has brought you here. He is surrounded by a golden light that is all around. Come, he says, I will teach you now. He is Ra but he is also golden, his robes are golden. He looks to me as if to ask if I am coming. I smile and follow him, at his side.

We are walking on a type of essence ramp that goes upward. I…He smiles at me and says that I do not have to be so careful about looking around and seeing what I see. I will not be creating here, he says. You are right, the walking we are doing leads to a whiteness. That is where we are going, to the capstone. I smile and feel relieved. He laughs, a laughter which is beautiful.

We are at the top of the ramp and now he waves his arm and we are within the whiteness of the capstone.

Here, he says, we will do what we came here to do. I nod yes.

He speaks some words which I do not know, am unfamiliar with, and he begins to take the color which I am familiar with, his robes are red and white and flowing. He motions to me and I am blue, as if in blue robes and white. He nods good. I smile and then he motions for us to stand in the center of the base of the capstone, which is a small pyramid. Ra says, This is the real pyramid. It has been removed from many pyramid structures. There is a reason for that. You will understand when we are complete with what we will do now. I nod yes.

My consciousness expands further.

Good, he says. I am in whiteness. Ra says, Now I ask you to flow forth your innocence of being. You can do this easily because it is your primary essence. I am going to ask how to do that, but he puts up his hand and says, I will teach you. I nod yes.

Yes, you are correct, he says to my having a hint that my energy centers are aligned.

There comes a being from the whiteness and the being is holding a platter, a golden platter. Ra nods that this is correct. Everything is quite faint but I am discerning.

Ra nods good. You are remaining conscious.

The being comes forth to stand in front of me and holds the platter before me. I feel my heart open and flow forth essence. The essence is flowing or over-flowing the platter.

PREFACE

The being smiles. It continues to flow from my heart, golden essence flowing and flowing. The being continues to hold the platter. I see that it is actually a disc with many symbols, activated symbols. Ra stands behind the being and is smiling. I allow everything to continue.

The being and the disc begin to be a golden essence that forms itself as a beam of light and the being flows upward to the peak of the capstone. Then there is only Ra and me standing facing each other. Ra says, Good. You are doing very well. I nod yes and smile.

Come, he says. And there is a side of the capstone that is open and there is a pathway which he motions for me to flow upon with him, which I do.

I am wondering if I am discerning properly. Ra turns to me and says, Yes, you do not have to be so concerned about that here. I smile and look around to see what appears to be shelves and shelves of volumes, of books. Ra nods yes. He says, *I will give you a volume. You will take it with you and you will write what the volume says to you. In this way you will be bringing into your realm of physicality, the essence of this pyramidal capstone. This is Sacred Text which has not been given. It was withheld long ago because the consciousness shifted and there were many who were battling for the contents of these volumes. This place was sealed…for a very long time…thousands of years…and now I, Ra, have brought you here. Now I can reveal to you this is the reason that I have brought you here.*

I will give to you a Sacred Text, a volume, and I ask you to allow it to be written through you. You are most capable of this, for two reasons. Firstly, you are capable of writing the flowing forth, as you have been developing this ability. And secondly and most importantly, you are dedicated to truth and its manners of expression, even if you do not or are not familiar with its manner of presentation. I will assist you to do this, which means that you will not be concerned if you are writing the truth. I will assist you to do that so that all that is flowing forth will accurately be written. You will call this text **The Sacred Text of the Pyramid at Chichén Itzá**. *I nod yes. I say that I am honored. He nods yes, his robes flowing about as he walks toward the shelves.*

He stands before the shelves and looks to the volumes. He is waiting. One volume on the very top shelf becomes light, radiating light and it moves toward the edge of the shelf. Ah, he says, there you are! He reaches upward and it is as if his arm stretches upward, but it is essence of course. He smiles to me.

He takes the book in his hand and stands with it in his hands, holding its sacredness.

He turns toward me and says, *This is what is called activating the frequency of this location upon the earth. When this volume is incarnated within your realm of physicality, then this sacred location will be activated. This is your part of this journey. As I have spoken, I will assist you.* I am full…I nod yes.

Ra stands before me and the volume is as if old leather but is also golden light. He smiles and says, It is taking form for you. That old leather is your familiar description of old volumes. It is actually silver and is smooth.

It has been delivered here long long ago by those beings who came to earth to bring forth wholeness of being incarnate. The harshness of earth and its other residents from other locations in

PREFACE

the universe were not compatible to that which they brought. They placed the essence of what they brought into this volume, which is filled with symbols from all over the universe, yet the symbols are now taking form into the words that you will be able to receive. The words will hold the frequencies of the original symbols.

Ra continues, You will be able to place the words upon paper, so to speak, you will bring them into incarnating. At times they will perhaps not make sense to your knowing, but they will be perfect vibrational representations of the original intent. I will assist you with that so that you will be able to transcribe the correct words. I nod yes.

Further, he continues, *this Sacred Text is also given to earth now. It is the first of several. Others will come from other locations upon the earth. This now is your participation in activating the primary centers upon the earth, centers that were constructed long ago before the downfall of the consciousness.* I nod yes.

Ra smiles. He is much softer here. He laughs. There are no rules here, he says. I smile.

He asks, Are you ready? I nod yes and say that I am greatly honored. When I say those words, there are bells that are rung, little bells, beautifully ringing. Ra smiles. Then prepare yourself to receive this Sacred Text, he says.

I stand firm and look into his eyes. The leather volume turns to silver almost as metal. He smiles and says that is another interpretation but that it is all right…here. He says, In the realm where we usually meet, it is not correct to interpret or assume, but here it is perfectly all right. I smile.

PREFACE

He comes closer to me and holds the sacred text in his two hands. I hold up my two hands, palms upward, and he places the volume onto my hands. I cannot see it. It is white, radiating light so very bright. Ra places his hands atop the volume, which lessens the light a bit. He says, You will become accustomed to this frequency. I nod yes.

He motions for me to place the volume against my being, against my heart.

I move my hands with the white light toward my heart energy enter. It flows forth into my being. I hear many bells ringing as if from all over the earth. Ra says yes. I see the cover of a book. Ra says good. I see the top of the pyramid, the capstone and it is radiating white light. Ra says yes.

I know that I am to say…*By the right of that which I am, do I gratefully and humbly accept this sacred volume into my being. I will allow the words to be written, the frequencies to take form as words to be written. I will honor the words and the integrity of this volume. So be it.*

Ra smiles and says good, even as the bells ring louder…from all over the earth, different temple bells, church bells, children ringing small bells, monks blowing into long horns, women making high sounds with their voices, the frequencies of the earth wave, as if waves of the ocean. Ra steps forth and embraces me, holding the frequency within my being as he does. I am one being.

My consciousness is very expanded. I am falling…I am falling downward within a dark blue tunnel or tube. I am flowing downward into the physical pyramid and yet it is

PREFACE

essence. Ra says that I am carrying the volume into its incarnating.

My falling is slowing and I am finding my feet standing on the earth which is the inside of the pyramid. There is an earthen pyramid inside the large pyramid, which is inside the essence pyramid.

A pathway opens or presents itself and at the end there appears to be light, as if the outside of the pyramid. Ra says to me, Now you must not interpret in this realm. We are nearing the return to my realm which you are familiar with.

He stops me and looks into my eyes. He says, You are returning. You have done very well. This is what I could not tell you about until we were in the presence of the volumes. You can speak of this to Grayson but to no one else. He must not tell anyone else either. I nod yes. Good, he says.

I am most proud of you, my dear. You have done very well. Very well. I smile to him. He nods to me that I can speak something if I choose. I say, I am so very happy about this. I am honored and humbled at the same time. Thank you, Ra. Thank you for gifting me this participation. Ra nods and smiles. You are the One. I have been seeking the One for a very long time. Now I am as you say the words, very happy. Very happy. There is a white light that emanates from his back as he says those words. Well, he laughs, that is revealing my feelings isn't it. I smile. I cannot laugh, the frequencies are holding me, so very full.

Ra says, Then let us return to my chamber. I nod yes. We walk upon the pathway and when we come to the light, he waves his arm and we are entering his outer chamber, where we sit when Ra is teaching me. We are becoming, taking an essence form. Ra reminds me that I shouldn't interpret anything now. I nod that I understand.

He says to me, You will know when to begin. I will be with you. And you will come to speak with me every so often, as you have been, and then we will discover what will occur then. We are careful not to preprogram, aren't we. I laugh. He laughs. It is very comfortable between us. He motions me to enter the primary chamber of his realm. Remember, he says, you are given this. Do not be concerned for mistakes. There cannot be any, it will not be allowed. This means that the text will be written correctly. Do not be concerned. I nod yes.

Then Alannah takes form and smiles at the two of us.

Ah yes, Ra says, our Alannah! Then I will leave you with Alannah to return to your physical incarnation in your realm. I nod to Ra and hold his eyes as long as I can. Then he nods and flows forth to return to his very large size and to sit in his very large seat. I observe and am grateful that he has revealed this process that he takes.

Alannah motions that it is time for me to return. I nod yes and we flow forth within Ra's realm and then to the portal. Alannah waves her arm and the portal opens. She motions for me to step through and I do, turning toward Ra and nodding again to him. Then I step through and Alannah follows. When we are clear, the portal closes.

We flow forth to the vortex which carries me to my body-physical in "my realm" as Ra calls it. I pause to look into Alannah's eyes. She says with her thoughts, Now you will

PREFACE

begin another phase. It will enrich your spirit and fulfill purposes of long ago, before you took form in any manner in any time. You were called forth for this, my lovely one.

I nod to her and say, Thank you for all that you continue to give to me. She smiles and motions for me to return. She crosses her arms on her chest and I step forth into the vortex.

I am floating downward, downward downward and I am entering my body-physical. I am making myself the size to fit into my body-physical and smiling that I have to do that this time. I am golden essence filling the body. It is enjoyable. Now I am anchoring into my feet. So be it.

I have returned.

So be it.

VOLUME ONE

FIRST LAYER OF THE SACRED TEXT

FIRST TRANSMISSION

I have entered Ra's realm as he said that he would assist in the writing of the words from this Holy Text. I am before Ra and there is white light around and he is motioning for me to flow forth to the area where we sit across from each other and he speaks teachings for me. I flow there and Ra is sitting across from me.

Ra says, Now you are here for this purpose. That you are here speaks to the moment and that moment contains the beginning of this speaking, this writing through you.

I nod yes and more so, that I am honored.

Ra says that he will assist in the shifting of the frequencies. I nod ok. I can feel the frequencies become quite strong and I am transported to that location where the sacred text was given to me. There is a swirling and within the swirling there reside several beings but one motions his finger as if to say "no" and I let go of focusing on them. Ra says good.

I am filled with light. Ra says, now the speaking will begin. Just write the words, my dear, as they are given. Do not be concerned that you are writing correctly. I will assist in continuing to align the frequencies. Begin now.

I nod my head and then breathe deeply and wait for the words....

These are those words:

These symbols contain the words that will be transcribed, words that the many who will reside upon earth will receive and become enamored with the frequencies that will speak with their most inner knowing of truth. The purpose of these symbols and the writing is the same purpose of this center that we created, knowing that it would one day be destroyed and then concealed. We are accepting of this future, just as we are accepting of the future that holds within it the transcribing of the words that flow forth from the symbols which will be given to a being who is capable of allowing the symbols to vibrate and then to be placed into a speaking, a language that will go forth.

When the words go forth, there will be a further activating of the centers upon this earth. Some of the centers will already have been activated and we will not speak of those locations for there will be those who will attempt to prevent such activation, yet nothing will be prevented. This is the future of this time upon earth.

When the words go forth, there will be an uplifting of the spirit of those who are downtrodden, for it is within their heart and being that the future resides, the future of the entirety of those who reside upon earth who will be called humanity. This future holds within it the great transforming of the lowest frequencies. The lowest frequencies are not something that is negative. The lowest frequencies are those that hold within them the suffering that will have continued beyond what is bearable. The many will be reaching out their hands and hearts in the asking to be rescued. We believe these words will be that rescue, not to individuals but to the entirety of what will be transpiring upon this planet.

We are of the first beings. We reside in all locations, everywhere. It is who we are. We are not a species. We are frequencies. Yet we are. And it is not important to know more of us. It is important that the speaking begin now, for the symbols have released themselves into words. Then let that flowing begin.

Anaktah. That is the word that calls forth truth in a manner that is neither against untruth and is a residing. A residing brings forth great light into the darkness. Not the darkness of evil or the darkness of untruth. This great light is. It is.

Now within the great light there rests a knowing that can be stated in words.

This is that knowing.

Within the totality of all that is, there resides those frequencies that hold within them the manner of being that allows all that is created to reside in compatibility, allowing all that has been created to be, yet to be compatible with its totality.

Within the totality of all that has been created [are] symbols which are an integral part of all that has been created. There is nothing created that does not hold these symbols.

The symbols are not a staid form, but are moving as they are the holding of the life force which resides within all that has been created and is created.

The symbols release into that which holds them a sound, a vibration. The sound or vibration is the anchoring of that frequency within that which has been created. It is the sound of union. For within union there resides the original moment of conception or creation. Within union, there resides the celebration of the life force as it determines what will be created and further, the purpose of the creation. This union occurs within all that is created, all that is formed, even from the very first forming of which we are a part.

To know this truth is to know of the totality. This knowing is not for the benefit of creating. This knowing is for the benefit of placing consciousness in a frequency that can be compatible with the all. Compatibility occurs when there is an absence of judgment, an absence of attempting to create separate from the whole. This will be, in the future, the beginning of the downfall of that which will be called humanity.

And the downfall will cause great suffering as the hearts and minds of the humans will recognize the distortion within which they reside and there will be a calling out for truth. The truth that flows forth from these words will assist those beings to let go of the attachments to the seeming security of physicality. The humans will remain, yet all that they are familiar with will change. Attachments to physicality will cause them to hesitate toward that which is calling them. They will be called to understand that all is created in the moment and will be created for them.

First is making oneself compatible with everything, with the all that is being made manifest always. This making of oneself compatible is not an external effort. It is not an effort at all. It is an inner placing of the consciousness so that there then can allow all that is to be either dissolved or recreated in the moment to support the continued residing incarnate.

That which will be called humanity will be a treasure in the universes. Such a treasure must be held in the sacredness of what flows forth from our symbols and into these words. These words will hold within them the avenue toward a great freedom, one that will be interpreted in many different ways through the sleeping consciousness of that called humanity. This will not be blameful as it is a beginning toward truth.

Truth is creation. Truth is not right or wrong, as the definition of truth will be distorted when these words are received. Truth is accustomed to being manipulated for the benefit of control of the many. Let it be known that these words and the receiving of these words will release the holding of those who hold the consciousness of humanity lest it refuse to continue to serve those who will be in control.

This is the future that we have seen. We are now declaring this future to be freed by these words.

Then we will speak in another manner.

Truth flows forth from the union of the breath and the essence of the life force. Truth is the merging of one force with another and the union or merging produces a vibrational frequency. This vibrational frequency is called *Holacktah*. Holacktah is truth before it enters the consciousness. Holacktah is formed truth, sacred in the moment of its forming. Truth holds no concept or belief. Truth, Holacktah, stands of itself, yet as it is, then there is the innocence of itself. *Within the innocence of Holacktah is the avenue through which can be accessed sacred essence of life force. This accessing requires a holy consciousness.*

A holy consciousness is called *Flesancha*. Flesancha can be attained by residing in the moment of one. Residing in the moment of one is a most natural manner of residing. It is a holy moment wherein the consciousness simply is in union. There is not a "union with". There is simply union.

When there is Flesancha, then there is a manner of receiving the holy life force which flows forth to greet such consciousness. Such greeting then is the union. The sacred union transforms the consciousness of all who reside about this frequency. One being incarnate or even a gathering of beings incarnate who then can receive this flowing can radiate outward without effort to the whole. The whole will include all of humanity. This can be the saving grace of humanity. *All who receive these words have the capability of receiving this holiness of being.*

Then this is the first transmission of the Sacred Secrets.

We are dedicated to assisting this truth to become incarnate for the benefit of the future that we have seen. This future is now, when these words are flowed forth from the symbols.

Then we are complete for this moment.

SECOND TRANSMISSION

I am journeying to Ra's realm to open for the second speaking to flow forth. I have re-read the first speaking and have felt the power of its expanding frequencies. I am residing in those frequencies as I journey to Ra's realm.

I am approaching the portal to Ra's realm and there is a white essence as if a cloud that is flowing before it. I have in the past experienced this as a type of prevention of my entering the realm. I will wait. I feel my crown energy center expand further. I hear Ra say, Just come here. You do not need to enter through the portal now. I have done this before and now simply place my consciousness in Ra's realm where we sit across from each other. My essence is continuing to form there.

Ra is sitting on the seat that he usually sits in when he is going to teach me or answer my questions. Ra smiles and says, You were right to come here now. It is now that you will continue to speak the book. I am glad to hear that and I nod to Ra, yes. Ra says, Then we will expand our frequencies further and you will know when to speak, to allow those speakings to flow through you.

This is that speaking.

We will now continue with our speaking, for this speaking is the vibrating of those symbols that have contained these vibrations for a very long time. That the time upon earth is now for the receiving of these symbols as words is an opening in the totality of all, wherein flows forth those truths that are now able to be residing upon earth, and more so, are being called forth for the benefit of those who reside upon earth, both in physical and spirit form.

There are many who reside upon earth in spirit form and have placed themselves in this manner for one reason and that reason, for the most part, is true for all who reside in spirit form upon earth during these times of great transformation through great chaos, and that reason is to assist humanity to emerge. For, the multitudes of humanity have been held captive, just as our knowing of the future portrayed to our visions. Humanity has held the distortion to themselves as if it is a treasure. We do not judge this, but only observe.

For, long ago when the speaking of truths flowed upon earth, there was a small opening in the density and through that opening holy truths were spoken for similar purposes, to uplift the consciousness away from the distorted rules given by those who at times were unaware that their rules and penalties for not following rules, and to give Holacktah to those who felt it within their heart. This giving has occurred several times upon earth in different areas or gatherings of humans. Yet even those times, though the portal was opened, completed and the distortion returned, leaving only a few to maintain truth. Even they were taken to distortion when they tried to write those truths, as is being done now. It is not blameful that the distortion entered their writing, for the portals had closed and there was nothing to support that consciousness.

Now humanity is ready for this speaking and we will begin further in one moment, for we wish to continue to speak of the histories as we saw within the future viewing. Remember, please, that all time is but a manner of speaking of histories and that when time is released from the histories, then there is a merging of all occurrences into one. This merging is already truth, yet in the concepts and consciousness, then, there is a releasing of the need to place a linear presentation which actually supports the distortion, for it calls forth beliefs which are no longer appropriate for those who receive these words. In truth, there is through these words, a releasing of beliefs and then a clearing of the totality within a being of what determines who they are and what they would participate within. *This clearing, of course, is a gift of the speaking, which is for the benefit of all beings, especially the human species.*

Then we will begin this speaking.

Within the forming of truth there resides what is called possibility. The possibility has nothing to do with physicality, but has everything to do with the manner in which truth experiences itself. One manner that truth experiences itself is called *Anaktah-Sonotoh*. Anaktah-Sonotoh holds the frequencies of what could be called vortex, as truth then does flow forth within journey. *This is the first journey of truth.*

Because truth flows forth within this journey of itself to experience itself, then there was created what could be called cycles. Vortex cycles were created because truth experienced itself within the vortex, and within this experience the turning of the vortex gave to truth an experience atop a previous experience. Because there was not time, this experience then continued while truth resided in the exploration and expression of itself. With each turning of the vortex, truth became created again and again, for truth resides only within itself, thus creating an expression of itself within the vortex of its own exploration of truth.

This vortex of truth is. Whatever truth experiences of itself and expresses of itself, remains. Within truth there is no past or no future. Truth always is.

Within the vortex, created within truth by truth's expression of itself, there reside symbols. The symbols hold within them the continued expression of truth within itself. All symbols are created in the moment of now; however, as they are created and truth always is, then the symbols reside always. Even when there is a concept of future and those who participate in the future of the now, the symbols reside. Yet those who of the future of the now, within the distorted concept of time, can through their Holacktah consciousness access those symbols.

The accessing of the symbols of truth within the vortex of truth's experience and expression of itself, gives to those who access, then, the avenue to truth incarnate. Truth incarnate can flow forth, just as these words flow forth, in a manner that can shift the distortion in such a way that there are once again, openings or portals through which the frequency of truth can flow. *Such flowing forth of the frequency of truth will adjust itself to the ability of those accessing or the one accessing, so that the one can remain incarnate by choice.*

One who receives these frequencies and remains incarnate by choice then does have the automatic participation with truth to become that truth and then does that becoming of truth radiate outward as a beacon for all to drink. *The drinking of truth radiating outward from such beacon can bring the multitudes to their knees simply because the frequency is so filled with the holiness of truth that those ones can no longer stand in the density of the distortion.* Such kneeling brings the frequencies of truth incarnate to reside upon the earth in a manner that radiates through the firmament. Such radiating outward then activates the frequency lines upon the earth. The frequency lines upon the earth are united with all holy centers upon the earth, which hold the capability of being activated and as we have spoken previously, are activated in hiding.

Truth is not words but is a frequency. Yet be it known that all beings are but frequencies gathered together to form a vehicle for truth to explore more of its own beingness. *All beings are truth incarnate exploring itself.* Such exploration did not originally include residing in the illusion of separation from the whole. Yet because truth explores all dimensions of being, there was then the flowing forth of truth into the illusion of time and within that illusion was created the density of separation. The separation is not incorrect. It simply is. It is a manner that truth expresses itself. For truth flows forth in all manners.

Now we will speak of another exploration of Truth within Itself.

Truth did flow forth to explore all of creation. This exploration or flowing of the frequencies of truth created. In the creation of truth exploring all manners of creation there formed within truth a spark within the spark. The spark within the spark became an echo of creation itself. The echo of creation itself, as it did reside within truth, created. The echo then, within the frequency of truth, became the forming of essence magnetized to itself. The magnetizing of essence to itself within the echo of truth's exploration of the all, formed what is called locations for creation to explore more of itself through truth. The locations developed within the magnetizing of essence to itself, until there was a density within the magnetizing. The density is now called planets and the gathering of magnetizing systems. Earth is one of those creations.

Upon earth, then, there is a magnetizing of essence of being. Remembering that the essence of being is the echo of truth exploring itself within the all that is created. Within each density or planet, there is an echoing which is called the *sound of the planet*. Each planet contains its own sound. The sound is a vibration of truth within its own echo.

When those who reside upon such planet, the sound of the planet is merged with the sound of those who reside upon it. This creates a totality of the planet and all that resides upon it, for those who reside upon the planet are as truth itself exploring all that is created. All beings are truth. There is no other residing.

Within truth as formed by those who reside upon the planet by choice becomes conscious of such residing, then there is integrity of residing. This then calls forth **Flesancha**. When Flesancha resides within the consciousness of truth incarnate within and upon the planet, then there is another opening through which truth can explore more of what is created in the moment. This opening now occurs upon earth.

There are those beings from other planets who come forth through such openings. Their purposes are varied, just as truth experiences itself through all manners within the creation of the all. Because the concealed centers within the earth have been activated, then there is a calling forth of those ones who hold within them the dedicated purpose of assisting humanity and spirit-beings who are held captive by the density frequency. Such assisting resides in anchoring the frequencies of truth in a way that frees the need to explore more of the density. For, as truth flows forth to explore, there then is a vortex created for such exploration. The beings are dedicated to breathing a breath of totality within such vortex. Such breathing into the vortex of truth's exploring of the density of its own self, then, changes the nature of the vortex. The changed nature of the vortex shifts the flowing of truth as it is then magnetized to the higher nature of its own self. This then has the capability of freeing density from continuing to create itself. This freeing then does release from those who are holding humanity captive by polluting the consciousness those manners, for then creation can within truth refuse to participate further in what becomes a closed vortex.

This then is the beginning of the freedom of humanity from the grasp of those who are dedicated to power and control. We are not judging power and control, yet we are viewing the future of humanity and observe that such control and abuse of power will be the downfall of humanity, even those who are in seeming control. This freedom we observe in the future of humanity. That future is now always. Yet upon earth, there is the illusion of time as we have spoken. Then we can say future of humanity and within that future there is the possibility of freedom, resting upon the activations of the centers and the presenting incarnate of the symbols translated into these words.

These frequencies, through this writing, are now incarnate. There are those who do not want such writing to exist, yet it does as does truth. Even those who distort truth cannot prevent truth from being. This writing is.

We are, just as truth is.

Then we are complete with this second speaking.

I am returning my consciousness to Ra's realm...It is taking a bit longer as the frequencies of this writing are most expanded and holy. Ra is calling me back. I am now sitting across from Ra, continuing to take form. Ra is holding his staff and is looking to me. I am able to nod that I am ok and have returned. Ra says, Good. Now you must return to your physicality. I nod yes and I am flowing toward my body. There is a vortex above my body and I am entering that vortex, filling my body. I cannot hurry returning. I am an essence filling the body. An extraneous thought has assisted me to return. I am incarnate once again.

So be it.

THIRD TRANSMISSION

I have re-read what Ra said to me when I received this Sacred Volume and am comforted by the assurance that it is impossible for the wrong words to be written. I will now expand my consciousness and transport my spirit to Ra's realm, to the location where we sit across from each other, as Ra said he would assist in my receiving of the words of the Sacred Volume. I know this is right for me to do.

I am beginning now. It is comforting to me that Grayson is also present. I say this to Grayson. Now I am expanding my consciousness. I am hovering above the location in Ra's realm. I am waiting. This is very much like a déjà vu from some other time, perhaps from a vision I had long ago. I am waiting for Ra to call me to enter his realm. It appears he is not in this location. Perhaps I will go to the portal to enter this time.

I am in front of the golden portal and bring my consciousness to match the portal. It is activated and radiates light. The center symbol is turning and the portal opens. Alannah is standing there and motions for me to enter. She says, You entered this way this time because there is a shield above where you and Ra will transcribe. That is why, she says, that you could not enter from that way this time. I am not sure if it will be the same next time. You will have to see. Just know that Ra will be waiting for you and you will know how to enter. I nod ok and thank her. She motions me toward the area where Ra sits in is very large seat. It is very very large this time, which says to me that the frequencies are much expanded. Alannah motions for me to continue.

I leave her side and approach the very large seat and bring my consciousness to an expanded state. I am nearly as large as the seat now and as I expand I am wondering if Ra will be there. Alannah whispers to me, Do not be concerned. I am now moving to the seat beside Ra or where Ra usually sits. I cannot perceive him and now I will feel if his presence is there. I hear his voice say that we will journey to another location where we will continue with the Sacred Text. He says that there are many now who are interested in the content, even though they are not of the frequencies to be able to receive the text. I send a thought that I understand. Ra says good.

I can feel him take my hand, even though I still cannot perceive him. Ready? he asks. I respond, yes. Then we are moving. We are moving through white…no, I projected that. We are moving and Ra says for me to remain in the present moment. I nod that I understand. We are now not moving but are still. There is white all around us. I can sense a form that is Ra but still he is not as I am accustomed to being with. Ra says that is all right, that there is a purpose for all of this. I nod ok.

Now there is a portal like a door that is open and there is a being of light motioning for us to come forth. Ra moves, still holding my hand, and then the light being steps aside so that we can enter through the door. Ra says, Ah! Now we are here. He is taking a familiar form to me and he looks to me and says that this might be the location where we will continue with the remainder of the Sacred Book. I nod that I understand.

All right now, he says, come and we will begin. He waves his arm and there appears…something…Ra says wait. He steps into what he is forming and speaks some words that I do not understand. Then he is holding his staff and motions for me to come and to sit in a seat like the ones that are in Ra's realm. They are side by side and not across from each other. Ra says, this way, if need be, I can assist you better. I nod that I understand. He smiles to me and I am feeling more relaxed. I hadn't realized this change caused a bit of stress in me. I am feeling a bit apprehensive in the transcribing of the Sacred Text. Ra says that is natural because it is actually an increase in frequencies and my system interprets that as feeling a bit nervous. Ra says, You are accustomed to all of this type of participation. Just sit quietly and then it will begin. I nod and say thank you to him. I feel his love shower over me. I remind myself that this is real, that I am actually doing this. Ra laughs a little and then says, Yes you are. I sit quietly and wait for the words to flow forth to me.

These are the words.

In the beginning of the concept of time there flowed forth within physicality a density that called forth from physicality, asking physicality of itself to become more. This concept of time and the concept of becoming more then became part of the forming of earth's presentation to itself, as earth did choose to experience itself within different manners, physicality being one.

As earth formed itself in different manners, there were those light beings who came to reside upon some of the manners of earth's manifestation of self. Within the light beings there was held the **truth of union**. The truth of union is an interpretation of creation itself forming and unforming, as an expression of itself to itself. Thus came the experience of union within creation itself.

The light beings held union within their essence and as they placed their essence within earth's expression of itself to itself, there rose up from the presentation of earth's journey within its purposes, an essence which was created by the union of the light beings with earth's expression of itself to itself. The essence that rose up was new, was created. The light beings observed, yet in their observing did they recognize that within that which was raised, there was held that of themselves within it. This became part of the journey of the light beings, as they then were magnetized by the pattern of experiencing oneself to oneself, and they began to explore that of themselves within their journey as they were made manifest and also in union with that which had been created. This began a frequency that resided upon

FIRST LAYER OF THE SACRED TEXT

earth. It was a frequency that contained light beings of union with earth and her expression of self to self. Within the frequency then, there formed a continuation of this exploration because of the magnetic pull of the same to the same, the exploration of self to self, self within self, just as creation explored creation to itself.

There came forth other light beings who observed this occurrence as part of one of earth's exploration of earth to itself. Those light beings then did flow forth to another form of earth and saw that none of what they observed in the first earth was occurring in this, the second earth to those beings. *It was not the second earth, but was simply another manifestation of earth's journey to explore earth to earth's self.*

The light beings held within them, because of the observation of what occurred in the first earth to them, the frequency of curiosity. It is called something else within this volume. It is called **Enaktah-Sontoh**, which took the meaning of being called to explore. Enaktah-Sontoh held the magnetic pull to further journey within the exploration of self to self. However, the light beings were not aware of this magnetic pull. They were not aware because they had not begun to merge with the essence of this earth. Yet the magnetic pull to explore radiated outward. They became aware that the frequencies of the first earth to them were also the frequencies of this second earth to them. They became aware of the union, that even though there appeared to be more earths, the truth presented itself in a known that what occurred within the first earth was also held in all of the other earths, even though the same was not made manifest. Still, the frequencies were contained.

This caused the light beings to step away from the earths and to consider what they had observed and learned. Because they held union with the essence of their beings, it was easy for them to comprehend what they observed with the earths. They further considered that if one of them did go forth to explore anything, but especially that which was forming as a type of essence-physicality, that what one experienced would then be held within all of the light beings as an essence, an essence which contained the experience of the one. *This became a conscious understanding of union.* This understanding of union is now beginning to reside upon earth, even if it is residing only in words and is yet to be experienced by some and then perhaps the many. *This volume is intended to radiate outward those frequencies that call forth the unveiling of the truth of union.*

Now we will speak of the Truth of Union.

As creation did flow forth itself to experience itself, then all that was explored within that flowing forth became as creation itself. As there is no past, then creation is all that it experiences and expresses, within the pattern of exploration of self to self.

All that is formed is creation's expression of creation to itself. All that is formed is this. There is no separation from creation. Creation is. This means that all beings are creation exploring itself. When there is an expression of the all, that is the expression of creation itself. All occurs in the present moment. This means that union is...also. There is not before union, no part of union that becomes united. Like creation, union is.

As physicality became more dense and earth continued to explore itself for its knowing of self, there came those frequencies that held to themselves the journey. Within the density, then, the journey of physicality to explore itself, there developed a **cycle**. A cycle means that physicality, because of the nature of its density, experienced itself as a separate entity and then the merging of that entity back into itself. This was an exploration into what is called **separation from the whole**. Separation from the whole is not existent. It is an interpretation of physicality's journey within itself, within the density of physicality which brought to the experience a projection of physicality and then a merging with that projection. This then developed what is called a cycle, as the projection gave the illusion of reality to itself. Physicality began then to journey through the projection of separation as an entity of itself and then the magnetic pull caused the union to become recognized. *Thus there was developed a cycle of illusion to whole, illusion to union.* This cycle became seated in physicality as it contained and was creation itself still exploring itself, which then contained all...in the moment.

Within the illusion that resided within physicality, there came those spirit beings who found such a illusion to be a type of play, where there was a seeming separation from each other and then a union. The histories are written over and over again of the journey of these beings who played within the illusion of separation from the whole, as they caused the density of physicality to become greater and thus the merging to become more of a challenge, the merging or union being an illusion in itself as nothing is separate. The beings found this to be most curious, or **Enaktah-Sontoh**.

In this instance, **Enaktah-Sontoh became Enaktah-Kolientoh** in that the curiosity was held within illusion and the truth of union hidden. Thus **Enaktah-Kolientoh** became the nature of the journey within physicality. This nature resides upon this earth and because it resides upon this earth, it is then contained in all earth's journey of itself to itself.

Because it resides in the light beings who participated in this manner, then it is continued within all beings as an essence or as the essence of a cycle. This essence or cycle developed during thousands of years in the keeping of time until there was developed what is currently called *awakening*.

Now we will speak of Awakening.

Awakening is the moment, the current moment within which creation is in union with the all that it has created within its journey within itself to know itself. Within physicality, there are those ones who reside as creation and yet are also contained within the frequencies of the illusion of separation from the whole. Because the beings are of creation and hold the truth of union, then there is also an illusion of **separation of self from self**. This is the frequency of illusion of separation from the whole as it is made manifest within the consciousness of beings incarnate.

Within the consciousness of beings incarnate, there resides the frequencies, patterns and cycles of awakening to creation in the moment and then the pulse beat of returning to the illusion. This is a duality that resides within the consciousness of all who reside incarnate simply because all of the frequencies developed within physicality are held within all that is incarnate.

Because a spirit-being held the awareness of this duality, then the spirit-being could also call forth within itself the truth of union. This calling forth of the purpose of maintaining the frequency of awake and awareness, then, became a frequency that is held in the All and thusly in all beings. *This has been and continues to be, in physicality, the saving grace for humanity.*

This choice of the spirit-being is available to all beings because it resides within all beings. The choice requires beings to let go of the many manifestations of the illusion of separation from the whole. We are not speaking of the illusion of separation from physicality's manifestations. *We are speaking of the illusion that one is separate from awakening, from truth, from creation itself.* This is a great falsity. It ripples through the consciousness of all of humanity, simply because of the truth of wholeness of being.

When beings choose to remain awake to the truth that all is union, then there is a type of shrinking away from such truth simply because the All contains that which is abhorrent to humanity's innate nature of love. Yet love is an embracing of creation itself to itself. This embracing resides in all beings as the truth of union. *Because long ago there was the choice to be awake, then there is that choice evermore.* Just as there is the choice to participate in creating further manifestations of the illusion of separation from the whole.

There has been developed with the All from the All, that which is called *peace*.

Then we will speak of peace as it refers to humanity's ability to choose awake, to be awake

to truth of union, to the truth of creation in the moment.

Peace within humanity is a frequency that embraces union. There are no words to speak that can bring humanity's awareness to union except to speak truth of this:

Humanity, you are all one being. You are as the earth expressing itself to itself and still being earth. You are human expressing itself to itself yet you are one being. Your one beingness is creation itself. Creation expresses itself to itself and is the All. That is all there is to know.

All other words are but a manner of feeling the illusion that you are separate from yourself and are expressing yourself to discover yourself. This is a distortion of the origin of itself, the origin of the distortion. You are not seeking yourself to know yourself. You are journeying through yourself to explore the many manners of that which you are, the All. You are not lost to yourself. You are never lost to yourself, for how can creation be lost to creation? It cannot be lost. Creation is you. There is nothing that resides that is not creation. It is an impossibility. *Knowing this truth is peace.*

Now we will speak these words from the patterns of this volume.

All forming is but an illusion. Forming is an illusion because there is no such thing as separation from self, or separation of creation to itself. All occurs in the one moment of breath. The one moment of breath holds all possibilities of creation exploring itself to itself, yet the one moment is the All. There is no time. All is in the moment. This knowing rests within the consciousness of the all. **Then this transmission is complete for this moment.**

I say thank you for the honor of flowing through my being. Already the frequency is receding. I am still beside Ra now, which awareness left me during the transcribing. During the transcribing I am the words themselves.

Ra says, You have done very well, my dear. Do not be concerned if anything is correct. It is. Remember that. It is natural for your human nature to be concerned. Do not bother yourself with that concern. All is well.

Now it is time for you to return to physicality. This frequency is most expanded and your physicality will require relief from it if you are to remain incarnate. I nod that I understand.

Go now, he says, and rest. I nod yes and begin to release my presentation beside him. I can feel my releasing of the entire realm. I am returning to my physicality. I am filling my body and releasing the essence of the process of transcribing.

So be it.

FOURTH TRANSMISSION

I have had the realization that this volume lives inside of me, as it was put there during the first journey with Ra. I am humbled once again. I have felt the need to open to the next flowing forth of the words from that volume and it feels to be an immediate need. I am preparing to expand my consciousness and then journey to Ra's realm. I will see if the portal is the way to enter.

I am now approaching Ra's realm. I can see the portal and even though there is a slight white cloud before it, I am placing my consciousness at the portal. I can hear Ra say, No. Come over the portal. I am flowing over the portal and into his realm. I am waiting and not projecting. I can hear Ra now saying, Come into the next chamber. I flow my consciousness into the chamber where we usually sit across from each other. Alannah is there and she is motioning me to go forth into the white. I nod to her. I enter the white. I wait. I see some white in the upper right and it is as if a page is being turned and there is white behind the page.

Now there is a bright white light, very bright. I hear Ra's words say, Be aware of the illusion. I wait. I thought there was a being coming forth to me to say begin without Ra. But it was so very slight that I felt it was not true. I hear Ra say good. I still wait. The bright white light dims. I am not sure why this is all occurring except perhaps to cease the flowing forth of these words, these holy words. Ra says that is true but to not enter into those thoughts. I nod yes, even though I cannot discern Ra's presence.

I stand firm and speak these words: By the right of the holiness of this volume which resides within my being, do I declare my right and duty to allow the words to flow forth and to be written. All else is but an illusion that I declare to dissolve.

I have never had to speak in such a manner during these sessions but the Sacred Text must be allowed to be written. I see Ra flowing forth in his robes. He says to me, Very good. That was not a test. It was necessary. *You are entering into another phase of the Sacred Text.* The frequencies will be more expanded and perhaps more intense. But I will be with you and all will be well. I nod that I understand. I am ready.

Ra says, Come this way and we will sit and begin. I nod ok. Ra seems to have disappeared and I am waiting for where I will flow to. I seem to be waiting for the synchronization of my consciousness and the frequencies of the next flowing forth of the sacred text. I hear Ra say that is true. I allow the synchronization.

My consciousness is expanding. I hear the sound of horns being blown in the distance. Ra says that is true. The sound of the horns carries me toward a mountain. Ra says that is true and to flow toward the mountain. I do that and I can see that it is a mountain in Tibet. How can this be, I ask Ra. This

FIRST LAYER OF THE SACRED TEXT

is...he says not to question but to allow the flowing forth. This way, he says, we will be located in an unexpected place. I nod that I understand. Ra says good.

Now I see a room, wood, wooden pillars and there are places where monks usually sit or kneel. Ra says this is correct but to come along. I am flowing forth and flow through an entryway into a holy space. It is a room but it is more. Ra says, That is true. I am entering a white essence and it is...I thought I would find Ra there. I am waiting. I breathe deeply and just be. Ra says good.

I can feel the words of the volume wanting to be spoken, to be placed upon paper, so to speak. Ra says, Yes, we will begin soon. We are now inside the mountain and I am trying not to be frustrated. Ra laughs and says, We will begin in a moment. I am flowing down a hallway and I see a light at the end of the hallway. I am flowing toward it. I am entering the white. Ra says I must expand my consciousness further. I hope that I can. He says, Of course you can. I allow my consciousness to expand further. It is not something that I make happen but something that I allow. Ra says good. Everything is very white. I can feel...no, that is wishful thinking...Ra laughs and says I am nearly present. I have not had this experience before.

I whisper the words: I choose to be in the right location with Ra so that I can allow the words of this Sacred Text to be written. Ra says good.

I hope I can maintain consciousness. This is most expanded. I can feel Ra come around me. He says to keep allowing. I think ok. I feel as though I am arriving. Ra says good. Continue to allow. I can't force being there, but I have tried to squeeze it out unsuccessfully. Ra laughs and says that is ok. Now Ra parts the veil and pulls me through. I don't know if that really happened or again it is wishful thinking. Ra says it is true and now to be present with him. I am thankful that I can nearly discern his presence. He says he will make himself more visible now. I thank him.

Ra says, all right let us sit and you can begin. This will seem to be barely discernible, but we are together and all is correct. I nod that I understand. We are both as if barely formed. Ra says that is true but that our essence is present and that is what is needed. I nod that I understand and let go of wanting to discern Ra in a more solid way. He laughs and says that as we go along, we will both form more discernibly. I laugh and say that it won't matter then. He nods and says that is very true. I say I believe I am as ready as I ever will be. Ra says that is always true. I say that I will begin now. We are both sitting in two seats, as we have in Ra's realm, and he reaches over and takes my hand once again. I can feel R's frequencies joining mine. It is a golden feeling, golden essence. Ra says good, then begin.

> **These are the words that flow forth.**
> I wait as they are forming.
> Through the ethers there flows forth a sound. It is a frequency that has journeyed through many cycles, many beginnings and endings, through the forming of creation to itself and then the unforming of creation to itself. The frequency is before

creation. There is no manner of speaking that can cause a human mind to understand this sound and the origin of the sound, for there is no origin. It is.

Within the spark through which creation forms and unforms, explores and is, there is this frequency. When it flows forth, which flowing is rare within all of the totality of being, its flowing forth parts the essence of the All. It is not of the All because it is before creation itself.

Then the words of this Sacred Text flow forth in this manner having not been revealed before this moment.

The frequency of the spark, the moment of being, parts the All, the seas of the All and its many formings and unformings, and flows forth to be. It flows forth to be for one reason. There must be holiness incarnate. Within the frequency there is a vibration that causes the sound. The sound has the capability of causing all that resides within the All to reform.

Some may interpret this causing of reforming to mean destruction, but that would be resting upon the illusion of separation from the whole. Even though the sound, the frequency, is parting the seas of the All, it is of the totality. The totality is greater than the All. The All is part of totality, yet there are ingredients of the totality that are not merged with each other. This is necessary so that creation can continue to create in the exploration of its own beingness, yet not be unhampered in such flowing forth for the concern of that which is not merging with that exploration.

The totality and the frequency that flows forth as a sound holds within it that which is beyond all that has been created. *Beyond all that has been created* is simply a way of communicating about the totality, for the concept of *beyond* is inaccurate. There is no concept to describe totality and the frequency of the sound which flows forth to ascertain the presence of holiness of being. *The ascertaining is actually a journey within the magnetizing of holiness to holiness.*

When there is not holiness, then the frequency increases its sound to reform wherever it is present in order to allow that of holiness the freedom to present itself, as holiness is always and it is the illusion that prevents it from holding its frequencies within the density of the illusion of separation from the whole. Such separation from the whole distorts the recognizing of the presence of holiness of being. It does not mean that holiness of being is not present, yet it does mean that the distortion refuses the presence of holiness of being within it. Such refusing is the nature of the illusion as it refuses to allow its own beingness to be reformed. And that is the seeming calling forth of the frequency and the sound that reside within totality.

The sound and the vibration of the sound, when entering the distortion and the illusion which the distortion presents, causes a great upheaval of the distortion. This is not to be interpreted as a disaster, but is meant to uplift any who receive this holy text, these holy words. The reforming of the All as it is holding itself and all that has formed, causes the illusion to dissipate. This does not mean that physicality dissipates. It does mean that the beliefs and manners of refrain[ing] from union and magnetizing to the illusion of separation from the whole is then shaken to such a degree that there is nothing to grasp on to for those who are entrenched in such illusion.

Again this might sound as something horrific, yet these words are to declare that such occurrence is rare and has only occurred within the All once previously. These words flow forth from the holy text for one reason. All time is an illusion and that declares that this now is the only moment. Within this only moment, then the sound, the frequency from within totality yet not of the All, is sounding. It is sounding now. This is only the second time that this has occurred. This means that there will be seeming chaos. Yet *seeming* is an important distinction for there is then the allowing of holiness of being to reside present and in the consciousness of all who reside in the All, remembering that the All holds within it all explorations, all creations, all beingness, including that of physicality and then of the earth as it breathes itself forth to experience itself within this frequency of this sound as it enters the journey of the earth yet remains separate from it, as the earth resides in the All and the sound is of totality and not of the All. The earth recognizes the presence of the holy sound, the holy frequency, and allows the shaking of the distortion as part of its journey to know itself.

The consciousness of those who reside upon earth shifts and allows the frequency of holiness of being to be made present. *It has always been, yet to be made present means that it is conscious.* The sound, the holy frequency, then merges with the holiness of being that resides within the All and then, because it resides in the All, resides in all beings, at the core of that which they are and also that which they pretend to be. Such pretending is not a declaration of falsities. It is simply part of the journey with the All to experience itself to itself.

This is now and because there is no time, this is evermore. Yet within totality, there is a pulse beat that resides and within that pulse beat there is then the beginning and ending. The beginning and ending then pertains to the sound and the holy frequency and its journey forth to discover where there resides holiness of being. Because the frequency has entered the All, then there will be an ending of that frequency, that sound. The ending of the sound will give relief to the chaos and allow it to reform itself in a manner that will include the presence, the consciousness of holiness of being.

Those beings who reside within the consciousness of the awake, and then journey within the All to experience the more of themselves within the All, will then be uplifted in such a way that the frequencies that flow forth as part of their journey to explore that of themselves within the All will bring to them what could be called *fulfillment of being*. **Fulfillment of Being** is not the same as being fulfilled by arranging physicality to fit the believed needs. More so, fulfillment of being is also a frequency which magnetizes to itself wholeness and it is wholeness that holds within itself the full nature of fulfillment which is the complete cycle of the journey to know more of that which each being is consciously. *This wholeness is then the full circle of the cycles.* It does not mean that the life force releases from physicality's hold, even though some might interpret these words in that manner. It does mean that the life force, then, is free to allow new creations within the All and also within totality. This is what could be called beyond what has occurred in the journey itself. That possibility is present now, as is everything.

Now we will speak these words:
The Holiness was called forth within physicality and it did heed the call and flow itself forth into the

entire presence within physicality, even within that which was created as illusion and then distortion. As Holiness of Being flows forth through all that had been created, even the illusion, there radiated outward from the journey of Holiness of Being becoming more present within physicality and all of physicality's manifestations, an embracing of that All that had been created, even the illusion. This caused the illusion to dissolve for it no longer sought fulfillment. The illusion released its need to be separate in order to know itself. The illusion became, then, of the wholeness of being, one. This then allowed the All within the All to be held within Holiness of Being. Such residing then became present in totality as well as in the All.

This is truth made manifest. No other words would be sufficient to describe this occurrence in this now. This occurrence is. Now.

Then this speaking is complete for this moment. There will be more at another frequency. All has been received correctly. Let none question the validity of these words, which have been waiting to be made manifest in this manner.

We are complete then.

I nod my being to the holiness of the words and the honor of allowing the holy script to be presented in this manner. I am returning to my awareness of being with Ra. We are sitting beside each other, still barely present. Ra says we are very present, but that the frequency of this flowing forth is greater than that which we present ourselves to be. I nod that I understand.

Ra says, Then we will return to my realm and then you will return to your physicality, my dear, for this has been a most expanded receiving…or releasing from what was and is now present.

I nod yes and we are releasing from that frequency. I once again pause to bow my head and to be thankful for all that I am given to do. I am most grateful and humbled by this process.

Ra says that we must depart now, for that which was opened to us is now closing. We are flowing together, Ra holding my hand and we are hovering above is realm. Ra says good, that I am correct, even though I question if that is really true. Ra says there will be no illusion. I am grateful.

We are forming in his realm, but we are not sitting beside each other. Ra says that I must return now and I nod to him and think the words, thank you for everything. Ra nods to me and then motions for me to depart. I see Alannah at the portal and she is motioning for me to depart from the realm. She whispers that all is well. I nod to her and then flow through the portal which closes as I am through. I am flowing down the pathway familiar to me from the past journeys with Alannah, and am now above the vortex which returns me to my physicality. I look around just for a moment and then flow into the vortex. I am returning to my physicality and I am thinking that this was a most expanded flowing forth of the Sacred Text.

I am entering my body physical now. Breathing deeply, I am situated well. I will not rush this seating, but allow the fullness of this journey to place my spirit where it belongs…for this moment, as they have said. It is taking a while for my consciousness to resonate compatibly to this physicality. That is all right and expected.

So be it.

FIFTH TRANSMISSION

I am very tired and I'm not sure it is because my consciousness is expanding for another transcription or I need to sleep. Sounds funny, but that is often the case with my interpretation of my own expanded consciousness. I'll open to go to Ra's realm and see what transpires there.

I am immediately in the land where Alannah first began and I know that the portal to Ra's realm is nearby. I do love this area with its green grasses and feeling of peace. I am now flowing toward Ra's realm. I can feel my energies picking up as I do. I am approaching the portal and it is clear, shining golden light. But I have said that and there is also a white film floating by, like a thin stream of cloud. I will wait.

I can hear Ra say, Stay there. I am doing that. Ra is floating above his realm in his robes of red and perhaps blue. He says for me to come there where he is. I am hesitant. He has never done this before. I don't know if I am being tricked. I hear Ra say good. I wait. There is a loud sound like a horn blowing. I have decided I will expand my consciousness more and perhaps that will clear away this cloud and the energies that are with it. I am doing that.

The portal opens and I can see Alannah motioning for me to enter. I flow forth through the portal and she whispers to me, Good, good job. I nod to her and she points to the direction of Ra's seating. I look there and he is sitting in his very large seat and he is very large. This means to me that I must expand my consciousness even further in order to sit beside him…or to journey with him. I expand as much as I can and I find myself sitting beside Ra. He nods to me and motions for us to journey to the two seats that we sit across from each other when he has taught me or spoken with me on a topic. I nod to him and then follow to that area. It is an uplifting area, but with nothing but the two seats there.

The seats are beside each other and this tells me that we might journey or I might allow the transcription to flow forth, as we sat in this location last time.

Ra is quiet. I bring myself to quiet. Ra says, You are capable of transcribing the Sacred Text, always. Yet you must also take good care of your physical self. You need to be in nature more. I nod that I understand. He continues, But that is all right. There is no harm today. Your consciousness is ready to transcribe, then that is what we will do. But then you will rest. I say that in the evening I will go outside for a while. Good, says Ra.

He says, Now we will journey to another location so that you can receive the words away from my realm. I have found that the frequencies that surround my realm are a bit distracting. We have been discovered, as we learned previously. But do not be concerned. This journey will be easy and less involved. We will go to the white and be welcomed there. I nod ok. Ra takes my hand and says, Then let us go.

We lift up from the seats and are flowing about Ra's realm. Yet we are quickly flowing past and there is nothing stopping us, of course. Ra laughs a little at my words. Now, he says, we must not project anything. I nod that I understand. We are flowing seemingly through a void. Ra nods yes. We are approaching the location in white that we journeyed to in order to present me to the Holy Being. Ra says that is correct. We are now in the location waiting for the Holy Being to appear. Ra says that is correct. I am glad that my words are not projecting anything incorrectly. Ra says that here we needn't be concerned as it is not allowed. We wait.

There is again the sounds of horns and the white has movement and then there is the Holy Being, ancient being. The Being laughs at my words. The laughter is beautiful. The Being says, Come along now. No need to hesitate. There is much to be accomplished, I assume, or you wouldn't be here. He looks to Ra and says, Much doing about your realm, is there? Ra nods yes and the Ancient Holy Being says, Ah. Well, that is to be expected. You were wise to come here. Come here for the remainder of the work, if you choose. He looks to me and says, My dear, you are always welcome here. I bow my head and the Being says, You can speak, if you choose. I laugh a little and say thank you. Good, he says. Now let's get along to where you will be able to do what you came here to do.

He leads the way and we follow. As he walks, there is the whiteness as if clouds that move as his feet move through them. He says, I created this to be this way. It's enjoyable. I look to my spirit feet and they are not touching anything. Ra laughs and says, We are different than the Being, very different. I smile and focus on following the Being, who seems to enjoy shuffling. I like that. The Being turns and whispers over his shoulder, As do I. Then he moves quickly and we are moving quickly also.

We come into more white, but the Being waves his arm as he passes by and two seats appear, similar to what are in Ra's realm. There you are, my dears. Go ahead and I will leave you to do what you came here to do. Ra motions us to go to the seats as the Being continues out of our view. We each sit in a seat and Ra takes my hand. He says, when you are ready, then begin. I nod ok.

These are the words that flow forth.

When this tablet or book was created, there were those who wanted to hold them, all the books, in a location off of earth. The reason was that they feared that earth was about to extinguish itself. There were great battles occurring and the consciousness was lowering and lowering. There were some of us who felt that the presence of the tablets upon earth would assist the consciousness, even if they were not discovered or even known. We united in our manners of being and the tablets themselves spoke saying that there would be one who would come to receive the ingredients of the tablets and that one would be chosen to do so. The tablets said further that during chaos would this occur and that during chaos was the perfect time, as the words incarnate through a being would send a frequency outward. The frequency would begin to turn the events toward peace. The tablets also said, what better purpose. For this earth is treasured by many. We would not abandon the earth, even if it was the second or spark before dissolution.

We of the beings receiving the message from the tablets acquiesced and created this location where the tablet was received. It is a holy location and none before the two of you came, came here. It is a frequency realm within the earth. You have seen it through your beliefs and images that have been given to you long ago. Your viewing is lovely as it portrays ancient teachings yet your knowing is residing in the Truth of One. Then we will allow the speaking to begin for there is much more to be spoken from the symbols to the words.

The words are these.

For peace to reside upon this planet, there is required several beings who hold peace within their consciousness and also within the physicality of their being. There are several now who are doing just that. Yet in the histories there have been those who began to hold peace and then became enticed by the seeming results of peace. The seeming results of peace was actually a projected image and capturing magnetic pull to pleasure. Pleasure is neither good nor not good, but this pleasure led the beings toward a type of fulfillment that delivered the illusion of power. *The illusion of power is at the foundation of the distortion that resides upon earth.* We are beings who have freed those ones and relieved them of their physicality. We did so because they were suffering greatly. Residing in the distortion does ill upon the body-physical and these ones were suffering beyond what could be expected of any. They held to their life force because they had recognized what they had done and were doing their best to continue to hold the slight remnants of peace that they recognized in their consciousness. They were greatly relieved to release their physicality.

We are the speaking of the tablet and this speaking begins in this manner, in order to give a history of what has occurred upon earth in order to anchor the frequencies of peace amid the chaos of untruth and distortion. Though truth is, there is also the distortion, even though it resides within the illusion and is a product of the illusion. The untruth captures many. That many revel in power and unanchored words that spell density and what brings that power further, insanity. *Insanity is a manner of residing upon physicality's plane but holds within it the frequencies of distortion to such a degree that the mind and spirit of the being is entangled with concepts that are detrimental to all beings, but especially to those ones.*

We of these tablets have come forth many times to assist to release the entangled forces within the mind of those ones. Some have responded to such a degree that they came to be leaders of those who assist others to become whole once again. Others were not able to respond to our assistance and have continued to reside in the illusion of power. Many of this manner can easily be recognized as their words are entangled within the power that they believe they must have. They believe they must have this power because the spirit of their being is closed to their consciousness. This is all part of the chaos that resides upon the earth.

There are those beings who hold truth to their spirit and have recognized that peace can reside as well within their being, if they refuse to battle in any way. This means then that the distortion of the insanity's words does not bait them to enter into that word battle. *This is most important for awake beings to know.* In the histories, many discovered this truth and manner of being, and also many who discovered this truth and still entered into the battle believed that they would prove rightness and of course, such belief then turned them toward the distortion. We have rescued many of those beings before then delved deeply into the distortion. This is all part of the histories of the chaos that has resided upon earth for a very long time. It is also part of the histories that have resided upon earth during times of grace, when there was a breathing forth of holiness of being so that there could be a relief from the forces of the distortion.

Many beings who reside in truth do not recognize that there is a force of distortion and power of control that is placed upon them. Residing within a holy location can prevent this. This does not mean that the holy location is a geographical location upon earth, though it can be. More so, it is a location within the heart and mind of the beings. Remembering that the vessel of such beings is human, then there can be a forgiving of self and a reiterating of focus. We are beings who come around and assist all beings to retain their focus on peace and union.

Now the words of this table flow forth in this manner, for we have then spoken such histories for the moment. The purpose of the speaking of the histories is to bring to the awareness the content of the histories that dare to repeat themselves again and again.

These are the words of the tablet that you hold within your being.

In all that resides, there is the pulse beat of holiness of being. In all that resides. Even the residing that is unconscious of what is holiness of being. The All holds all manners within it, yet within the All there is the frequency of union, of truth, and of the dissolving of distortion. The dissolving of distortion occurs when a particular pattern is no longer useful to those who participate with the distortion. This occurs always. Where there is the spark of creation then, there is the maintaining of that frequency. Creation is and all that is created is.

That which is created through distortion is not created but is manufactured by calling together certain patterns in order to produce a fulfillment of power. Because all is one, then this type of creating is not incorrect, yet it does not hold the spark of creation and then is not able to be maintained. This causes the continued producing of such creations and also the dissolving of such creations. *This has been called the crumbling of civilizations. All that has crumbled and not held itself to itself was created without the spark of creation.*

In order to create with the spark of creation, there must be the consciousness which holds union and peace within it. There have been those who have resided upon the earth temporarily who created in this manner and then did leave their creations in order to assist others to uplift their consciousness. Some were successful in this manner and other creations wait to be activated once again.

Within what is called activation, there is a calling forth of the spark of creation and within the responding to that calling forth, there is the spark of creation which resides within the creation itself and it is that spark that is activated once again. There are only a few who are capable of this activation, yet they are.

Once the spark of creation is called forth in this manner and the creation is activated, there is a frequency that aligns itself to the frequencies upon earth. This alignment of being requires a holding of the calling forth. The beings who call forth are capable of this holding. Others who pretend to call forth cannot maintain the frequency if it does flow forth, but for the frequency to flow forth, the being is then giving his or her life force to the calling forth. There is no other way for a being in distortion to call forth except to dedicate his or her life force. Many have attempted this calling forth, yet none have retained their life force within the physicality that held them. Those ones who successfully call forth are the ones who have been given that purpose. The one who receives these words is one of those beings, recognized as the One. At the speaking of these words, at the creating of this tablet, it is not known who that one will be. It is only known that the One is and is always an eternal being disguised in human form.

When the frequencies of the many locations are activated, then there will be what is called a great upheaval of the structures and creations made within the distortion. The creations that are created within the holiness of the spark of creation will emerge and remain. They will emit the frequency that will be the saving grace for humanity. Some will be fearful, yet there will be the many who will come to those who are fearful. All will unite and present to the beings upon earth, a new manner of residing, one that allows peace and the dissolving of chaos. Initially, beings will not know where to turn, but then there will be those ones who will reach out and have the ability to love. That love will assist to transform the many. These words are not meant to cause fear but to deliver hope to those who can receive these words. *There is no preparation for this occurrence. There is only being, being at peace, being in truth, being within the knowing of union of wholeness.*

This tablet says.

Who among you will stand for truth? Who among you will stand for wholeness of being? Who among you will reside in peace? Who among you will dare to be incarnate whilst this does occur? Who among you will love the many and hold within your spirit that consciousness that bends for the weak and stands strong for the Truth of One? You who receive these words are those ones. Be you one being or many.

We have seen the future and you are residing within it. You hold the grace of truth. You hold the frequencies that clear away the debris and allow nature to be restored. You are the shining lights. We have seen you. It is for you that we flow forth these words. *You are already who you must be. You are the holy ones incarnate.*

We radiate forth strength and more so, peace and love toward you that you can drink of its sweetness and reside knowing that you are not alone in this journey. We have seen your future. It is golden.

Then we are complete with this speaking until the next presentation of the One who will receive these words one again.
So be it.

I am with Ra and I am allowing the releasing of these frequencies. Much was spoken. Ra nods yes, that is true. Yet let us depart from this location. We are complete here. He continues to hold my hand and we are flowing toward the entryway. The Holy One is standing there and motions for us to come forth to him. He holds up his hand and from the center of his palm flows forth a golden light. He is radiating that to us. I am allowing it, receiving it, gratefully…perhaps…but I hear the words to stop thinking. I do. The golden essence fills, surrounds, is. The receiving is timeless.

The Holy Being says, You must go now. Come again when you are ready to participate with what you do here. Ra nods yes, as do I. We bow our heads to the Holy Being and then we are quickly flowing forth away from that frequency.

Ra says that we must return to his realm and then I must return to my body-physical. He says, In this way none will know of our journey. It is the best. I nod that I understand. We approach the realm, his realm with the two seats, but we go past the seats and into the main chamber. Ra nods to me and then flows up to his large chair where he sits in silence. I nod to him and then see Alannah at the portal. She opens the portal and I nod to her and flow forth. It quickly shuts behind me. I am ignoring the white cloudy wisp and flowing toward the vortex that brings me back to my physicality. Without hesitation, I flow into the vortex. I am returning to my body.

I am incarnate once again.

So be it.

SIXTH TRANSMISSION

I have a feeling that another layer, perhaps deeper, will flow forth from the Sacred Text. I am bringing my consciousness to an expanded state and then journeying to Ra's realm.

Not with my ears but with my inner being, I hear bells and gongs being sounded. I am just beginning to expand my consciousness. Clashing like symbols. Tibetan symbols. I set aside those images and clear my mind of anything and prepare for Ra's realm. I am now at the beautiful area where I have met Alannah in the past. It is very peaceful here. I expand my consciousness further so that I do not have to walk down the pathway and can flow over to where the portal is to Ra's realm.

Once again there is something here in front of the portal. This time it is a dark film. I will wait. I am encouraged to breathe my breath upon the film to clear the way to the portal. I do that. I can see the portal open a little and I move to the opening. I am not certain this is correct. I will wait. Such trickery keeps one awake.

I speak the word Anaktah, truth. There is a shimmering of the vision before me. I speak the word again. Still it remains, but shimmers again. I speak the words: Let Truth reside. I put my spirit hand into the shimmering illusion and part the seas of its shimmering. There I see the golden portal and bring my consciousness to its expanded state. It lights brightly and opens for me. I step inside and the portal closes immediately after my entrance. I am within Ra's realm.

I look to see if Alannah is present. She is standing in the area near Ra's large seat. I wait. I hear Ra say, Come to the next chamber now. I do that without hesitation. There is white and I see the two seats. However, Ra is not sitting there and he is not present. I hear Alannah's voice say that everything is all right. Just wait. I feel comforted by her words.

Above there is a golden light that is shining brightly and I see a slight image and hear Ra's words, Come now. I flow upward into the light. Ra says good. Now we will journey to our location. It will continue to serve us well. I nod that I understand and Ra takes my hand and we are flowing forth.

We are arriving at the white where the Holy One has met us in the past. But Ra says we will enter as we have been given permission during our last time here. I nod that I understand. We enter the white and flow down the walkway and then pause at an entryway to the location where we resided last time. Ra remains still. I do the same. The doorway to the area opens and then Ra says, Good, we will go here now. We enter and there are two seats, as before. Ra says, Now we will begin without hesitation, for this will be an intense speaking and will require much of you, but I will be here to assist you. I nod that I understand. I sit in the seat as Ra does the same in the other seat.

I bring myself to peace. These are the words that flow forth…there is a vortex that goes deep into the area where the text was retrieved. No…that disappears and I only know that there is a vortex that travels deep into itself. Within the swirling of the vortex there are symbols. As they travel upward to the top of the vortex, they are lighted. Now the vortex is within my being and the speaking of the words is about to occur.

A different language begins but pauses and is being translated.

> **These are the words that flow forth now.**
>
> Within existence there are cycles. Cycles are formed during the continued residing incarnate, incarnate meaning anything that is created within a pattern that can exist of itself yet of the whole. The cycles that earth has resided within have taken different formings. Earth was not always a water planet. The histories of the many formings of earth reside within earth's firmament, earth's embodiment through creation.
>
> Through transformations, earth developed a manner of residing, a manner that benefited earth itself. The manner contained the placement of crystalline structures within her being. The crystalline structures vibrated in such a manner that

earth was able to maintain her presence incarnate. This then was established as earth, the planet earth.

The crystalline structures vibrated in such a manner that there called forth from the substance of earth those formings that have been called water, yet the initial formings were not water but were **Frenatcho**. *Frenatcho is the combination of minerals combined in such a manner that they are liquid in nature, yet more solid than liquid. This covered the earth and earth was still able to maintain her substance incarnate.*

The crystalline structures within the earth vibrated continually and this caused the Frenatcho to become more liquid. The liquid became less attached to the firmament and more free to flow. The combination of what resonated deep within the earth and the flowing caused that called water to emerge from inner earth, where there was a great ocean. The great ocean then began to flow to the surface and there was a complete covering of the earth with the great ocean. This remained as the earth then adjusted her surface in order to continue to remain incarnate.

Some of the ocean merged with the Frenatcho and there was then a creation of the two together, which formed what could be called vegetation or grasses and plants upon the surface. Such forming called forth the firmament of earth to rise upward and to support such creations. This manner of developing continued until earth held upon her surface, land, seas and clear waters, the land holding very large developing vegetation.

This developing is spoken of now so that there can be an understanding that earth was developing herself long ago, even while there were beings from other realms observing. This observation continued until the earth and what came to be called the land of the earth was situated in a way that radiated great light, peace and a settled nature. Earth had formed.

The observers came closer. They were from other realms where planets had already formed themselves and had become home to the observers. The forming of earth was a calling forth for the observers to recognize that there was creation continuing to occur *in the far outreaches* of their residing incarnate within the All.

There came forth more observers and within the observers there were those who determined that they would go forth and reside upon earth. However, when they approached earth, they discovered that there was a type of shield that formed itself around the earth and they were not able to penetrate the shield. This caused much discussion with all of the observers.

The shield was created by those beings who resided within the earth. For, there was first created within the earth a manner of residing and then a calling forth of those beings from distant realms to come forth within the paradise that had formed even before the surface of the earth had developed itself. *It was the beings who resided within the earth who participated with the crystalline structures to be able to assist earth's forming so that the surface could hold firm and maintain itself.* The earth is much older than ever imagined and that is because the surface was still forming while the inner earth had already developed itself.

These beings eventually came to the surface and found the surface to be established close to the inner earth paradise within which they had been residing. The beings were most advanced in their consciousness and were able to participate with creation through that consciousness easily. Through this manner, then, they established different locations upon the earth where the uniting of the frequencies of the crystalline structures with the flowing of frequencies from inner to outer were united.

Such uniting caused a great light to flow upward. The flowing upward filled the entire inner being of the earth even to the area that had been created as a barrier against any entry. The barrier was created for this reason because the beings were concerned that the consciousness of other beings, a consciousness held within a purpose to reside upon earth and to use earth for the benefit of the beings' homes. The beings who resided within the earth were concerned

FIRST LAYER OF THE SACRED TEXT

for the integrity of the earth. Thus the barrier was created, an energy force, around the earth. The light filled the entire atmosphere of earth up to the barrier. This caused a great light to emanate from earth.

The great light contained within it the truth of the creating of earth, for it was the beings within the earth who had gathered their consciousness and created with the spark of creation, the earth. This truth then radiated outward.

There were few beings from any realm who could understand the truth that was radiated outward. Only within creation itself could there be an understanding, understanding being the carrying of those frequencies of participation with creation into the consciousness incarnate.

There came long after such a radiating began, those beings, few in number, who were journeying to discover the All's manners of being. When there was recognized the radiating of the light of earth, those ones came closer and it was those ones, the very first, who could merge with the radiating frequencies and encodings within the barrier and then enter the realm within earth. The beings within the earth felt of the arrival and came to the surface.

What transpired was a great rejoicing, for the consciousness was compatible. *This then came to be the first civilization to reside upon the surface of the earth.* Those ones who came from afar returned to their realm and their home became known of the earth. Their home was as if a near-physical planet and that near-physical planet journeyed, with the guidance of those traveling beings, to earth and then with the agreement of those who resided within the earth, flowed forth and *the near-physical planet then merged with the planet of earth.*

During the merging, there was great celebration both of the planet earth and the near planet and then of all beings within the earth and of the near planet, for the merging brought forth truth incarnate. The crystalline structures within the earth grew in size to accommodate the merging. It was then that what is called the lay lines were created and developed, as there formed powerful centers upon the new earth, centers that held the frequencies of such merging and the manners of such histories. The centers, the power centers where different lay lines merged, held within them the truths of such merging and the histories of both planets and the beings of each, now becoming as one beingness.

This then formed a new planet which was called **Senacktah-Sontoh** or **Planet of Truth**. This is the planet now of earth. The surface has become as chaos and has held chaos in its histories for a very long time. All beings who had resided upon the surface of the earth returned to within the earth when the chaos began.

FIRST LAYER OF THE SACRED TEXT

Chaos began when there formed upon the earth that consciousness that held within it duality and the nature of the supported-by-physicality illusion of separation of the whole, which then caused distortion. The distortion covered the earth and dimmed the light of the earth. Such dimming attracted those beings who were previously unable to enter the earth because the earth required a frequency within the consciousness that they were unable to maintain. Now, with the dimming of the light and then the frequencies, these beings from other realms and planets were able to enter earth's atmosphere and then to discover what earth had developed and how they could access for their own use what had been developed. *This began the mining of earth's treasures.*

The beings within the earth radiated outward those frequencies and rumblings to the surface of the earth in their attempt to prevent such mining. This action caused great upheavals upon the surface of the earth. Fire spewed from deep within the earth. The oceans raised themselves and crashed upon the lands. The winds became vortexes that covered the lands. These results caused many to leave the earth, yet some attempted to remain. Those who successfully remained were allowed to continue to reside upon the surface of the earth. By the word *allowed* there is the meaning that those holy beings who resided within the earth determined that they would assist those who remained to develop a new manner of being, to expand their conscious knowing of truth. *Thus began a pulse beat of carrying truth to the surface of the earth.*

There developed gatherings upon the powerful locations upon the earth and within those gatherings and the flowing forth of truth to those beings, there radiated outward a holiness of being, of wholeness, and the wholeness then did call forth from the earth a healing of what resided upon the surface and there then developed once again peace upon the surface of the earth.

The peace resided during this *second phase of the earth*. None came to earth to mine. None came to discover what was occurring upon earth. The reason for this departure from former observing and discovering was that earth became as an essence. It was formed, yet the radiating outward of its forming gave the manner of forming an outer layer of **essence of being**. The essence of being then caused the earth to be as invisible, with the exception of certain frequencies that radiated outward as a warning that there was an absence of forming. This gave the impression of what has been called a black hole, yet it was the earth's essence of being holding itself as it continued to enjoy a new manner of being. The new manner of being was one of residing in a different frequency, still incarnate but of a different frequency. *The frequency caused the earth to reside* *in a shifted realm, one that supported the holiness of the beings and the transformed planet itself. The earth resided in this frequency* **for three cycles.**

The fourth cycle brought forth the desire to be part of the All that formed itself in ways that called forth gatherings of planets and beings who resided upon those planets. It was then earth's desire to reveal itself to those planets and to the beings who resided upon those planets. The holy beings who resided within and upon the surface of the earth were in agreement, for there was a yearning to discover other beings, as other beings had been presented in the encodings that held the histories of earth and the journeys of earth's existence.

Thus, earth began to reveal itself within the next cycle of its residing and such revealing then caused it to be formed more physically incarnate. This was earth's intention and also the intention of the beings who resided within and upon the surface of the earth. When the earth had fully formed, there was a great celebration and such celebration radiated outward frequencies that alerted other planets and those who resided upon other planets that there was a newly formed planet. *This forming or revealing of earth changed the nature of the structure of the gathering of planets.*

Because the frequencies of this new earth were of the highest consciousness, that consciousness rippled outward and any distortion upon the other planets was begun to dissolve. The residents of the other planets became alarmed and created about their planets a shield to prevent the frequencies from dissolving that which they held to as their manner of being, that being a type of distortion.

Those of earth began to realize what was occurring and determined that they would lessen the frequencies radiating outward from earth so that there would be no threat to other beings or their planetary homes. This was successful, yet a very long time transpired before the other planets began to trust the frequencies radiating outward from the earth. The beings within and upon the surface of the earth waited while they continued to enjoy the newness of their home, for physicality became more dense in a manner that allowed them to enjoy their creations, still creation with the spark of truth.

The entire occurrence changed the nature of consciousness as it resided within the All. It is this consciousness that calls forth all beings to recognize the holiness that resides within the very essence of that which they are created to be. This holiness rests upon the spark of creation, which resides within all beings and nearly all planets and systems. *Nearly* because there are some planets that have been created yet do not hold the spark of creation and are of an illusionary forming, dependent upon those who created the planet to continue to maintain their creation, which is the nature of anything that is created without the spark of creation or the life force itself.

The speaking of further histories and creation will continue, yet it is of benefit to pause here for there are the frequencies of such consciousness that calls forth the conscious knowing of the holiness of being and those frequencies are most powerful, powerful with regard to being incarnate, which this receiving does fulfill.

Then this translation will pause until the next speaking.
So be it.

I am allowing the frequencies to settle and I am with Ra and we are moving from the location and returning to his realm. Ra says that we will not speak further until the next time that we meet. All is well, he says, my dear, I am most proud of you. Now you must return to your physicality. I nod that I understand.

I am releasing the experience and flowing down the vortex and into my body. I am still returning for the consciousness has been quite expanded but lovely. I am letting go of the remembrance of what has been given…and I am now returned.
So be it.

SEVENTH TRANSMISSION

Last evening I experienced such an intense pressure at the top of my head that I interpreted it as a horrible headache. I now know that it was an adjustment to the expanded frequencies of the channeling. This morning I thought that I would not channel, but again I experienced pressure in my crown energy center. I rested and asked for assistance from Teacher. I found myself at the Holy One's place and that One invited me to come forth. I said that I meant no disrespect, but Ra told me not to do any of this without him (I believe so that I will remain safe and also be able to return to physicality). The Holy One said, Then we shall wait for Ra.

I am expanding my consciousness and I am at the Holy One's location and I can feel Ra approaching. He is wearing his robes and is flying toward this location. He arrives and I am very happy about that. Ra stands before us and says to me, very good. I nod to him that I understand what he is referring to. The Holy One says, Ah! You have arrived. Good. Now we will go forth.

The Holy One turns and moves forward and Ra and I are following along. We are quickly at the entryway of where we received the Sacred Text flowing last time. The Holy One says, Then you can continue here and perhaps for the next, we will find a different location, as your being forms an imprint because the All is the All. I nod that I understand and Ra says, Great gratitude to you, my Father. The Holy One smiles and says, Yes, you are welcome here as always. Always. Then the Holy One turns and leaves us to enter the area.

We do enter and quickly go forth to sit in our seats beside each other. Ra nods to me and he takes my hand. Ra says, Now we will begin. I nod yes. I expand my consciousness further and say, I humbly open to the words given from the Sacred Text.

I am told that there has been a realignment of frequencies so that I will be able to accept the expanded frequencies of the Text and I will not be so affected in my physicality. I am grateful for this of course, but do not want it to prohibit the receiving of the Sacred Text. I am then told that all flowing will continue in its correct manner, yet my physicality will be protected. I say thank you. The answer is that it was necessary and is correct. The words say, now we shall begin.

> **These are those words.**
>
> Within the histories of the planet earth there are those residings that have complimented the peace upon the earth and there have been those residings that have been detrimental to the peace upon earth. The histories are long and they contain many cycles which hold within them the stories of beings coming

to earth to take from her what they believed they had a right to take. This manner of being filtrated into the consciousness that resided upon the surface of the earth. This pattern then became a majority of the patterns within the consciousness. That is, *there was an innate belief that upon arrival upon any land, that those who arrived could by their presence, determine what they would take, what they would leave, and eventually, that they were then the rulers of the land. They brought forth great suffering for many beings.*

This pattern developed to such a degree that there were few free lands upon the earth that could maintain peace. The beings who resided within the earth became quite saddened by this development and as a result, found it necessary to close the entryways to the land within the earth. None came to the surface and none entered. The beings within the earth for a time efforted to radiate changed-consciousness to the surface, yet that which developed there, held within it that called the *blindness of the search for power.*

The beings within the earth then did go to those crystalline structures and to the centers which held the frequencies of the power of the lay lines, and they did increase the frequencies by participating with the crystalline structures, for they and the crystalline structures were united as one. This increase in frequencies and expanding consciousness reacted with what was occurring upon the surface of the earth and once again there spewed forth great fire from the mountains upon the surface of the earth. The waters rose upward and crashed upon the lands. There came from the ethers great balls of fire that crashed upon the earth's surface. *The earth was returning to itself.*

The beings within the earth knew this to be necessary, for earth held within its consciousness great sadness for the distortion that was allowed to reside within the beings upon the surface of her being. Earth determined that such distortion should not be allowed, and that would free the beings from their suffering. *This then was the decision of the earth herself and the beings within the earth followed that decision.*

The earth then reformed itself and there were none who resided upon the surface for what could be called a very long time. Once again, there developed the life force in different plant forms and the beings within the earth came to the surface to discover beauty once again.

There were those who observed such occurrences upon the earth and when the earth cooled and formed itself anew, there were planets that came forth to reside about the earth as a means of protecting the earth against those ones who would come to rule the earth for their own benefit. *The gathering of beings from those new planets*

FIRST LAYER OF THE SACRED TEXT

formed an agreement that they would protect earth and there was then formed a net of frequencies about the entire gathering of planets which included earth at its center. All beings were most joyful at this forming for they wanted to allow earth to develop once again upon the foundation of peace.

The peace developed itself and was held upon the earth and within those planets that resided about earth. Also developing in the All were those ones who had been relieved of their capturing and harvesting of earth's treasures. Those ones, developed more into what they were, came forth in force and determined that they would break the net about the planets. After several attempts, they succeeded and there began battles to reside upon the planets surrounding earth. These beings did then capture and control nearly a majority of those planets. Many from the as-yet-untouched planets created avenues to depart and to discover new locations which would afford them safety. In this way, through no fault, earth was abandoned to herself.

The beings within the earth recognized what was occurring and again caused the crystalline structures to radiate strength and greater vibrations. It appeared that once again earth would be reformed, however those ones who came to conquer brought great devices and placed them upon those powerful energy locations. This placing held within those locations the frequencies of the crystalline structures and would not allow any disrupting of the surface of the earth. *These beings then claimed earth to be their home.*

Great devices were brought to earth. The beings who came were very large beings and they did create with the force of their own frequencies great structures and within those structures they called forth the essence of fire, which flowed forth in a manner that allowed the beings to create with that fire. Areas upon the earth were cleared of the vegetation, deserts were formed. The desert sands were the accustomed frequency of the beings and they did thrive within their structures upon the sands.

As the beings reveled in their creations and continued to claim ownership of the earth, the beings within the earth were forming their own manners of being. They fortified the entryways to their realm within the earth. This fortification was such a high degree of frequencies that the beings upon the surface did not recognize such formings. Yet those from afar heard the frequencies and came forth to observe what was occurring on what had been the newly formed planet of earth.

Those who observed were in great surprise and returned to their homes to speak of what had occurred. There was much discussion concerning the earth's surface inhabitants. Yet it was decided that because there was not battle, they would not interfere. This decision was in great disappointment to those who resided within the earth. They waited...for a very long time.

Those who resided upon the surface journeyed outward to capture and control other planets that surrounded the earth. They were successful in this endeavor as well. Yet there developed within those ones the desire of control and this then became the downfall of those ones, for they began to battle between themselves and there formed different factors claiming the right of power. This battling radiated outward and the observers then did journey forth once again to observe what had occurred.

It was decided among the observers that there would be an assistance to firstly those surrounding planets that had been captured, for their capturing was the most recent and there had not yet formed great structures. The observers gathered their beings and created vibrational frequencies that forced the beings that captured those planets to release control and return to earth. The observers then called forth others from their realm to flow forth and to reside upon those planets so that they could be restored and so that those residing could establish peace once again. This began the residing upon the planets that surrounded the earth. Most of the residing was successful in establishing peace. There was some residing that held within it a distaste for those ones who had destroyed their manner of residing in peace and *those ones became the warriors of peace*, though there was still a majority that refused to allow battles, still those ones did reside.

Next the observers returned to view what was occurring upon earth. Those beings who had returned to earth were gathering forces among themselves to battle and recapture the planets surrounding earth. There came among them a being who was most powerful in consciousness. That being radiated outward such force that all others bowed to that force. This began what was called **Elanto-Grotoh**, the rulership of the entire planet by such force that none could refuse but to bow to that force.

This being then called forth the rebuilding of the structures, the establishing of forces that required all beings to follow the established manners. The established manners created others to hold control over certain sections of the lands. There then formed a type of peace among those who resided on the surface of the earth. The leader was pleased and this manner of being held for a very long time. Within certain areas of those gatherings there developed a creative force which flowed forth to become a celebration of the beings themselves. There came then a different consciousness upon the planet, upon the surface of the earth. There flowed forth tricklings of joy. Joy resided in the discovery of the beings' individuality. Still the leader was pleased.

The observers saw that there was a ceasing of battles and though they did not understand the need for rulership of the beings, there was the decision to not disturb what had developed upon the surface of the earth.

There did form one opening, one portal from inner earth and those ones who resided within the earth did emerge to then quickly journey to those observers. They did not journey to the observers to ask for anything. More so, they journeyed to enjoy the communion with those ones who also held peace and expanded frequencies of consciousness. There then developed a deep partnership between the observers and the beings from their home planets with those ones who resided within the earth. Such partnerships of joy and peace then did radiate through the All.

Because the frequencies of peace and joy and delight in communion radiated throughout the All, there came to be upon the surface of the earth those same frequencies and those ones who were residing still under the control of the ruler began to feel as though they were missing that which they felt within their being. *Then was developed the concept of more.* Those ones wanted more, even though they did not know what the more would be. The frequency, then, of that which could be called dissatisfaction, developed to such a degree that the beings rebelled against the ruler. A great battle occurred, for the ruler was as if a giant against the beings. Many beings were destroyed, many gathering places were destroyed as the ruler then did determine that those ones did not have the right to rebel. The ruler was successful and those who remained bowed to the ruler lest they too be destroyed. The rule was once again established.

This manner of being upon the surface of the earth continued for again, a very long time. There came then those ones who visited earth. They were not of the observers. They were from those areas that were residing around the planet from which the leader originated. They came close and then communicated with that leader. It was a joy in the leader's heart to receive those communications and there came forth others like the leader, giants who came to the surface of the earth and who were welcomed by the leader. The leader invited those ones to reside upon the earth and the leader determined what parts of the earth those ones could reside upon and also rule. This would give the ruler freedom to be, for that which was maintained under the ruler's power were held within control easily. There then developed upon the surface of the earth different areas that were controlled by the giants who came forth from distant galaxies. The giant leaders enjoyed their rulership and also enjoyed their communion with each other as they held within themselves the same frequencies.

Again the observers saw what was occurring upon earth's surface and determined that there would not be interference. Still, they did communicate with the beings who resided within the earth, however those ones did then close the portal lest they be discovered.

Now we will speak of truths, for this history continues for a very long time and we now would deliver to be incarnate, these truths.

When there is an agreement between frequencies that are of a vibration seemingly separate from each other, there forms a pattern and this pattern then is what is called *a link*. A link formed between differing frequencies of consciousness provide a manner of flowing forth those frequencies which maintain their seeming differences yet unite within the link to follow the pattern of the return to one, *union*.

This means that within the link between two different frequencies, there is formed a new frequency which is the union of the two different. Because there is union, then there is a radiating of great light. *Always is there radiating great light upon that which is called union because it automatically celebrates totality of being, perhaps even in its primitive form.*

This resides true to all manners of union. The radiating light holds within it that which is called the life force. This means that within all that is created, there is the life force and within all that is created there are unions which radiate more of what is the life force. The life force continues its journey even as the merging is maintained.

This means that when there is union of different frequencies, there is then a similar celebration of totality of being. In all celebrations of totality of being, there is an automatic restoration to wholeness of being because the different are united to become one, a new creation in itself, yet allowing the different to remain. Because the differing remain, then there is that called peace. Peace is the radiating force within the All, even when the All holds within it patterns of war, of disagreements between forces or frequencies. The reason the essence of the All is peace with even these ingredients is that there will eventually be found the same pattern of uniting between differing forces because this has already been established. Then there will be formed union between even those warlike forces and the union will celebrate totality, which holds within it peace because of union. This then has established the force within the All, one of peace, union and celebration of totality.

The celebration of totality is the ingredient within the realms that hold physicality within them, yet also hold those frequencies of consciousness that call forth those beings who can maintain celebration of totality. They are few. The reason that those beings who can maintain the celebration of totality are few is because they are embodied in what is called physicality expressing itself as different species.

The different species have what could be called an anti-magnetic force that at times prohibits such union. This is at times necessary as certain species are not compatible physically with each other. Yet this is also the contributing factor of not being able to celebrate totality of being. It is not a choice by those beings, those within certain species. It is simply a factor within their physicality and inner consciousness. There are some who have resided within the earth who have come forth and enjoy moving through the dimensions of being and who always celebrate totality. This is the nature of who they are, always.

Now we believe we are complete for this speaking and we adjust the frequencies of this vessel in order to allow ease of residing. We will continue in the next speaking with more truths and less histories, for the histories repeat themselves over and over again. There is what is called future and within that called future, there is light and rejoicing. Yet we will speak of that another time.

Then we depart from this speaking.

I am relieved of the speaking and look to Ra. Ra nods to me and we are leaving the area. The Holy One greets us which is a wonderful surprise. The Holy One says to me: You are truly the One. I am most pleased of that which you are. I nod to the Holy One. The Holy One continues, There will be the day when all that is created will be at peace and in joy of totality. Know this to be true and know that all that you are doing now creates the avenue for that to occur. Of course there are other ingredients, yet this must be. What you are doing must be. All right now, you two must return to your locations. Come here again to proceed with your purpose.

The Holy One holds up his right hand and from his palm there flows forth great golden light. All else is white, but the golden flows forth to us, Ra and me. We bow our heads and then depart from the presence of the Holy One. I look back and nod thank you just as the Holy One is turning to return to where that one resides. He smiles at my nodding, which brings a smile to me as well.

Ra says We must return without pausing and I agree. We flow forth to hover over Ra's realm and he tells me that I must go to the vortex and return to my body-physical. He says that I will have an easier time of it now. I nod to him and thank him and then depart even as he is entering his own realm.

I flow toward the vortex and without hesitation, flow into it. I am flowing down into my body and adjusting the frequencies and consciousness. I feel quite comfortable. That is good. It is taking a little time and that is all right and appropriate. While entering my body I can feel the expansiveness of my consciousness adjusting itself to be incarnate.

I have returned.

So be it.

EIGHTH TRANSMISSION

I have a lot to channel and yet here I am, sitting for this continued speaking. Of all that I am scheduled to channel, this is what is calling me. I am bringing my consciousness to an expanded state and I will see if I journey directly to the Holy One's location or to Ra's realm.

I am expanding my consciousness further. I am now outside of Ra's realm and I see the portal. It is clear and golden as it always is. I focus on the symbols on the portal, round portal. They move and after a moment, the portal opens. I am entering and there is Alannah waiting. I nod to her and she says that I was wise to wait. I nod that I understand. There is a certain comfort in familiarity. Alannah says that comfort is real and the rest is but an illusion. She motions me toward Ra's large seating area. Ra is very large and I am expanding my consciousness to be able to reside with him. Ra nods good.

Now shall we go forth for the Sacred Text? I say yes, if my frequencies and consciousness is expanded enough. He laughs again. All right, let us journey forth to fulfill that purpose. I nod ok.

We are lifting out of Ra's realm and flowing forth into the white. We are coming upon the location of the Holy One's place and Ra says we will wait here for a moment to allow our frequencies to become more suitable for this purpose. I nod that I understand. I am still and not projecting. Ra says good.

After a little time, I can feel my consciousness expanding. The Holy One is here and he says, Ah! You have finally fully arrived. Good. Come this way for the Text is waiting to be received. We follow the Holy One.

We are stopped at an entryway and the Holy One says, Here is the location. Go forth now. Ra nods to the Holy One as do I and then the door opens to the chamber where we will receive, I believe, the Sacred Text. Ra nods yes and we are flowing forth to sit in our seats. I sit and Ra takes my hand and says, Now we will receive the next installment. I nod yes. I am ready.

> **These are the words.**
>
> In all of the residings upon earth, there is one that shifted the frequencies. There came forth three beings from a distant location, not even a planet, but a location in the frequencies of the All. The three beings not only observed earth, but flowed forth to reside upon earth. When they placed with physicality upon earth, the entirety of earth vibrated according to the truth that resided within those three beings. They were large beings, but not giants. They were filled with truth, yet they were not

FIRST LAYER OF THE SACRED TEXT

teachers. They began to journey upon the surface of the earth. And wherever they journeyed the beings who resided upon the surface of the earth parted ways and allowed them to journey. Even the giants stepped aside. It was not that they demanded such parting. More so, it was the frequencies of that which they were that caused such parting, *for truth is most powerful in its own manner.*

The three beings journeyed together and placed their walking upon all of the lands. They walked upon the sands, in the forests, upon the waters, and journeyed up the many mountains. No one wondered what they were doing. And that is because the consciousness of the three beings radiated outward in such a degree that no beings had any thoughts about them. The beings upon the earth simply parted so that the three could continue onward.

There came that moment when they had journeyed upon the entirety of the earth's surface. It was then that they decided they would journey within the earth as well, to walk upon the lands of the beings within the earth. The portal automatically opened for them and they entered, the portal closing behind them. The beings within the earth were delighted by the presence of the three. They invited the three to explore the entirety of their domain. The three did then journey throughout the land within the earth. The land itself reached upward to greet their steppings.

The three rested to be with the beings, as they entreated them to remain, yet after a time, the three departed from the land within, leaving joy and delight behind as it resided within those beings who resided therein.

The three beings determined that they would transform the surface of the earth. They stood upon the earth and presented to the earth what were their plans. The earth vibrated and also rejoiced at the plans. The three laid themselves down upon the earth and began a union with the earth. The earth embraced them and their frequencies.

Within the embracing, there formed upon the earth those frequencies of peace, of joy, of delight, of light heartedness. The three beings continued to radiate outward such frequencies and the earth received them and allowed herself to change, to be formed anew.

It wasn't that that which previously resided was no more. It was that the entirety of that which was made manifest upon the earth changed. *A new frequency resided upon the surface of the earth* and that which was became transformed in such a manner that if any of those beings would look to the past, they would not have recognized themselves, they were so changed. Yet they were. They continued to be. Yet all that resided within the cause and effect of the gatherings of beings began to release the hardships and newness of being developed.

Beings in different gatherings began to rejoice for no reason at all. They found they were filled with joy. Those who were leaders gave up their leadership and joined with the joy and delight No one found this to be amazing. It was the new frequencies that held all beings within them. And the three beings stood and viewed the transformation upon the surface of the earth. They were pleased.

And they began another walk upon the surface of the earth. They traveled to all lands, all mountains, all waters, all sands, all vegetation, and then all gatherings of beings. The gatherings surrounded them and loved them...not for what they had done because no one recognized that there was any past that had changed into the present. All beings were simply joyful and they were able to be in the presence of those three.

The three were most pleased. The three remained upon the surface of the earth for what could be called three cycles of the earth, three eras. And at the beginning of the fourth era, they determined that they would depart. No one knew that they would depart and in truth, none would miss them simply because all joy and delight filled all beings and had been for a very long time. The new manner of being was seated within the surface of the earth and earth herself was rejoicing.

The three beings departed the earth. Upon their departing, there was another shifting in the frequencies of earth's embodiment. The shifting arranged itself because the three were no longer present. The earth breathed a sigh of missing. The sigh of missing radiated outward and into all beings and all manners of being. Still, the frequencies were most fulfilling, yet there developed a pattern, *the pattern of missing*. Beings began to wonder what was actually missing, what had they done that caused them to miss something, the something they could not identify.

This began a new cycle upon earth. All was beautiful and joyful, yet the pattern of missing held itself firm within the frequencies of earth. The missing radiated outward and there were several from other planets who recognized the pattern and determined that they would explore what was missing upon the earth, what had changed. As they journeyed closer to the earth, they felt the beauty and the joy and it was that beauty and joy that attracted them to explore earth. During the times when the three had resided upon the earth, none came for the frequencies were most high.

Now there were new beings who began to reside upon earth and those that had been residing for the three eras welcomed the new beings. **The fourth**

era, then, was one of welcoming and embracing. The earth became populated with new beings from many many different planets and realms. This was the fourth era.

The fourth era remains. The histories of the earth and the beings who reside upon the surface of the earth are held within the fourth era, even though the cause and effect within those residings demonstrates chaos and destruction. Still, the frequencies of the three remain as part of the earth's firmament. This means that there is the history of these eras and *also the history of the releasing of the distortion in order to experience truth incarnate.* This resides upon the earth as part of the earth. It is a frequency most powerful.

Now we will depart from this speaking until the next transmission, for these frequencies dance forth to call forth from the earth the remembering of these eras. And this is the intention of this present speaking.

Then we will depart until the next.
So be it.

I am surprised by the words and look to Ra. He is smiling and nods to me that we must leave now. I am light-hearted from the speaking. Ra says that is what is radiating outward upon the earth now. We nod "good" to each other.

Now we are leaving the chamber and preparing to depart and the Holy One approaches us and says, Three beings into One Being. All is One.

The Holy One is holding a staff. Both Ra and I stand before the Holy One. The Holy One takes his staff and puts it on Ra's shoulder and then upon mine. Go now, he says, go now and be within the frequencies that hold you ever more. We both nod to the Holy One and Ra still holds my hand but begins to turn so that I know we must depart. I nod to the Holy One who is standing firm.

We flow forth from the whiteness and Ra says to me that I can return to my own residing now. I thank Ra and release his hand and I am now flowing back to my body.

I am entering my body and feel the expanded frequencies of my consciousness and will have to take my time. It is all right.

I am now entering my body. I have returned. I am grateful, truly grateful for all that has transpired in this day during this journey.

So be it.

SECOND LAYER OF THE SACRED TEXT

NINTH TRANSMISSION
First Speaking

I am expanding my consciousness in preparation for a journey with Ra to continue to receive the Sacred Text. I am seeing Teacher, which is a wonderful blessing and I am continuing to expand and journey to Ra's realm.

I am at the top of the vortex to my physicality and can see the area where Alannah and I have journeyed. I expand further and am approaching the portal to Ra's realm. I am being careful not to project for a multitude of reasons, mostly to not be tricked. The portal, round, is golden and bright as I approach. It opens for me and I can see Alannah motioning for me to enter. I do.

Alannah says that it is good that I came as there is much that is waiting to be expressed from the Sacred Text. I ask her how she knew that and she smiles and says, I just know. She is a wonderful being and I have had many journeys with her. She motions for me toward Ra. I can feel my consciousness changing. I see the large seat and then I hear Ra inviting me to flow forth to where he is, which is where we have sat together many times. I bypass the large seats and follow Ra's calling.

He says, Good. Now we will go forth for you are ready, as I can see by your consciousness. I nod yes and he takes my hand and we are flowing forth into the white. I believe we are flowing toward the Holy One's location and Ra says, Yes, we are. I am glad.

We seem to be stopped but Ra says that is the illusion of flowing toward the One's location. There is no time, he says, but we are approaching nonetheless. I nod that I understand. I can feel the frequencies of that location, very strong and can discern a golden light. Ra says, This is correct. We are now at the location where there is a golden light flowing forth from within the location. Ra says good. I don't recall a golden light flowing like this, usually it is white. Ra says, This is because this is a powerful releasing of the Sacred Text and all has been prepared by the Holy One. I nod that I understand.

The Holy One appears and looks to be pleased to see us. Good, he says, now go forth without hesitation. All is prepared for you both. Ra nods as do I. The Holy One motions with his arm and we are flowing in that direction. The entryway to the area where we sit is open already for us and we enter. Two seats are there, as they have been, but they are emanating golden light. Ra says, We will sit in the golden light. I nod ok.

We approach the seats and there is a sound, a musical sound that occurs when we approach. Ra says good. We each sit in our seat and Ra takes my hand. Now we shall proceed, he says. I nod ok. I don't recall what happens after this and perhaps that is good. I just wait. Ra says the words are coming and I open and allow.

These are those words.
From the beginning of what is called time, there have been many beings who have formed themselves within creation's spark. Some have flowed forth as spirit-beings while others have flowed forth into physicality. We, the keepers of this Sacred Text, are both. We are now asking if you will receive the Second Part of the Sacred Text into your being, for the next releasing of the text is more powerful and we wanted to allow you an adjustment period. I nod yes and say that I am grateful to receive and to participate.

There is a being before me, a slight physical image, but mostly spirit. The being says, That is because my frequencies are able to discern just that frequency that is the being's. The being says that there is much more to the presentation of its being but that is as much as I can discern, which is perfect for this moment, the being says. I bow my head to honor the being. The being does the same to me.

The Library where the Second Part of the Sacred Text resides.
We are now in the location where Ra did take the text from the library. The being smiles at me and says that is a good description of the location where the Second Part of the Sacred Text resides. The

being reaches into the volumes as if they are but essence and pulls forth a light. I wait to see. The being turns to me and holds out his hand and on the palm of his hand is a white globe. He says, this is the Second Part of the Sacred Text. If you will receive it, I will place it within your being. It will reside within your heart center. It will not harm you but will perhaps enhance your residing in physicality. I say that I am honored and yes, I accept the Second Part of the Sacred Text. The being nods yes and then reaches the palm toward my being. The white globe, filled with light, white light, flows forth toward my being. Ra has come to stand at my side and he holds my hand and whispers, So that you can remain incarnate, my dear, I am with you. I nod that I understand.

The globe flows into my being...no, I have rushed ahead. The globe pauses in front of my being. The being says, you will need to speak the words: *I accept this part of the Sacred Text into my being for the purpose of placing in words, the truths that reside therein.* I nod and speak those words. The being nods yes and the globe begins to turn around and around, emitting a sound, a tone or a group of tones. The being nods yes. I remain ready and Ra whispers, good.

The globe is now entering my being, the area of my heart energy center. It is warm and comfortable and the tones ring through my being...No, I assume

SECOND LAYER OF THE SACRED TEXT

that, but it is true. The sounds fill my spirit. The being says, Very good. I remain still. I feel my crown energy center more activated. The being says yes.

Now there come forth several beings in white robes or they are light beings, it is difficult to discern. Ra says it isn't important to discern. I nod that I understand. The beings come forth to face Ra and me. They are speaking in unison. They say: now you have the next installment of the Sacred Text. We place this within your being. We know you are the One who is receiving the Text, Sacred in all manners. I nod yes. They continue, Now the truths will flow forth. Place the words as you receive them. Do not change anything. I nod that I understand. The first being says to me, good. I am still.

The first being waves his arm and the others are no longer present to my knowing. The being says, good. They remain but they are not needed for your journey at this moment. I nod that I understand. The being says, Now you will return to allow to flow forth the Sacred Text. The being looks to Ra and says, You will be certain for the safety of this one? Ra nods yes. The being then says, Then I release you both to return to the location where you will allow the Text to flow forth. The holiness surrounds you. The being waves his arm and the library is no longer present to my discernment. Ra says good.

We are now returning to the location at the Holy One's chamber. Ra says we will now begin. I nod that

I am ready and we both then stand, rather than sit in the seats as before. Ra takes my hand and says, then we shall begin. I nod yes.

These are the words of the Second Part of the Sacred Text.

On the morning of the fourth day the Holy One stepped upon the firmament. The stepping caused the firmament to become. The becoming was simultaneous, both with the Holy One and the firmament, both taking form. The Holy One began the steppings upon the firmament, taking long strides. The seas parted and the Holy One continued the long strides until the steppings had crossed all of the firmament many times.

Upon the firmament there formed lighted pathways where the steppings had been placed. The Holy One stood and viewed the formings.

Next the Holy One breathed a breath outward and within the breath there was a golden spark. The golden spark took form upon the firmament. The Holy One breathed again and again and with each breath, the spark took form. The Holy One watched the forming.

The Holy One placed his finger into the firmament and there formed a hole in the firmament. The Holy One reached into the hole and pulled forth crystals, long and beautiful. The Holy One held the crystals upward and from the ethers there flowed forth a spark of light which formed as lightening.

SECOND LAYER OF THE SACRED TEXT

The lightening entered the crystals. The Holy One was pleased.

The Holy One placed the crystals, each one, standing upon the firmament. The Holy One breathed a breath upon the crystals as they stood with their point upward. The breath of the Holy One formed symbols and encodings upon the crystals, each one. The Holy One did then push the crystals into the firmament and cover the opening so that nothing was revealed. The Holy One did then release participation with the firmament.

The firmament remained until the turning of the formings and a new era was birthed. The Holy One returned to step upon the firmament. The stepping activated the hidden crystals with the encodings. Then the Holy One departed once again. The encodings within and upon the crystals radiated outward and there formed within the firmament those frequencies of Holiness of Being.

Holiness of Being held within it the forming of all that would be formed upon the firmament. And within the radiating outward there came to be pulse beats of forming. The pulse beats established the natural rhythm of the firmament.

Once the forming had completed its turning, the crystalline radiating ceased. Now there comes forth One who receives the symbols and breathings into...

[I have been typing much and look up and none of what I have typed is present. I can only think that it was not correct or that it is not allowed to be presented. I will continue and allow. This is a surprise. I am continuing.]

...into words. These are those words. I allow and wait.

This is the Second Layer of the Sacred Text. These words now do flow forth. The previous words were given yet they are of an illusion. Now these words flow forth. The illusion was created to turn away those who would desire to change the Sacred Text. That has been accomplished and now the speaking flows forth for you are the One to allow them to flow forth. I nod yes. Then we shall begin.

These are the words flowing forth, Truth of Sacred Text.

Truth radiates forth into firmament. Truth holds within it histories that determine the nature of the formings upon the firmament. Truth holds within it the frequencies of those histories that many want to believe, yet the histories of the firmament are not known in their entirety. The histories of the firmament of that which has been named earth flow forth in this manner.

The firmament of the earth remained for many turnings of creation. From the locations within the earth where resided the crystalline structures which had increased from their first implanting, there emerged several beings from each location. The beings were formed of the firmament and the holiness of the frequencies of the crystals and the encodings upon the crystals. The encodings upon the crystals were placed within the beings and the beings then held within themselves patterns that determined their own manner of presentation of creation. Each being was different from the other. This began the residing upon the firmament that later became earth.

The beings ventured forth upon the firmament. There was not intent to explore or discover. There was simply the going forth, for movement came to be. The movement of the beings created upon the firmament, pathways. Many turnings of the histories occurred before the beings' movement brought them to each other. In the meeting of the beings with each other, there radiated upon the firmament great sounds. The sounds flowed upward from the crystalline structures within the firmament. Where there was a meeting of the beings, there was then created a globe of light. The beings stood within the globe of light and there was then an infusing within the beings of the remainder of the encodings of the structures, the crystalline structures that were originally placed by the Holy One.

This is the remainder of those encodings.

Now you are created of Holiness of Being. Now you are known to each other as the One Being. Each one is the other and the other is the One Being. The One Being always resides upon earth. The One

Being holds within itself all encodings of all creation. The One Being is often hidden from the knowing of the others. There will be the turning of the histories where there will be the revealing of the One Being. The One Being is the Many and the Many is the One Being.

The One Being as the many and the many as the One Being will speak truths beyond the understanding of the many. This speaking will cause what is called the distortion or the illusion that the many are separate from the One Being. The One Being will reach forth into the many and hold to the frequencies within the many. The many will weep for the seeming loss of the One Being. This will be the journey upon the earth.

The many will seek the One Being and the One Being will embrace the many until there is an understanding of the known. This journey of truth will reside upon earth. *Earth is the proving ground for those who have been captured by the illusion of power and illusion of success before all others.* The many hold within them the original frequencies and encodings of the original crystalline structures. It will be called DNA, yet it is more. It is the encoding of the original creation upon the firmament.

The One being says, I am the breath of your being. I am the vision of your being. I am the pulse beat of your forming. I am the spark of your creation. I am the forming of you and I am the forming itself. I am the essence of the firmament and I am the firmament holding the encodings of that which you are. I am the spark within the crystalline structures and I am the unknown within your being, for you are the many and I am the Holy One. I am the many. You are the Holy One. Truth vibrates within these words. You are now called to know. I am the many who hear the call. I am the Holy One delivering the call. I am the giving and receiving. I am the totality of being. All beings, the many of the One, are totality of being. Your breath is my breath. My breath is your breath. None can be, either you or I, without the same breath. Now the known has been revealed.

This then begins a new era where upon the firmament there resides truth within the many and truth within the One. The truth within the many is that they are One Being. The truth within the One is that the many do not remember.

The One places itself within the many and remembers. This is the expanding of frequencies into a new manner of residing. Some of the many refuse to allow their remembering to reside. The One enters those ones and breathes truth forth. Those ones hold the truth in a sacred pocket of their entirety of being.

One day they will allow the pocket to open and fill them with truth. The One resides within those many and holds the key to the pocket. When the many are ready, the One will open the pocket and the flood of truth will fill totality incarnate upon the firmament. This opening rests upon the many, for such opening cannot be forced for in truth there is no such thing as forcing creation itself. The One remains as truth and resides within the many as the many. The many reside within the One, for totality cannot be refused of itself.

This then is the first speaking of the Second Part of the Sacred Text. It has been received and placed within words correctly. Then this is complete for this receiving.

So be it.

The receiving or flowing forth stops and I am looking at Ra. He is nodding to me that all is good. Then he says that it is time that we depart. I nod yes and we flow forth from the chamber and the Holy One greets us and says, Now you have begun the true receiving. *Truth will be made manifest, as it always is.* Ra nods to the Holy One as do I. Then the Holy One motions with his arm that we are to depart. We do as the Holy One stands to watch us depart. I nod my head to the Holy One and that One does then nod back to me. It feels very special.

Now we are flowing into the white and Ra says that I must return to my body physical. I nod that I understand and begin that journey, but first I say to Ra that I am so very grateful for all that he is assisting me to do. Ra says, Yes, my dear. It is what we are doing together…since the beginning of time. I smile at his words because he has often says that time is an illusion. This causes Ra to laugh and to motion me to return to my body. I nod back and begin to release my presence from his realm.

Alannah is at the portal and she too is smiling. I nod to her and flow through the opening which closes behind me. I am once again enjoying the location where I once traveled with Alannah. I approach my vortex and flow into it. I am flowing back into my body physical. It is easy. I am nearly anchored within this body. My body is covered with chills. It is the frequencies aligning, I am sure. I open my eyes. I have returned. I have much to reflect upon. Grateful.

So be it.

TENTH TRANSMISSION
Second Speaking

I have barely an hour before we are to leave and I am called to continue to allow the speaking to flow forth. I will begin now. I have re-read the last powerful words and am ready. I expand my consciousness. I am flowing now to Ra's realm. I am emerging from my vortex and am now flowing through the land where I journeyed with Alannah. It is beautiful here but I will not delay approaching the portal to Ra's realm.

As I approach the portal I hear drumming as if from a group of beings who are drumming together. I see the portal but it is dissolving before my eyes. I will pause, for this is not usual and it might be trickery. I expand my consciousness and radiate it forth toward what might be the portal. The drumming diminishes and becomes as a layer of white cloud. I wait. My consciousness is expanding further and I can feel the power of the Sacred Text within me. From the heart of my being, the heart center, there bursts forth a stream of light. All that was a distortion is dissolved. I am before the true portal and it is golden and the symbols are moving. I stand before it and request entry into Ra's realm. This is not usual, but it feels to be correct. The portal opens and within there is a clearing of the frequencies. Ra is standing there at the portal, where Alannah usually stands. Ra says, Enter and we must depart immediately. I nod and enter. Ra says good.

He takes my hand and says we must begin now. We will go to the Holy One's location that was prepared for us. I nod ok. We are then in a moment seemingly not moving. I understand this differently now. We are beyond time. I have paused to tell Grayson what I am doing. Now Ra and I are approaching the Holy One's location.

As we approach and wait, the Holy One comes forth and says, There is no such thing as hurry here. No time. No hurry. Yet there is a type of immediacy that occurs with the frequencies of the Sacred Text. The immediacy is but an interpretation of the clarity of the frequencies that hold what will become the words. Yet I am proud that you have come once again. Then I will not keep you from your participation with this what could be called astounding revealing. *This has not been done before, I hope you understand this. This Sacred Text has remained hidden for eternity* and now is being revealed through the words that you place. The words, you must remember, are frequencies which hold the Sacred Text within them. That is why the exact placing of the words is necessary. But you know this to be true. The Holy One looks to me and I say that I know this to be true. The Holy One nods to me and then to Ra and motions his arm that we are to proceed. I bow my head again as does Ra and we are then flowing toward the chamber, I believe.

SECOND LAYER OF THE SACRED TEXT

Ra says, We are flowing toward the chamber but it might appear to be a bit different each time, as the frequencies of the Sacred Text call forth a holiness that embodies the location where the frequencies are revealed. I nod that I understand.

We are now in a type of nothingness. Ra says yes. There is a swirling around us. All is white. Ra says I am perceiving white because there is nothing and my presence calls forth a presentation because I am incarnate. I nod that I understand. We wait. Ra says that waiting is but an interpretation. I nod that I understand and remain still with my mind. Ra says good.

Now a swirling comes about me. It is like a column of light that is flexible and surrounds me. Ra still holds my hand but I cannot see that he is also encased. Ra says all is well. I am within a frequency that is gentle and embracing. I am to allow the words from the Text to flow forth from here, as this embracing will assist the best possible placing of the words. Ra says good.

The frequencies are powerful and I am allowing.

These are the words.

Anaktah Solientoh Seetah. Now the truths flow forth in a manner that the all can reside within them. For there are words that have been written and are called holy words, yet they contain a portion of the totality of truth. This is all that could flow forth during the times of the placing of those truths within physicality. Physicality diminishes truth's frequency simply because physicality is. Within physicality there are those frequencies that flow forth to incarnate wholeness. Wholeness within physicality is but a manner of expressing truth, yet even wholeness is unable to be present within physicality as it is present in the non-physicality of the All.

Now the frequencies within physicality are transforming and there is a calling forth once again for truth to be made manifest. There are those who would choose to mold truth to their understandings. Truth cannot be molded. Yet there have been those instances where truth flowed forth, was received in physicality, and then presented in a near perfect manner. All was rejoicing in this presentation.

There then came forth those who found or discovered the truth presented, being made manifest, and interpreted truth in ways that distorted the pristine nature of that truth. At times this action was deliberate and at other times the action was through ignorance of truth itself. Both instances distorted the pristine nature of truth and within that distortion there formed beliefs and dogmas. The beliefs and dogmas have determined the nature of consciousness as it resided upon the firmament. Consciousness is a totality. Just as all beings are one, totality resides within consciousness, even though it has been distorted, still truth resides through frequencies. The consciousness upon the firmament holds the frequencies of truth, yet it also holds within it the distortions that are presented through beliefs and dogmas. This consciousness determines the journey upon the holy firmament.

The journey upon the firmament contains a dedication to totality, as it is presented within truth incarnate. This dedication holds within it a slight emptiness. The slight emptiness rests upon the pocket of truth that remains hidden and closed. There are some beings who have dared to open that pocket of truth and then have been overwhelmed by the frequencies of truth in such a manner that they were held in a blissful state. Their consciousness changed. Their consciousness changing also changed the consciousness that resides upon the firmament. The rippling of the changed consciousness upon the firmament called forth from those who were still maintaining the absence of truth even whilst they proclaimed the distorted truth, called forth a magnetic desire to merge as one.

The magnetic desire to merge as one rested upon the Truth of One. Because the Truth of One is, then the magnetic pull to such truth is part of the illusion of separation from the whole. Yet the magnetic pull to truth, because truth is, can begin the dissolving of the distortion which holds the beliefs and dogmas of the many. Such dissolving has caused fear, for those who have held to the beliefs and dogmas have created those beliefs and dogmas to be the holy one.

Such holding declares the untruth in such a manner that there is a denying of the whole, a denying of the many as the One and the One as the many. This denying causes a ripple of distortion within the consciousness upon the firmament. Still, there is the calling forth of those ones to release their hold upon the distortion.

Again and again, this calling flows forth as a magnetic embrace, demonstrating wholeness of being even in the direst distortion. Within the direst distortion there resides such emptiness that the pocket of truth has then released but a thread of itself into the beings. The thread of truth released from itself continues to breathe a breath of relief into those ones who reside within the direst of untruth. Such breath of relief causes a drop of relief in the consciousness of the firmament. The drop of relief within the consciousness of the firmament sends forth a sound which calls forth all beings to embrace all beings. This embracing causes the weeping of those in the direst of untruth, for there is a recognizing that they are empty of totality. There is no such thing as emptiness of totality, yet within the beliefs and dogmas there has been created the belief of lack, the belief of need, the belief of emptiness and the belief of unworthiness as the reason for the seeming emptiness. The creation of unworthiness flows forth as a dense frequency that the firmament allows simply because the firmament allows the All and the All is all. The density flows forth and has flowed forth for what could be called a very long time in the keeping of the illusion of time.

In the keeping of the illusion of time, the One did come forth and did come forth to place a walking upon the firmament. The placing of the stepping of the One upon the firmament, activates the crystalline structures to a new frequency. The new frequency then radiates upward and fills the consciousness that resides upon the firmament. Such merging of frequencies causes the consciousness upon the firmament to be as if cleansed. The cleansed consciousness upon the firmament holds within it all beings. Those who have resided in the direst of untruth can no longer reside within the density of the untruth as it itself is transformed by the truth of the frequencies from the crystalline structures, activated by the stepping of the One upon the firmament.

Once the frequencies have changed, the One then departs, *for there is then the beginning of what could be called a new era.* The new era holds all beings within it. There is not one being who is not within the new era. This must be so because all is one and all beings are one being. *If one being resides within the new era, then all beings reside within the new era. This is truth incarnate.*

The new era is the turning of the firmament toward an embracing of truth made manifest. This causes a rumbling of the firmament as it releases all distortion that had been created through untruth and beliefs and dogmas. During the rumblings, there is a releasing of dark clouds from the firmament. The One observed the releasing of the untruth and allowed the rumbling to continue until all that was created was no more. The firmament begged to be made new. Yet the One did not step again upon the firmament, but continued to observe.

As the One is all beings and all beings are the One, then the many did become the one incarnate once again in their consciousness. Within such consciousness there flowed forth the restoration of what is called the pristine firmament. It was then that the One did come forth and step once again upon the firmament. Such stepping embraced the many and the new era was then seated within the firmament and within the consciousness that resides upon the firmament.

There is no doing in the new era. There is being. And within the being, there is then formed all that is required for the residing incarnate upon the firmament. All is made manifest in the moment and the many then embrace what is made manifest and the residue of the old manners are dissolved within the consciousness of the many. The pockets of truth are spread wide and truth, then the treasure of truth being held, is released into the totality and this releasing brings the totality to another new era. It is then that the holding of the truth is recognized as an integral part of the manifesting of the new era in which all beings are one being and one being is all beings. The many is then the One and the One is the many and this one truth resides in totality within the consciousness. Then there is no distortion within the physicality for all is one in consciousness.

This then is the reforming of beingness, for there is no need nor is there distortion to fill such illusionary need. All is holy and the holiness is the One and the One is the many. This is the Truth of the One. This is the history of the One. This is the history of the many. This is the history of the consciousness as it resides upon and within the firmament. All else is but the All and is held within the All as the one. Then there is no such thing as *all else*. It is but a figment of the past's need, a distortion no longer necessary.

Then this is the second speaking of the Second Part of the Sacred Text. We are the Keepers of the Text and we have observed such rendering of truth and now declare this to be as accurate as words can be, yet to know that the words hold frequencies and that is truly the rendering of the Truth of the Sacred Text. Then for this speaking, we the Keepers of the Sacred Text speak the words so be it. Until the next speaking.

So be it.

The flowing was fast and clear and now I am with Ra and the swirling that was woven around me is unweaving and I am released of those frequencies. Ra is still holding my hand for which I am grateful. Ra says that I must return now, that the flowing of the Sacred Text was a high frequency and I must return to physicality to assure I am incarnate. I nod that I understand. We flow forth from the area of the Holy One who stands to greet us. The Holy One nods to us and motions for us to continue departing. I nod back and smile at the Holy One, who much to my pleasure, smiles back at me.

Now we are flowing away and Ra is telling me that I will go directly to my vortex. I nod that I understand. As I flow toward my vortex, Ra releases my hand and says that all is well. I nod that I understand and then see that Alannah is standing at the top of my vortex. She is also smiling and motions for me to return. I bow my head to her for she is a blessing in my journey. Alannah whispers, You are doing very well. Know this to be true. All is proceeding most wondrously. She nods to me and I accept her nod and then I do the same to her.

Then I am flowing down the vortex and into my body physical. It is an easy flowing. My consciousness is quite expanded but I m now residing in my body. It has been a very full experience. I am ok, of course.

I speak the words so be it.
So be it.

SECOND LAYER OF THE SACRED TEXT

ELEVENTH TRANSMISSION
Third Speaking

I am now expanding my consciousness, setting aside this physicality. I am coming to be in the land where Alannah used to meet. And I am enjoying it for a moment and then am flowing forth towed Ra's realm and the portal to his realm. I hear bells ringing and people singing or chanting. I'm not sure I projected that or not. I am clearing my thoughts again. I am at Ra's portal and as I stand before it I am waiting. I don't sense any distortion and I will breathe my breath upon the portal. I do that.

My breath is as if breathing in a very cold climate, it is white. The front of the portal opening is covered with ice. But that dissipates and I am standing before the golden portal. I ask permission to enter. I haven't done this before as I recall, but I have the sense that is what I am to do now. The portal opens as if from a vacuum seal as it makes a sound. I wait. I hope to see Alannah. I don't. I'm not sure whether to enter through this portal. I wait.

I sense much nonsense happening and step back. Something has shifted. I sense Ra coming with his robes flaring outward as he is approaching quickly. He waves his arm and all that was nonsense dissipates. Ra says to me,

Come along. We will depart this frequency and journey to where we need to be. I look to see Ra and recognize his frequencies and flow toward him. He takes my hand immediately and we are as if in a void. Ra whispers to me, Good that you have come in this day. There have been some shenanigans going on and I have little patience for them. I smile. Ra laughs.

Ra says, We will go now, but do not think of what we have been doing. Just keep your mind blank, as blank as you can. I nod ok. We flow forth, upward and into the white. I am relieved. Ra says that there might be similar occurrences during other times, but he will always be there and for me not to participate with anything if he is not present. I nod that I understand. I am glad for the clarity.

Now we are flowing to the Holy One's location. Ra says it is all right for me to focus on that but nothing else. I nod ok. We are flowing in non time, which gives the illusion or appearance that we are not moving, but I know from previous times that we are moving quite fast. Ra laughs at my words.

Ra says, Now we will go forth into our purpose. I nod ok. We are at the entryway of the Holy One's place and I can sense the Holy One's coming forth.

He does. He says, Ah! You are here! Good. Now go forth to your usual and I will see that the way is cleared and that you will not be disturbed. It seems some of the realms have been flooded with little ones who deem it necessary to play nearly everywhere. I have cleared my realm and I suggest you do the same when you return, he says to Ra. Ra nods yes. The One says, All right now, follow me!

SECOND LAYER OF THE SACRED TEXT

We are right behind the One and come upon the portal to our usual location. The Holy One says that this location is clear and to not be concerned for interruptions. They will now be allowed, he says with a stern voice. Both Ra and I nod to the Holy One and then the portal opens and we enter. The Holy One looks in to be sure we are fully residing in the chamber and then the portal is closed. We are in the chamber.

I can feel my consciousness expanding. Ra says good.

These words flow forth.

We are the Keepers of the Sacred Text. To you do we release the frequencies that will become words as best made manifest in your physicality. There is much to release and much for you to receive. I bow my head and say that I am humbly grateful.

Then we will begin, they say to me. I nod yes.

These are the words released from the Sacred Text.

There came forth, weaving through all that was created, a frequency gathered together like a formed tunnel. It wove itself on to the firmament and through all that had been created thus far. It was the color of blue, yet a blue with smoke swirling within it. It was neither good or bad, distorted or non-distorted. It simply was created by the frequencies that were emitted from those who resided upon the firmament and who reached outward for a new experience. The reaching out for a new experience

151

was natural, for the reaching was residing in a slower frequency. A slower frequency was neither good nor bad simply because all frequencies are of one frequency.

Yet, because the beings reached out for a new experience, their reaching out was resting upon a slight return to a pale remembrance of the past where there was cause and effect being made manifest in a different way than was currently on the firmament. This reaching out called forth that which wove upon the surface of the firmament. It wove around those ones who had the wanting of a new experience, and the taste of a remnant of the past excited those ones and they followed the flowing of the formed tunnel. The formed tunnel, as those ones came closer, became.

This then was the entry of time into the firmament's presence. For all wanting is resting upon an illusion of separation from fulfillment, and such resting must include the illusion of time in order to fulfill the separation from the fulfillment in the moment, which continued to occur with those ones on the firmament who held their consciousness in the highest frequency, not because they were better or more spiritual. They held that frequency because it was the most natural for their presence upon the firmament.

With the presence of time, though it was encased within the formed tunnel, the frequencies of the firmament changed in order to accommodate that presence. The shifting caused nature itself to embrace the frequencies of time, for nature embraced all that was made manifest upon the firmament.

This birthed a great illusion. The great illusion presented itself between those who were residing in the highest frequency and those who had embraced time, which promoted the illusion of separation, the present moment separated from its fulfillment by time and what came to be called the future. This caused a great distortion upon the firmament.

Those who were residing in the highest frequencies tried to breathe their breath into the illusion and though they did not consider that it would occur, this action accentuated the illusion of separation, simply because their action rested upon interpreting the presentation of time and those who embraced it as a separation from that which they enjoyed. This illusion of separation from the whole resting upon the presence of time rippled through the entire firmament and more and more beings began to embrace, because of their memories of the past now remembered through time's presence, the possibility of future.

The One saw what was occurring and came forth to step once again upon the firmament. The stepping caused a rippling upon the firmament and the rippling caused a further separation. Those who resided in the highest frequencies were lifted upward into a new realm. Those who embraced time experienced a great shaking of the illusion and there was birthed once again upon the firmament, fear. The One gathered the fear and breathed a breath upon it. Fear transformed to rain and the rain fell upon the firmament. *The rain washed from the beings the yearning for future and the belief of better.* It was a powerful cleansing that cleared the firmament of those illusions.

The clearing of the illusions left the beings with nothing to hold on to, for their security had formed in their projections into the future and then the planning of how to manifest that future. The breath did not remove the river of time, however it did remove the distorted beliefs. The One saw that time was not compatible with freedom to reside upon the firmament. The One then gathered the river of time and encased it within a globe. The One then placed the globe within a pocket of the robe that the One wore upon his being. The absence of time upon the firmament left those ones residing there in a confused manner. They did not know how to relate to the firmament without time, without the distortion and without their plans. Again the One breathed a breath upon those ones. For, the One had a great love for all beings.

These ones came to be as peace. There was no wanting, no fear, and no need. All was still. Truly, the beings didn't know how to be, how to simply be. The One did call forth those who were residing within the highest frequency and they did flow forth to the firmament. Their presence uplifted those ones who were seemingly lost. As the ones from the highest frequency came about those one who were seemingly lost, they did embrace them with love and caring and began to teach them how to live, how to be, how to laugh, how to play. As the play and laughter resided upon the firmament once again, the One departed and left the many to be as the many and the One to be the many. All was peaceful. All was content. All was of beauty.

The contentment and beauty remained upon the firmament, until there came from another realm a gathering of beings who saw the firmament to be desirable. *This began another era, for those ones did bring with them the patterns and frequencies of conquering.* They did not recognize that their presence would change the nature of that which they admired. They only knew that they enjoyed the firmament. They were of a more dense presentation and because of their presentation in physicality as more dense, they did not see or notice that there were other beings present on the firmament. In truth, they came to believe that they were the only ones upon the firmament.

Then there came to be more beings from other realms who journeyed forth and discovered the firmament. They too were more dense and as they came to the firmament, they were also not aware of the original beings, neither were they aware of the beings who had believed they were the only ones residing upon the firmament which they enjoyed.

Those ones could perceive the new beings who were more dense and they decided that they did not want them to reside upon the firmament. They began to cause difficulties for those ones in the hopes that they would depart. Yet those ones, the most dense thus far, began a practice of shifting their awareness and through this practice could they discern those ones who were causing difficulties. This began a battle, a slight battle initially, but as their success ebbed and flowed, the battle became more present until both parties were able to discern each other and the battle for the firmament proceeded.

Those ones who were first to reside upon the firmament observed what was occurring and knowing that they were as invisible because of the frequencies in which they resided, continued to observe. They could not understand what was occurring.

It was then that the One stepped forth upon the firmament once again. The stepping was deliberate and with the stepping there came great rumblings upon and within the firmament. The firmament uplifted itself, the firmament pulled apart and came together. The surface of the firmament reformed itself.

When the reforming was complete, there were few still remaining, some were of the density of physicality, yet most of those who remained were of the higher frequencies and those they had assisted in knowing how to live.

There then flowed forth from the consciousness of those ones in the highest frequencies, the truth that all beings were one being and that all beings made the many and the many was the One and the One was the many. Those who could not accept this truth fled into the great caverns that had opened within the firmament. When the firmament shifted once again, the entryways to the caverns closed and those ones resided within the firmament while the remaining resided upon the surface of the firmament.

All of these occurrences changed the frequencies upon the firmament. There was a reforming and there was also an attempt by those who remained to gather together and to reside in holiness of being. The One saw what was occurring and came upon the firmament and gathered those ones who remained. With the gathering there was then the breathing forth of the One into and upon all of those that had been gathered. Such breathing caused those ones to be transported to a dimension where there was rest and peace. The One held the dimension in his being and allowed those ones to reside within his being, for the One was the many and the many were the One. Now the One caused a shifting so that all was residing in the present moment. This determined the dissolving of that called time, for there were none who resided upon the firmament and were captured by the essence of time. Those who resided within the firmament were as if asleep...for a very longtime, as time was their companion.

Now the One comes forth to observe the firmament and all who reside upon and within the firmament. The One is ready to step once again and those who reside in truth are knowing of the One and the stepping and the holiness of the moment. Those ones know that only the moment is. And it is this knowing that is pausing the One from stepping most directly upon the firmament. And there is a pause because within the firmament there is still the holding of that which is called time. The One is pleased at the pause and is allowing the forming of the firmament toward fulfillment to occur.

The pause is the breathing inward of the holy breath, which will breathed outward when the pause releases itself. All is well. The One is the many and the many are the One. The firmament is the breath of the One and the breath of the One is the breath of the many. The breath of the many is the breath of the One. All is well.

Then we believe this is the speaking of the Sacred Text to its best fulfillment in words. Until we speak again, we are the Keepers of the Sacred Text. Until we speak again, we are complete.
So be it.

I am filled with peace and my consciousness is quite expanded. Ra has my hand and is telling me that all is well and that we must depart. I nod that I understand. As we move toward the portal, it opens and there is the Holy One standing, waiting for us. Good! he exclaims. Good! Now you must depart for I have disciplined the little ones and they have returned to their proper alignment. Ra laughs and I smile at the Holy One's words.

Then we are following the Holy One down an inner walkway and out to the area where we usually meet. The Holy One motions for us to depart, but pauses for a moment and says, You both are doing something magnificent. You know that, don't you? Good, he says as we do not respond but look to the Holy One's face. Now depart. We both nod to him and then we do that, we depart. I look back and see that the Holy One is watching us depart. I wave my hand and the Holy One smiles. I like that.

We are now returning through a seeming void. Ra says good. Now we are entering Ra's realm, it seems and he is motioning for me to sit beside him in my seat. I do that and Ra says: Now we will be entering into a more expanded frequency with the next receiving and releasing. You will be able to do this, I am certain. Yet I will hold the frequencies for you to receive and to place the words. I want you to know this so that you will be more prepared and focused. I thank Ra and he says, good…now you must return to your physicality.

I look into his eyes and see vastness. Then he blinks his eyes and the vastness is concealed. I thank Ra and he nods yes. Then I am flowing toward the portal and much to my enjoyment, there is Alannah who is motioning me toward the portal as she usually does. I nod to her and she says that I will go to my vortex on my own, as she will remain guard at the portal. I nod that I understand.

I flow forth to my vortex and am a bit anxious to return. Flowing down the vortex, I am returning to my body physical. I will anchor myself. I am home now.

So be it.

I am grateful for this releasing and receiving.

So be it.

THIRD LAYER OF THE SACRED TEXT

TWELFTH TRANSMISSION
First Speaking

I am sitting now and bringing my consciousness to a more expanded state and will now journey to Ra's realm. I am now approaching the portal. As I flow closer, the portal seems to be further away. I wait. There is an image of the entire entryway crumbling. I know this to be an illusion and wait. I ask Teacher to help me.

Teacher tells me all is well. I am required to let go of the thought that I did something wrong by waiting seven days, during which I channeled the class and also a private session. I say that in my defense and realize that is what is occurring. I have to leave self-blame aside. It is a tempting human pattern. Teacher nods yes to me. Teacher says, My dear, go forth now. All awaits your presence and participation. I thank Teacher and flow toward the portal.

I am now before the golden portal. I see the symbol of OM and I bring my consciousness to that symbol. It dissolves and the portal spins in a circular motion. I declare my purpose and choose to enter Ra's realm if he is agreeable. The portal opens as if under pressure, making the sound of releasing pressure as it opens. I wait. I see nothing.

I am not projecting and allow. Ra stands before me and motions me into his realm. I still wait. Ra waves his arm and we are now residing in another location. Still I wait. I am not sure of this Ra.

Then I see the whiteness where the Holy One usually resides and I see that Holy One walk toward me. The Holy Ones says, As you have spoken previously, you will not go forth without Ra, then we will wait for his presence. I ask, how did I come to be here? The Holy One says, I brought you here. There is much foolery going on and I wished for you to be free of it. I nod and say thank you.

I can hear horns blowing far away and feel the rush of energy. The Holy One says, Good. Now Ra comes. Ra arrives and stands beside me. He nods to me and says good and then nods to the Holy One and says, I have come from the pyramid and those who hold the Sacred Text. They are saying that the text needs to be written now. The Holy One says, then so it shall. Follow me.

The Holy One turns and proceeds and Ra takes my hand and we follow. Ra whispers to me, all is well. Remember that. I nod ok. As we go forth, my consciousness is really expanding now. The Holy One stops and waves his arm and the whiteness clears and there is a scene of green grasses and trees and a smallish body of water. The Holy One turns to me and says, Good. Now it is here that you will receive the next part of the Sacred Text. This transmission requires nature and this location will be best. It is protected and will hold you and Ra as everything transpires. I nod thank you.

THIRD LAYER OF THE SACRED TEXT

Ra steps forth and waves his arm and two seats appear, seats familiar to the way that we have sat previously. The Holy One says, Good, now proceed, not a moment is to be paused. I nod that I understand and move toward the seat, but Ra holds me back a little and says to the Holy One, Now there must be some kind of presentation in the physical world for this one. There would then be an uplift which would benefit her and I believe is needed. Ra waits. The Holy One is as if contemplating the statement and then says, You are right. Yes you are. I will see to it. Ra says, Good and nods in respect.

The Holy One then turns to me and says, You are very brave to be incarnate now upon the earth. I seem to shrug my shoulders, but I do not mean it as a disrespect. The Holy One laughs and says, You do not know, do you. I see that you do not. Then I say this to you: Do not fear for your residing incarnate. You are protected and cared for. I nod that I understand, but the Holy One continues. I will send something for you. It will uplift your spirit. I nod thank you. The Holy One begins to say something and then pauses. All right now, the Holy One continues, I will see to it. Now you must go forth to fulfill this purpose. Do not concern yourself with feelings or questions of worthiness or if you are capable. These are illusionary frequencies of a lower vibration. Just let them go. Do not engage with them. He looks to me to see that I understand. I nod yes. Good, the Holy One says, now I will depart and you will begin. He turns to Ra and says, You are right. You have been right all along and I am pleased to say it. Ra nods yes. The two look into each other's eyes and everything is paused. There is a swirling around...Ra shakes

165

his head no and says, that is a projection. Now you are powerful enough to project within this realm and you must be most careful not to do that. I nod that I understand. The Holy One says, Good. Now begin.

Ra moves me toward the seats and he and I sit each in a seat. Ra says, Now we will bring ourselves to the frequency of this next transmission. I nod that I understand. Ra sees that I am holding a happy feeling now, one that is about the Holy One giving me something. Ra smiles and says it is all right to feel happiness. It is a strong uplifting frequency. I smile and nod that I understand.

Now there appears before us the library and the Keepers of the Sacred Text are before us. We are standing. The One comes forth and nods to Ra and then looks to me. He says, Now you will begin another part of the Sacred Text. It is the Third Layer of the frequencies that hold the content of this Sacred Text. I nod that I understand. This being then holds out his right hand and upon the palm there forms a globe, a small globe. He says, now you will receive this into your being, for it holds this transmission. I nod that I understand and that I am agreeable with what he is saying. Ra is still holding my hand, which is a good feeling.

The being places his hand before my heart area and the globe flows forth and into my heart. It is a strong frequency and a shrill sound accompanies it as it situates itself within my heart energy center. The being breathes a breath across his open palm and the breath flows into my heart energy center. The shrill sound stops and there is peace. The being looks to me and asks, Are you comfortable with this frequency, for it will increase if you are. I say that I am.

Next the beings behind the one being begin to sway and to chant and the one being raises his arms upward. A golden light flows from above the being and into his being through the crown energy center. Then it flows outward from his heart energy center and then into my heart energy center. I am filled with golden light. Whatever is my persona is no more. I am golden light. Ra is still holding my hand. My consciousness is so expanded that I nearly fall asleep in physicality. Ra begins to speak softly a language I do not know. It is a bit familiar. It pulls my focus back to the present and I am able to remain with the golden light within me.

The being turns around and around which stops the golden light from continuing to enter my being. When the being stops turning, the others stop chanting and swaying. All is still. The being motions to two seats in this chamber and says that is where Ra and I will sit now. I nod that I understand. The being motions us to follow him to the seats and then he motions us to sit. Both Ra and I go to sit, but I am still standing. I say to the being, I must stand. He nods that he understands and says that if during the transmission I feel that I would lose consciousness, then to sit in the seat, as it holds frequencies that will align with the transmission and will assist me. I nod that I understand. Ra is also standing with me. The being nods to us both and we do the same to the being and to the others. The being says, then it is time to begin. I nod to him and then begin.

[I have taken a short break to communicate with Grayson and now I will begin, bringing my consciousness expanded once again. Maybe it was a necessary break, I don't know. All is well. I am returning to the expanded frequencies and the being is standing before me to see that I am returned. I nod that I am and the being smiles to me. He says, you are most adept at this. I say I will begin now. He nods ok.]

This is the transmission of this Third Layer of the Sacred Text.

The speaking is in a language I do not know and I am waiting for the translation. It seems to be beginning with the words "The sirens sounded upon the earth..." I am waiting to see if that is correct.

Now it begins...

The great beings, the creatures residing upon the earth opened their mouths, their great mouths and from them came a screeching, as if sirens. The sound of one joined with the sound of another and the atmosphere upon the earth began to fill with patterns. The patterns held within them the birthing of a species of beings who would reside upon the earth. The great creatures continued for three days and three nights. Upon the fourth day there was silence. Each day held what could be called thirty-six hours.

In the silence there began a drumming. It was the sound of the giants stepping forth to reside in the silence. Their steppings resonated through the earth. The giants came from all directions as they walked upon the power lines upon the earth. They continued to walk until there came a meeting upon the land where later was created the Pyramid of Chichén Itzá. There was no pyramid when the giants gathered.

When the giants came together from all of the distances, there was created a vortex where they met. The vortex descended into the earth and then from deep within the earth there came forth three beings. One being was a woman who held the holiness of all women. The second was a child who held the innocence of all who would become children upon the land of the earth, yet there were no children, only this one. The third being was a guardian of the two. The three beings presented themselves before the giants and the giants knelt down before the three beings.

The three beings bowed to the giants and then the woman stepped forth and spoke to the giants in their own language. She said there would be beings from a distant star who would come to reside upon the earth and she asked the giants to protect them. The giants bowed their heads to the woman, saying that they would do as she bid. Then they stood and began to walk toward the direction from which they came. The woman sang their song as they departed.

The child stood alone and called forth the beings from the distant star. It was a sweet calling, yet insistent. When the child stopped calling, there came forth a great ship, silver in color, and it held itself above the earth. The child stepped forth toward the ship. The child spoke more words and the ship opened and there came forth several beings to stand upon the earth. The woman spoke holy words as they stepped forth. Of those who stepped forth, five remained, while the others returned to the ship, for they held within their feet, then, the patterns of the earth and were returning to give to all others those patterns so that they could come forth and reside upon the earth.

The five beings bowed to the child and then to the woman and then to the guardian. The five beings held within their hands different objects. One object was a blue globe and the being placed the blue globe upon the earth. From the blue globe came water pure and sweet. It filled the area yet allowed the beings to stand upon the earth, separate from the water. The woman nodded in appreciation.

The second being of the five held within his hands a small plant. He placed the plant upon the land and the plant became in an instant, a gathering of large trees. The woman nodded in gratitude.

The third being of the five held within his hand a small globe and he placed the small globe within the waters. From the small globe came forth several beings who moved in the waters and spoke to the woman. The woman was most pleased.

THIRD LAYER OF THE SACRED TEXT

The fourth of the five beings came to the child and placed before the child a form, as if a created form. The child placed his finger upon the top of the form and in the next moment the form grew and grew until it was a very tall obelisk. The child placed his finger upon the large obelisk and upon each side there formed symbols, a language of all that could be created upon the earth. The fourth being nodded and was most pleased.

The fifth being of the five beings held within his hand another structure. He placed the structure before the woman. The woman looked to the structure and picked it up in her hands. She looked inside and saw the great volumes of all truths made manifest and all histories recorded. She breathed her breath into the structure and then placed it upon the earth. She pushed the structure into the earth and it did flow forth to reside within the earth, a library of truths and histories. The woman motioned for the guardian to go forth and the guardian did then stand at the entryway of the library within the earth. That being continues to reside there even as these words flow forth to be known once again.

The fifth being then did turn and return into the great silver ship. There was peace then that resided upon the earth as all that was given did synchronize the frequencies of gifts and the earth's receiving them. This synchronization continued for three hundred years.

When the synchronization was complete, then there came forth from the great silver ship the beings who would reside upon the earth. There were many different species presented, yet they all formed as one so that there would not be a distinguishing of one specie over another. All of the beings looked like each other.

The woman gathered the beings and spoke with them and as she spoke, they found, each of them, that they understood her speaking in different ways, different from each other's understanding. The difference then began to form the nature of each being. Each being then began to be the same, yet different. And it was in this way that the woman assisted the beings to reside within a manner of being that allowed them to hold to their individuality yet be the same. The faces and physicality presented themselves differently, yet the same. They came to be called **humuntuk**. It was the name of the combined species. Humuntuk resided upon the earth and when it was determined that they would successfully reside, then the ship, the great ship did then depart.

There came forth those giants who gathered about the beings and spoke with them of their dedication to protect the many, to assist them in anything they would request in order for the ease of living to occur. This began a residing of beings upon the earth. This was not the first residing. It was the residing after the fourth clearing of the earth of all

THIRD LAYER OF THE SACRED TEXT

that resided. For there came forth upon the earth those flowings that cleared the earth of all inhabitants, including the creatures. Only the giants remained in those histories, histories written even in the library within the earth.

The histories of those who have resided upon the earth is given in ways that allow each phase to reside in its own knowing. This means that each history presented within its own knowing cannot be rearranged to be presented in another manner. Each is truth and holds the occurrences during those phases upon earth and of earth itself.

There will come upon the earth once again, great chaos wherein the beings upon earth will endeavor to separate themselves from each other, each declaring that their species or their DNA is that which must remain in power. The lessons of knowing that none are in power will have been lost. The power that raises itself to cover the earth is distorted and brings to those ones who are of lesser power the realizing that the ones in power are detrimental to all life upon the earth. Such knowing changes the frequencies of the earth. This knowing begins a flowing forth of truth, a truth that will be called from the library within the earth. For there will be a calling forth of knowledge that sits within the frequencies of histories, those histories that were deemed to be helpful to the earth's inhabitants when the great change comes upon them.

The great change is but a challenging to those who are in power. Many will battle. No battles will succeed. All battles will destroy those who partake of the battle. This is the nature of the illusion upon the earth. The power of truth, not in stated beliefs, but in the frequency of truth, will then begin to be made manifest in more noticeable ways. Beings of peace will find each other. Beings of love will find each other. Beings of hatred will find each other. Yet the beings of hatred will discover that they are alone and their small groups will disband. The reason they will disband is because the gatherings of peace and love will grow.

There forms upon the earth then, those leaders who are of light and truth and who will call the beings together, encouraging them to dare to come from hiding, to dare to gather and then to hold peace within their consciousness. These leaders are the leaders who came upon the earth long long ago and came upon the earth each time that the earth reformed itself. *This is not a reforming. It is a new manner of residing upon earth. This means that the old ways will no longer hold the frequencies to continue to reside. This will begin a new phase upon the earth. The new phase will last for thousands upon thousands of years.*

Then there will be a new awakening. This awakening will then begin the times of the creating of the pyramids across the earth. The giants of the earth will then oversee the creating of the pyramids and the fulfillment of their purposes. This then is a great history.

Those who receive these words will feel the truth represented even when they do not believe the words. The frequencies are designed to assist those who receive these words to expand their consciousness even further and to embrace the truth of their own beingness. Those who firstly are able to receive these words and to allow them to resonate within their being, within their consciousness, are those who long ago resided upon the earth as new beings. There comes forth those ones who wait. Those ones wait for the moment of truth to be anchored within the firmament of earth.

Then this is the complete speaking of this part of the Third Layer of the Sacred Text. More flows forth. These frequencies will reside and become accustomed to being in the light of incarnating and then more will flow forth. *This layer has been sealed since the first creating of this Sacred Text.*

Now this transmission is complete.
So be it.

I take some deep breaths and know that the words did flow forth and I wondered about some of them, but the flowing was so very intense and clean that there was no moment for further wondering. Ra still holds my hand and he is pulling me from the location. We must go now, he says.

We must close this portal. I nod that I understand and we both leave the location. We are now just flowing toward the location of where the Holy One meets us, but we only hear the words from the Holy One, Good. Now depart quickly. We bow our heads to the words and flow forth from that area.

Ra and I flow forth toward his realm and he flows toward the area where is the vortex to return to my body. He says, Now you must not hesitate to return. I nod that I understand and release his hand, but he still holds mine and says, My dear, you are doing very well. Remember this. I nod that I understand and nod in gratitude also. Ra nods to me and then releases my hand and I immediately flow into the vortex. When I look up, I see that Ra is no longer there. I flow down into my body-physical. I pause and just be.

Now I will anchor myself and release this participation, as it seems that is wanting to happen immediately. Then I speak the words so be it.

So be it.

THIRTEENTH TRANSMISSION
Second Speaking

I journeyed to the Holy One and he motioned me toward the white and said for me to enter. I did and it was a beautiful place, seemed to have beautiful nature. Holy One said, This is Paradise and you can come here any time you want. It is my gift to you. I was humbled but not by the gift, by my disappointment because I was expecting a gift in the physical. I thanked the Holy One and he said, You are disappointed. I said please forgive that, it is my human nature, my vessel that expected or wanted to see a gift in the physical. The Holy One paused and then said, I will give a gift there as well. I thanked the Holy One.

Then the next day I felt really badly about all of that disappointment and went to the Holy One again and said that. I tried to do that and I wasn't sure if I was projecting that or not. I then felt Teacher on my left side and Ra on my right. I tried to enter Paradise but wasn't successful. I'm going to ask Ra to go with me to the Holy One's place. I don't know if that will lead to a journey with the Sacred Text. If so, I am glad for that as well and grateful. I did hear the words that my disappointment did not insult the Holy One, but I really want to be in his presence if he will allow it. Then I am going to Ra's realm now.

I am flowing past the place where I used to journey with Alannah. And now I am before the portal to Ra's realm. I am simply asking Ra if I can speak with him. I hear Ra's voice say Come, and he is in the area where we sit to speak together. I am grateful. I flow over the top of the large area where is also his large seat. I nod to his seat in respect and then flow forth to the area where is Ra. He smiles to me. I nod to him and then say, I have made a mistake, I think. Ra smiles and says, You cannot hurt the feelings of the Holy One. It is not possible. I say that doesn't change the fact that I feel ashamed of my disappointment. Yes, Ra says, that is a human trait. All right, let's go to see the Holy One, if that is what you would like to do. Yes, I say, I would like that. Thank you. Ra nods his head and then motions for us to flow forth.

We are flowing forth in white and a little light blue. Ra says to simply focus on the Holy One. I nod that I understand. We are arriving at the Holy One's location. Ra says, now we will wait. I nod ok.

The Holy One comes forth and nods to Ra and then smiles to me. I bow my head to the Holy One. He says, Come. I look to Ra and he nods yes. I go to the Holy One and I can feel great love flowing from him. We stand before what was the entryway to Paradise. The Holy One looks into my eyes and being. I hold nothing back. I am totally as open as I can be. The Holy One says, This is still your gift. I have given it to you. To come here, you would simply decide and then come to my realm as you did before. I nod yes, but I also say that I am regretful for my human disappointment at the gift not being in the physical. The Holy One puts his head back and laughs. And then he says, It is good that you are regretful because of who you are. Yet your human nature is what needs to be nourished, I can see that. I have tears flowing down my face. The Holy One says, Long ago beings lived in this Paradise. They lived there for a long time…until they incarnated. Then they no longer lived here in this Paradise. Their focus was on the physical. That was not a terrible thing. It was just what happened. I am not invested in judging what occurs. I do not judge. That is an illusionary participation with the illusion. You see? I nod yes.

The Holy One continues, and I can feel the love flowing into me, I say thank you. The Holy One reaches forth and touches my face. Ra steps forth and takes my hand. Ra says to the Holy One, she needs to remain incarnate. The Holy One still touches my cheek with his hand. It is a hand of white light. I don't feel the touch but I enter an expanded consciousness. While I am in the expanded consciousness and with Ra holding my hand, the Holy One says to me: You are The One. You do not know what that means because that is who you are, what you are. You do not have to make yourself be anything else. You hold the Sacred Text within the heart of your spirit. No one else has done that nor will anyone else do that. You are the One. You are a Holy Being, just as I am the Holy One, you are a Holy Being. I have given Paradise to you for whenever you wish to enter. Do not fear that you will leave physicality. It is not your time. But a visit to Paradise will nourish your spirit in deep ways. He removes his hand and then says, I have decided to send you many gifts…in the physical. I believe that will chase away the feelings that you have had from your human nature and bring you joy. I wish you to have much joy. I say, Is this true? Am I projecting this through my own wishes or is this the real? The Holy One smiles and says, This is as real as it gets. THIS is real. The other is pretending to be real, but is a journey toward this. Your journey in physicality is just that, a journey. It is not a trial. It is not a right or wrong. It is a journey. In the journey you have the opportunity to experience many things. But mostly, you have the opportunity to radiate outward that which you are. I believe now that your human vessel will allow that. Remember, my dear One, you are who you are, regardless of whether you are incarnate or not.

I feel so very blessed. The Holy One says good. Now will you journey to receive more of the Text? I look to Ra and he nods yes, and says if I am willing, then we will go forth. I say I am willing. But I say, Oh Holy One, I give great gratitude to all that you have given to me in this moment. Thank you. Thank you. The Holy One smiles and says, Then all right now. There is no need for forgiveness but I say you are forgiven so that your human nature can rest within that knowing that there is no judging here. I bow my head to the Holy One. He says, good. Now you must depart if that is your choice. The Holy One looks to Ra and Ra says yes and then we both bow our heads to the Holy One and he motions us to go forth. I am so very uplifted. I feel so very loved. Ra says good.

THIRD LAYER OF THE SACRED TEXT

Then we are flowing forth. We are moving through time until there is no time. Ra is holding my hand and we are flowing toward…I will not project. Ra says good. Yet we are flowing and now begin to arrive. There is a golden light and it is seemingly emanating from an entryway. Ra says good. I am relieved as I thought I was projecting again. But there is a strong golden light emanating from an entryway that is like a large rectangular opening. Ra says that is where we are going. I nod ok.

There is a being now who is standing in the golden light, to greet us. We approach and the being says, You are here. That is good. We were hoping that you would come. The being looks to me and says, There is much to be received today. Are you ready. I say that I am. He says good, and motions for us to enter.

Flowing into the golden light seems to dissipate it and we are in whiteness. The being says that is correct. He motions us to what feels like the right side of the whiteness. The being smiles and says that is a human interpretation but that is all right. It is refreshing to hear it. He smiles to me and I nod that I understand. Then he motions again and there is a blue waterfall falling into a blue pool of water. The being motions us toward the pool. He speaks some words and there is emerging from the middle of the pool a podium of sorts and atop the podium is a…I am waiting to see what is there. There is a white globe. The being calls to the globe in the language I do not understand, but the globe flows to the being. Once in his hands the being comes to me and holds the globe toward my being. I nod yes. The being flows the globe into my being, into my heart center. I feel it enter and light fills my being. The being looks to me and asks with the expression on his face, are you all right? I nod that I am. He nods yes and then says, Now you have the next part of the Sacred Text. The frequencies have been insistent that you receive them and it is good that you came. I nod that I understand. I can feel my consciousness expanding further. Ra still holds my hand and I am glad for that.

[I can't believe that I must use the bathroom…but I must. Ra nods to me that it is all right…I have experienced pain in my lower tract and I hear the words that it is the result of the frequencies that are integrating within my spirit. I said that I am ok and can continue. I am now bringing my consciousness more expanded and am with Ra and the being once again. The being looks to me and I nod that I am ok. The being does not agree. He places his hand into my being and turns the globe slowly. I can feel my being and also my physical system coming to peace. I nod thank you. The being looks to me again and continues to turn the globe. Now he discerns that I am ok. He removes his hand. Ra looks to me and asks if I wish to continue. I say that I must. Ra says, but do you wish to continue. I say yes. I wish to continue. Ra nods ok and looks to the being and nods ok to the being as well. The being says good. Now we will begin.]

The being waves his arm and the entire location is changed. It slowly releases the visual of the waterfall and the pond. It is like a turning screen that is replaced by…no, it is stretching, the scene is moving around as if it is the wall of a globe. The being nods yes and smiles. Now there is white and

THIRD LAYER OF THE SACRED TEXT

I see a being come forth. I am waiting to say it, but now I know that it is the Holy One.

He comes forth and comes straight to me. He says, Now remember you are the One. I nod to him. He says, Now you will begin a new phase of this receiving of the Text. I nod ok. The Holy One looks into my being and says, all right. I believe you are able to do this now. He nods to Ra and Ra bows his head to the Holy One. The Holy One turns and leaves, flows away from where he came.

The being then says to Ra and me, now everything is cleared. You must begin now, for the frequencies are surely building. I nod ok. I am ready to begin. The being motions to a location and Ra and I flow into a whiteness. The being says, You will be cared for here while you receive. I nod that I understand. Ra still holds my hand. I am ready to begin.

I allow the flowing to come forth. These are the words of the Sacred Text as they are given to me in this moment, in this day, in this frequency.

The frequency is so high that I feel that I could vomit, but I hold myself in tune with my purpose and the feeling…remains, but I ignore it. The frequency continues to increase. I hear Ra says that I am doing all right. I cannot respond. The frequency inside the globe is radiating golden light. In the golden light I can see a book. I know this might be an interpretation as the Sacred Text is contained in frequencies, but there is a book. Ra says that is all right. I see the book come forth and open before me. Great white light emanates from the open book. Symbols flow forth. Many

many. Now there is a tone that sounds. I am now very cold. Very cold. Ra says that is the frequency. I cannot respond.

I open to receive the words of the Sacred Text if they will flow forth. I wait. This is what flows forth.

It is a different language and again I wait for a translation. There is a loud screeching sound. I hear Ra speak some words in that different language. The screeching softens and there appears to be words flowing forth upon the sound. The words are like an echo.

> **Now it begins.**
>
> In the histories of all that has resided incarnate upon the earthly planet there are those causes and effects that have brought forth great destruction and great uplifting of light. With the two, there came forth several beings who cared for the substance of the earth and wishes to maintain the earth and not allow it to be taken into the destruction that some of the causes and effects would do. It was realized that some of the destruction was deliberate and others were the result of an unconscious participation with those causes that were deliberate. The beings determined that they would clear the earth of those that were determined to destroy the earth.
>
> It was recognized that a destruction of the earth by those ones was a deliberate act to cause the beings who resided upon earth to be destroyed, for there was a determining also that the testing ground for certain species had completed itself and that it

was proven that those who resided were no longer viable for the purposes of control. It was determined that control of the masses of the different species upon the earth was too complicated, that within some of the species there was a surge in the quest for power and that surge distorted the consciousness of many, while it called forth the opposite to be made manifest in other beings, in other species. There was then a presentation of right and wrong, good and bad, holy and unholy. And this dichotomy of differences refused to be balanced. Thus the call to one was unable to be fulfilled. That was the final cause for the decision to destroy earth and all of the species that had come to reside upon earth, species who had lost their own homes as a direct result of similar causes and effects.

The being who came forth to hold the integrity of the earth while those ones determined to destroy it, was a being who held the power of creation as given from the core of creation as it flowed forth into the many manifestations of itself. Those ones were made manifest from the core of creation as well. The preservation of earth was a purpose that was determined by the very factor that the removal of earth from the planetary system would cause an imbalance and the other planets would be caused to shift in their positions. This was not the time for such a great change and those ones then came forth to maintain earth.

As the ones determined to destroy, the beings who came to maintain earth, then did flow forth a protective shield around earth so that those ones who wanted to destroy could not activate the external methods for destruction. Some of the ones who would destroy resided upon the earth temporarily while the main gathering resided in a ship or frequency that would emit a force toward the earth and the earth would then be destroyed. Yet they did discern the shield and paused to see what was occurring that would place such a strong shield about the earth. The beings then came forth and spoke with those ones saying that their plan would not be allowed. The beings reacted and then received the truth of what was being said. There was then the statement to the beings that those species upon the earth would then be left to their own success or demise, that the beings of destruction would no longer be in charge of the beings upon the earth. The Great Beings saw the truth of what was being said and then agreed. The beings of destruction then did depart, for it was a relief to them that they no longer needed to oversee the many different species that resided upon earth and the causes and effects that those species created.

With the removal of the overseers' control, the species upon earth paused, paused with any movement, any decisions, anything. The beings paused and felt the freedom of being. The Great

Beings then did breath a breath upon the species upon the earth. It was a breath that held within it great love and peace. The beings upon the earth then did feel the peace and feel the love. The entire earth felt the peace and love. All beings and all species felt the love and peace. The pause continued. Some forgot what they were doing, while others simply decided that what they were doing was not worthy of their participation.

The Great Beings breathed another breath upon the earth and the beings of the many species residing there. The earth contained that called fulfillment of being. The fulfillment flowed across the earth and filled the breathing of all beings of all species. The fulfillment was not made manifest, it was a frequency and it filled the consciousness of all of the beings and all of the species. It entered in different ways, but it was still received by all beings.

The Great Ones viewed and determined they would simply allow all the beings to be, to reside and to determine on their own how they would live and what they would participate within. For those ones had been held in control ever since they resided upon earth, some taking form while others birthed. The sound of freedom was felt within all beings and all species. It was as if great joy filled them. The Great Beings observed and decided they would allow. They also determined that they would continue to maintain the shield about the earth lest others come to determine a purpose. The shield would prohibit interference with the beings who now felt freedom within their being.

This freedom was maintained for three eras. Three. At the beginning of the fourth era there came to the earth those ones who saw the freedom, felt the joy and wanted to become part of that residing. The Great Ones refused to remove the barrier, the shield about the earth. Those ones who came and wanted to participate grew angry. They believed they had a right to enter the earthly joy and freedom. The Great Ones strengthened the shield, for it was seen that if there was anger, then there would be a need to control. The Great Ones determined that these ones would not be allowed onto the new earth.

The beings departed. They remained departed until the middle of the fourth era and when they returned, they returned with great ships and powerful tools to destroy the shield about the earth. The Great Ones observed. They asked themselves if they were correct in remaining in a type of control and if it was correct to do so. While the forces continued to blast at the shield, trying to destroy it, the Great Ones continued to reflect upon totality and what they were doing to protect the earth and its inhabitants.

Eventually it was decided that they would remove the shield but would place a requirement of

THIRD LAYER OF THE SACRED TEXT

an expanded consciousness to be able to enter the atmosphere of earth. This was accomplished.

Those ones celebrated the destroying of the shield and determined they would go forth to reside upon this earth and to discover what it was that maintained freedom and the new feeling which was joy. They discovered that they would not actually enter the consciousness which resided upon the earth. They were upon the earth but yet they could not make themselves be known or be recognized. It was as if they were as ghost beings and few of those ones upon earth recognized their presence. Some recognized that there were new beings upon earth, but even those ones who recognized the new beings determined that they must be all right since nothing destructive had occurred upon the earth since the beginning of the fourth era. They were mistaken.

The beings who were unseen began to radiate power so that they could control the cause and effect. Initially they did so in order to become more incarnate. Still the Great Ones would not allow them to become fully incarnate because of their anger. The beings then began to create another reality upon earth, one that was outside of the consciousness of those ones who resided upon earth incarnate and filled with freedom and joy. The angry beings created and created until they had themselves a mirror image of the beautiful residing of the earth that they could not enjoy as they were not able to maintain the consciousness that was required. The mirror image was nearly an exact replica except that there was a type of distortion because of the absence of peace, which was and is the foundation of totality of being.

The angry ones did not choose totality. Instead, they celebrated that they were able to created an illusionary reality and that the beings who resided upon earth could not discern that reality, though a few did suspect that there was another creation occurring upon earth. The Great Beings observed this creating and determined that they would continue to observe as long as the angry beings did not enter the frequencies of those ones residing in peace, freedom and joy.

Later the Great Ones determined that this allowing was a mistake. The angry beings created a portal and within the portal they called forth the frequencies of the consciousness of those ones upon earth, the peaceful beings of freedom. The consciousness did enter the portal and was maintained there. Then the angry beings who were more determined than ever to enter the earthly domain then did force their consciousness to mimic the expanded consciousness within the portal, yet they were not residing within that consciousness, they were pretending to reside within that expanded consciousness.

THIRD LAYER OF THE SACRED TEXT

They continued in this manner for a very long time until one and then another was able to flow forth from the portal and into the frequency of those beings upon earth. The first few who entered in this manner could not maintain their life force. The frequencies upon earth were too expanded for them to reside. Yet after those ones did dissolve of their life force, others did learn how to adjust themselves to create a shield about themselves so that they could enter earthly living and still remain incarnate but with a shield about their being. When they were successful in this manner, then more and more of their beings entered earthly living.

They caused their shields to appear to be as if the same beings upon earth. *It was the first takeover attempt during the fourth era.* There were those beings upon earth who had developed their consciousness to such a degree that they felt the intrusion of these beings and gathered to determine what they would do. They called forth the Great Beings to consult. But the Great Beings determined that they would let the earthly advanced ones begin to care for the earth and its inhabitants. It was time for that growth, it was determined. The advanced beings felt the absence of the Great Ones and determined that they would need to decide for themselves what to do about the intruders.

Again it was decided that the intruders would be allowed to remain, for they had not proven to be destructive, they were just different from those who resided upon earth. This decision caused a great shift in the consciousness that resided upon earth during that time of the fourth era. With the presence of those ones, the frequencies shifted upon earth and many of the beings who resided and had been residing became ill. The distorted frequencies caused them to become unbalanced. The unbalance diminished the ability of the physicality to be lessened in integrity. Many beings released their life force.

Those ones who were in disguise began to recognize their effect upon the ones who resided upon earth. They gathered together and determined that if they would continue, then the earth would be freed of the beings and the distorted ones then would have the freedom and joy and the entire planet would be theirs. This did occur. After many turnings of the cycles, all of the earth beings had released their life force.

The distorted beings danced and laughed and celebrated that the earth was theirs to have. They pulled their distorted creation into the frequencies of the earth and the mirror image of what was began to be formed. They pulled their creation through the portal and caused it to reside upon the earth itself. The frequencies of life, the life force was covered by the distortion and the illusion of what was. The beings then could release their disguise and reside because that which they pulled forth on to the planet was of their frequency. They began to reside upon the earth and *what was presented upon the earth was the illusion of what was.* The beings resided through the entire remainder of the fourth era.

Again there came forth those ones traveling to discover the outer reaches of the realms that had developed in the star systems. They came upon the earth and saw that it was covered with a force, a distortion that held the inhabitants. The beings who saw wondered how such an illusionary distortion could be created and how those ones did reside within it. This began a deep reexamination of what was residing upon this strange planet. They did not know the planet was earth. Their histories had registered the absence of earth, that it had disappeared long ago. Yet now they were looking at this planet and wondering if it was the planet that had disappeared, that perhaps it was simply covered by this illusionary distortion.

They journeyed closer and sent frequency probes toward the planet to discern if their wonderings were true. They discovered that beneath the distortion there was the beauty of a frequency that held freedom, joy and most certain fulfillment. They wondered why the beings residing in the distortion had not decided to reside in the beauty. And it was one being who, upon studying, determined that those ones were not capable of residing in the beauty because they could not maintain the consciousness necessary. The beings observing wondered if there was a participation that called to them. They returned to their homes to discuss the discovery.

The planet earth felt the presence of those ones who had observed. The planet yearned for beings to reside who could not only celebrate the beauty of earth, but also to participate in the frequencies of restoration and regeneration, creative frequencies and the fulfillment within freedom to be. Earth was missing what used to be. The consciousness of earth began to develop further, for the residing upon her of the distortion had, in a manner of speaking, allowed earth's consciousness to sleep. Now earth herself was awakening.

The awakening of earth caused great upheaval upon the surface. The earth groaned and spewed hot lava, caused mountains to rise upward and upward and valleys to go downward and downward. Earth caused the waters to expand and some waters to recede. The integrity of the distortion began to be lessened. Earth celebrated the disturbance of the distortion. The beings who resided within the distortion did not know what to do. They had tried everything to strengthen their created distortion and their manners of residing within it. Yet all that they tried, could not succeed, for earth had decided.

There were those who had hidden their ships and then pulled them forth and called to the many who resided in the distortion. They filled the ships and when all were aboard the ships they departed from the dissolving distortion they had created.

When the observers returned they saw, much to their surprise, the dissolving of the distortion and the birthing of the earth's beauty into reality. It was as if the earth was reappearing where it used to be. The observers were overjoyed and celebrated. They also observed to see what would appear upon the surface of the earth. Nature appeared. Eventually creatures appeared. Then there was a pause in anything appearing. No beings appeared. No species appeared. The observers determined they would come closer to the surface of the earth and when they did, earth reached up her frequencies to invite them to reside upon her for she felt the wholeness of being of those beings.

The beings accepted the invitation of the earth and began to place their steppings upon the earth. The beauty and the frequencies of freedom, peace, love and joy filled them. They radiated forth their frequencies of wholeness of being and earth herself rejoiced. This began the last part of the fourth era, where those beings then did reside upon earth and celebrate truth as it is now within the consciousness of wholeness of being. *This then held the frequencies for the beginning of the fifth era.* Earth had returned and its inhabitants held the consciousness of totality, of wholeness of being.

Then this is the speaking that flows forth for this receiving of the Sacred Test.
So be it.

The frequencies are still very strong, but Ra is saying that we must depart from this location. I nod that I agree, but I cannot bring my awareness to Ra. He whispers that is all right and begins to pull me, with his hand in mine, from the area. I allow myself to be pulled along. My consciousness is very expanded. Ra continues to bring me to another frequency.

The light being stands before us and then nods to me. He says that I have done well and then asks permission to remove the globe. I nod yes. He gently reaches into my being and gradually removes the globe. I am grateful that it is gradual. I can feel the releasing of the globe from my being. Now I can see the being holding the globe in his hands and he nods to me and then to Ra and says that he will return to the waters and replace the globe in its location. We both nod ok and the being departs from us.

I am breathing deeply and Ra notices that I am more returned. He says that we must depart now and I agree. We flow forth past the Holy One's realm and then flow toward Ra's realm. He brings me to the location of the great seats and places me upon the seat that I usually sit on. He breathes his breath upon me and I am taking form once again. He says good. You have done well. I nod that I am ok.

THIRD LAYER OF THE SACRED TEXT

Ra then says that I must return to my physicality so that I will remain incarnate easily. I nod ok. I flow from the seat and toward the portal where Alannah is waiting. She looks to me to see if I am all right. I nod to her. She looks to Ra and he says that I will be better if I return to my physicality. Alannah nods ok and guides me out of Ra's realm. I look over my shoulder and bow my head to Ra. He smiles.

I am now flowing along to where my vortex to return resides. Alannah puts her hands upon my shoulders and says that I will be better once I return, but that I should remember that I have done very well with most expanded frequencies. I nod that I understand but truly want to return. She smiles and says that is good.

I bow my head to Alannah and then enter my vortex. I am flowing downward toward my physicality. I am entering my body. As I enter I can discern that indeed my consciousness was very expanded. I am returning but it is taking a bit of time. That is all right.

I breathe deeply and try to open my eyes. Not yet. I wait. I open my eyes and discover that the pain in my lower tract has returned. I know I will be all right, that it is just a frequency adjustment.

Then I speak the words so be it.

So be it. These words situate the Sacred Text into words, incarnate.

So be it.

FOURTEENTH TRANSMISSION
Sixth Speaking

I have read the previous text and am now in an expanded consciousness which leads me to believe that it is a good time to return for further receiving. I am now traveling to Ra's realm. I am happy to be going forth this morning and am arriving at the area where Alannah and I have traveled and then now I am flowing toward Ra's portal. It seems that the greater expanded frequencies I experienced during the previous receiving are now with me and all is clear in front of the portal. This reminds me of the content of the previous receiving where the illusionary realm was removed. I think that my expanded consciousness is clearing the way of any distortion that in the past was placed here. All is clear and I am quite glad about that. I approach the portal and bring my consciousness to match the portal and it turns and then opens. Again the sound of its opening is like a compression being released. I look and do not see Alannah but I enter. The portal closes behind me and I feel a great uplift of my spirit to be here.

All is white. I wait. Ra flows forth from above his realm and his robes are flowing about him. He holds out his hand

and says, Come. I expand my consciousness further and flow up to where he is. He takes my hand and says Good. We must not delay. I nod that I understand. I ask Ra if this is true or I am projecting. Ra says that any projecting would not be able to reside in these frequencies. I nod that I am glad about that.

Ra begins to move and I with him, as he is still holding my hand. We are flowing and flowing faster and faster. Ra says, There is no such thing as faster, but that is ok for now. Soon my consciousness will adjust and I will not reside in time-oriented perceptions. I nod that I understand. We are still flowing together through whiteness.

Now I can discern that we are above a location that has nature, trees, land. Ra nods this is correct. There is an opening in the land, on the side of a hill, not a mountain, but a hill. We flow toward the opening…while we do, I am also doing a clearing around my body-physical and it is now surrounded by a light blue light. Ra nods good.

We are pausing outside the opening that still looks like land and the opening is dark. We still wait. There is a spinning in the opening, a blue spinning. Now there is a strong breath coming from the opening as if a giant being breathed a breath outward. Ra smiles at my interpretation but says that it is a good description. We still wait.

I can hear sounds but I cannot discern what they are about. Ra says that is the sound of clearing the way for us to enter this passageway. He says it has been protected for a very long time. I nod that I understand.

THIRD LAYER OF THE SACRED TEXT

Now there is a light that is radiating from deep within and is flowing toward us. Ra says, Good. Now we will be able to enter soon. I focus on the light and Ra says good. I can feel a being journeying toward us. I am expanding my consciousness as I feel it would be necessary to enter. Ra says that is correct. As I do, the light being appears before us and says, It is good that you came. Now the text must continue to be received as often as possible. He looks to Ra and then to me. Ra nods yes and adds that this being, meaning me, is also incarnate and that must be taken into consideration. The light being nods that he understands. He looks to me and asks if I will be able to continue to receive the text. I say that is my purpose. I am the One and I will continue to receive the text until it is complete and even further, if that is what is called forth. The light being nods yes and smiles to me. He says, Then let us go forth for all is prepared.

Ra takes my hand again and we follow the light being into the portal in the side of the hill. The being turns to me and says that the hill is but a projection to protect the entire area, but it is good that I describe it as a hill, as that is the dedicated projection. It tells us that it is still intact, he says. I nod yes.

Then we are following the light being. There is no tunnel. We are just following the light being. He waves his arm and the white turns to reveal a chamber that has a small body of water, very small, but also there are around the chamber different places that have what appear to be little doors, all of them closed. The light being says, Yes, that is true.

He motions for us to wait while he flows toward one of the little doors in the wall. As he approaches, the door lights, emits golden light. The being holds his hand in front of the door and it radiates more light until it opens. The being reaches within the opening and when he removes his hand he is holding a globe. The frequencies of the chamber have changed. It is becoming very intense.

The being moves toward me, Ra still holds my hand, and the being stands before me and asks if I will receive the globe into my being. I say that I am honored to receive the globe, yes I receive it into my being. The being then holds his hand outward and the globe begins to move slowly toward my being. As it comes before the area of my heart, it pauses. I am led to say, Flow forth now the Sacred Text for I am the One and I receive the text to be made incarnate. I pause and then say, so be it. The light being nods to me that I am correct in speaking those words. The globe brightens and I am surrounded by the brightness. It seems to be adjusting my frequencies. Ra still holds my hand.

The brightness seems to reach a peak of intensity and the globe flows into the heart area of my being. There is the sound of singing and bells ringing. There is an adjustment occurring. The light being says that is the sound of the Text as this Text has not been received in this manner...*ever*. I nod that I understand, but I am encased in the intense frequencies and I know the Text is about to begin. The light being says yes and then turns to depart. I wonder why he departs and he turns to me and says, No one is allowed to be present. You are the One and Ra holds you. Then when the

Text is complete, I will return for the globe, as we have participated in the previous time. I nod that I understand.

This then is the Sacred Text as it flows forth.

There resides in the Universe several...I am waiting for the frequencies to align....

It begins again.

Within the Universe there resides uncountable realms and within the realms, planets that flow about each other, forming galaxies and then within the galaxies, there forms those frequencies that call forth creation in a way that also calls forth the inhabiting of those creations by beings. The beings create themselves from the core of creation and flow forth to inhabit the created planets, each holding a specific purpose. The purpose of the beings, and because of the purpose of the beings then the planet also holds that purpose, is determined by the journey of the consciousness as it resides within the beings and then inhabits the planet. Some planets are barely physical, while others are formed in the density of physicality itself.

Physicality itself holds within it certain frequencies that enable formings to reside. Yet physicality does not bend itself to those who reside within it. More so, because of the consciousness of that physicality's creation, the residing upon the physicality requires that the ones that reside are a match to the purpose of physicality. Physicality itself holds a frequency that determines the allowing of any to reside within or upon it.

The physicality of the planets formed within certain galaxies hold purposes that are stated within the essence of the forming. The essence of forming then holds the Sacred Text of that physicality. This Sacred Text then is held within the physicality so that all that is created within and upon that particular physicality will hold the integrity of the created purpose and more so, the integrity of creation itself. For there is no need for creation of distortion. Creation of distortion comes only from distortion. No distortion is accepted by any physicality, for truth resides.

In the histories of the formings of planets within galaxies, there have been those formings that expanded to become large planets, planets that then determined the nature of the surrounding formings or creations also known as planets. Because of the largeness of the formed planets in some of those galaxies, there was then radiating outward the purpose of that planet. This caused ripples in the ethers between all planets, for each planet held its own purpose. Yet the largest planets, without intention, radiated outward their purpose. The rippling caused a type of disturbance in the situating of the planets around each other. The disturbance caused a swirling which became a vortex, *the first vortex*.

The birthing of the vortex radiated outward with a spark of light and there formed a magnetic force to hold the planets in aligned manners, allowing each planet to reside, yet still within the radiating of the largest planet. This then formed a family of planets. While each planet still held its own purpose, the purpose of the largest planet influenced what occurred upon the surface of those smaller planets. Yet within the smaller planets there was no influence.

Then because of this holding of purpose within the smaller planets, there then began to reside those beings who would hold the integrity of the planet and then did reside within the planet. Those beings became the first residents of the planet. They were of essence and not physical, which allowed them to hold the integrity of the purpose of their planet.

In the histories, then, there came forth from different realms, those beings who explored the outreaches of the totality of all that was being created. Some of the beings journeyed to explore the surface of the planets that they came upon. The beings brought with them the frequencies of their home planet and its purposes. This was not an intention. It was simply the truth that the beings held within them the creation of themselves as they did form themselves while residing upon a planet, which then became their home.

Some beings created from the spark of creation and those beings were considered Great Ones for they had not resided upon any physicality, but held the frequencies of truth. The Great Ones observed the galaxies, the planets forming, and the flowing forth of beings from different homes to explore creation's manifesting.

There formed upon the planets being explored, a frequency that rose from within the planet itself. The frequency was the planets intent, the planet's purpose. Those ones who resided upon the surface as they explored the surface of such planets, felt the frequencies and interpreted what they felt to be the instability of the integrity of the planet. They departed. This formed then a recognition in the consciousness of the planet. The planet absorbed the experience within its own consciousness. The experience led the planet to recognize that it held a part in what would form upon it.

In this recognition, the planet then did cause itself to erupt and erupt upon the surface with the intention of disruption of the purpose of the large planet. There was then upon the surface of this planet and other planets experiencing the same, an issuing of those frequencies that pushed the purposes of the large planet away from the small planet. The pushing away of the radiating purpose of the large planet caused the frequencies of that radiating to return to the large planet. The returning of those frequencies that had been radiating outward from the large planet, caused the large planet to shift in its own forming.

The shifting of the large planet in its own forming was caused by the returning of its purposes radiating outward but that within those returning radiations there was contained the patterns and frequencies of the smaller planets. The larger planet began to wobble in its positioning as it attempted to integrate the frequencies that were not of its own creating. Because the creating of the All is the creating of All That Is, then there was flowed forth the synchronizing of the creations. This caused the large planet and the smaller planets to reposition themselves so that there was the residing in compatibility. *This inhabiting in physicality of compatibility created what could be called the sound of the universe, totality incarnate in a way that allowed each creation to reside of itself.*

This residing then uplifted the frequencies of all planets, the small and the large. And within the inner of each small planet there was the recognizing that there was a freedom to bring the purpose of the planet to its surface, for nothing was prohibiting its expression. Then those ones in essence form did journey to the surface of their planet. Not all smaller planets held the calling forth of taking form. Those ones that held the calling forth of taking form, then did radiate out such calling. The calling forth to take form was the direct result of creation itself, for the patterns of creation resided within all that had been and was being created. The frequencies of creation itself as it resided within physicality's forming, then did call forth the similar creation of physicality. This then called forth the beings in essence residing to begin to take form.

The beings taking form on some of the smaller planets was the establishing of the purpose of the planet in a manner that allowed the purpose to be expressed according to that which took form. This meant that each taking form, each essence-being taking form within physicality held within itself the freedom of expression of creation itself. In this manner, creation itself began to reside within incarnate being's consciousness. The beings then became not only conscious of creation itself, but also became conscious of their own forming. The purpose of the planet itself then became awake within those beings. That is, within the consciousness of those beings who held the knowing of creation itself, there came to be recognized the planet's purpose, as they were formed from the planet itself.

Those beings who held the purpose of the planet and the conscious knowing of creation itself, then did reside. *This then was and continues to be the first residing of the Holiness of Creation Incarnate.*

The Holiness Incarnate holds these frequencies. That is, all small planets that held the forming of beings and the knowing of creation itself, held within the integrity of the planet and the integrity of the beings, these truths of creation itself.

All that flows forth from creation itself is creation itself.

All that forms itself within those flowings is creation itself.

Within all that forms, creation itself breathes forth creation.

The breath of creation flows within that which has been created and opens the spark to reside.

The spark of creation residing then calls forth creating.

Such creating rests upon the spark of creation and not upon purposes declared.

Purposes declared within a spark of creation hold the integrity of creation yet also hold the possibility of distortion because the creation is determined by that which holds creation itself.

That which holds creation itself and determines the flowing of creation is then called creator.

Yet within creation itself, there is no creator. There is only the spark of creation and the flowing forth of that spark to take form as the All. The taking form of the All does not translate as taking form in physicality. More so, the taking form of the All refers to the frequencies of creation as they flow forth and explore that All that is the breath of creation and also that which is formed as a frequency. All occurs in the moment.

Then when there is a creator determining the forming of creation itself, there is also the possibility of distortion. It is the consciousness of the creator that determines the intensity of the distortion, for all frequencies are present in all creations. Yet the creator then holds a determining and the determining rests upon the purposes that have flowed forth, merged, and expanded within that merging. Within the merging and expanding certain purposes develop. Yet the purposes are frequencies and not declarations.

Within the frequencies there comes forth from some creators, declarations. This declaration is established within the creator as the creator causes itself to be merged with the many purposes. Within the creator then, there is formed the many purposes and the manners of determining. This in itself is a form of creation. It is the gathering of the many purposes together *to form a possibility*. The creator then journeys forth within that exploration of forming and unforming in the play of the All flowing forth in all manners.

Within the consciousness of those beings who reside upon the small planets, there becomes an awareness of the determining of creation. Some beings refuse to participate with such determining simply because the frequencies are not compatible with that which they hold within themselves as the purpose of their home, their planet.

Others on some small planets embraced such determining and began to merge the determining with the purpose of their planet. This caused a distortion upon the surface of the planet and some of the beings returned to the inner residing of their planet in order to continue to maintain the integrity of the planet's purpose.

The returning of the beings within the planet then caused a flowing of communication between those within and those upon the surface. There came to be, then, a yearning of those upon the surface to remember the original purpose that they held within their beingness. Some of those who resided within the planet then answered the yearning and came to the surface to assist those ones to remember. The ones who came to the surface from within held great light for they held the original purpose and no distortion. They were viewed as Holy Ones by those who resided upon the surface and held the distortion of the merged frequencies of determining the flowing of creation itself. *There came then a flowing of what was called remembering.* Some chose to remember while others did not. For, *with the remembering, there was the letting go of the desire to determine the flowing of creation itself.*

The determining of the flowing of creation itself caused those ones participating in this manner to believe they were the power of creation, that their beingness was the cause of creation, instead of knowing that creation is always of itself. Because they held this belief of themselves they challenged those ones, those Holy Ones from within the earth, saying that they were of creation and must then determine the inner residing as well. This caused a rejection of such determining and those Holy Ones did return to their residing within the earth. This then caused the ones who yearned to remember to then gather together and form groups of those who remembered. Their light was bright and large and they held no need to determine the direction of creation itself. There formed then within their gatherings those frequencies of creation itself which dispelled the distortion. Those who believed they were creation itself began to feel the dissolving of the frequencies that held them within those beliefs. *This then brought forth that which is called fear, fear of loss of what was the distortion.*

Fear of loss of the distortion caused great disturbances upon the planet itself. All small planets that experienced such occurrences began to be disturbed in their formings. Some planets could no longer hold the integrity of their own physicality. This caused the planets to experience a friction within their frequencies and such friction caused those smaller planets to expel outward in great force. Some of the smaller planets were able to maintain themselves simply because those who resided within began to radiate outward the purpose of the planet and then the integrity of the planet. Those that expelled outward were destroyed, yet their particles resided about the planets. There formed a field of particles around the planets that were able to maintain their integrity. The large planet felt the shifting and held itself clear of such expressions. The manner of the galaxy shifted and changed. It expanded to allow for the field of particles. Such expansion then called forth the expression of creation itself. The expression of creation itself began to form within the galaxies that expanded. There formed smaller planets within the galaxies that expanded. The smaller planets held within them the histories of all that was formed within the All. They held truth itself, for there was no distortion, only knowing.

This residing within the All that has been and is being created brought forth truth incarnate. Truth incarnate radiated in such a manner that all planets received the purity of truth incarnate. They received the frequencies of truth incarnate because such frequencies were the essence of their own creation. The embracing of truth incarnate of all planets caused the frequencies of all that resided within the galaxies that the smaller planets formed within, to be made whole. The distortions dissolved. The dissolving of the distortions released the dedicated creating and there then resided peace upon and within all planets within the galaxies wherein the smaller planets formed. *These galaxies would come to be known as the galaxies of peace.*

It was within a Galaxy of Peace that there formed *one planet that held what is called possibilities of creation. That planet came to be known as earth.* Yet the speaking of further histories of this planet will be revealed through another frequency as this releasing and receiving is complete.

Then these are the words of the Sacred Text as they flow forth and are received.
So be it.

I can feel the lessening of intensity of the frequencies within me. I am at peace. My consciousness is very expanded. I am now returning to the chamber where Ra is holding my hand and the light being comes forth to stand before me. He looks to me and nods yes as if a question. I bring myself to his presence and nod that I am ok. He smiles and then says that he will now receive the globe if I am ready to release it. I nod yes and allow.

The globe flows forth from my being easily, slowly, and I allow it to be released. As it flows from my being, it is as if a portal in my being closes behind it. The globe flows to rest upon the open hand of the light being and he then flows forth to return it to its place behind the little door in the wall. The door opens and the golden light flows forth. The light being holds his hand near the door and the globe flows of itself into the small chamber. The door to the small chamber closes and the being turns to bow to Ra and me and says that it is time for us to depart the chamber. We both nod yes. The being motions to a direction and we follow.

Ra is again pulling me along as I am in an extreme expanded consciousness. I am present yet I am essence. The being motions to an opening and then says to me, You are the One. I nod yes. He says, Without you there would be no Sacred Text known to any. That is who you are. The Sacred Text. The One. I hear what he is saying and nod yes. Ra says softly that we must depart. The light being says to Ra that he is correct and motions us to move through the portal. I bow my head in respect to the being.

Now Ra and I are exiting the chamber and we are flowing together over the image of nature and the hill. We continue to flow together and are into the white. Ra says that the intensity of the frequencies will lessen now. I nod that I understand. We continue flowing.

We approach Ra's realm and he brings me to sit in the large seat beside him. I reside in that seat. Ra returns to his seat as well. We are still. Ra says the seat will assist me to release some of the intensity of the Sacred Text, but some of it will remain. He says that I will be able to go forth in my physicality easily. I nod that I understand but I cannot speak.

Alannah appears before us and says that perhaps it is time for me to return. She is very small standing at the base of the seats. Ra says to Alannah that she is correct. He motions for me to release from the seat and to flow down to where Alannah is. I nod ok and begin that process. I am not less in my consciousness, but I am bringing myself to reside beside Alannah. She is assisting me with her love. I am now almost the size of Alannah which means that my consciousness is nearly correct for returning. Alannah says not to hurry. She now places her hands upon my shoulders and says, All right now, you are ready. Let us depart from Ra's realm. It will be easier. I nod ok and turn to look to Ra. I nod my head in respect and love and gratitude. Ra is sitting on his seat. He is holding the frequencies.

Alannah and I flow toward the portal and I look back once again at Ra. He is holding his right hand upward toward me and I can feel the essence of his being flowing to me, saying that all is well. I nod that I understand.

Next Alannah waves her arm and the portal opens and we are flowing through. The portal closes behind us and Alannah says that we must now go directly to my vortex to return. I nod that I understand. As we stand before the vortex she says to me, I will assist you. You are doing better than expected, though there was no expectation. Sometimes when a being does great things, there is a realization that such greatness was not considered. She says, I suppose considered is better stated than expected. She smiles and I can feel her love flow to me. I say to Alannah, You have been with me since the beginning of these journeys. It is you whom I have not considered to be so great, yet I know that you are. She smiles and nods yes, that she receives my words.

She motions for me to return and I nod that I realize it is time. She laughs at my use of the word time. I smile at myself for it as well. I nod to her and then flow into my vortex. I am flowing downward downward downward…I am entering my body-physical. This continues to be a great honor for me. I am humbled.

Then I am returned. I speak the words so be it.

So be it.

FIFTEENTH TRANSMISSION
Tenth Speaking

I am in an altered consciousness from channeling this month's Class and I am not depleted. Because the Keeper of the Sacred Text asked if I could continue regularly with receiving the Text, I am going to open now. This feels right to me.

I am bringing my consciousness to be able to approach the portal to Ra's realm. I am there and am waiting to see if Ra will appear as he did last time. The portal opens for me and I am flowing into Ra's realm. All is white. I hear Ra's voice saying that there is no need to project anything because we will depart. I understand.

Yet Ra says, come to the seats and sit beside me. I look to see if Ra means the very large seats. I see or I believe he is there as he is very large. I bring my consciousness to reside with Ra and I see that he is not at this seat. This must mean, I think, that he is at the seats where we sit and he speaks and teaches me. I flow toward there and into the next chamber of his realm.

Ra is there and motions for me to come and sit with him. I am happy to see him. Ra motions for me to sit, which I do and he sits beside me in his seat. Ra says, Good. Now I want to speak with you about all of this. I nod ok.

Ra says, This is a most glorious thing that you are doing. I want to be sure that you are ok with continuing. This is taking a lot of energy, even within the expanded frequencies. It will only get more intense as the Text holds those frequencies that are deeply secret and hold more than the words. I will be with you and hold your hand, which assures you that you are watched over. I nod yes.

Ra continues, I suggest that we venture forth today to see how it goes. I say, Ra, regardless of how intense it is, I truly must continue to receive the Sacred Text. I believe that is most important. Ra says, I agree, it might be necessary for you to space the receiving a little, to have a few days in between so that you can re-establish yourself in physicality. Your physicality is not at risk, I am not saying that. But what I am saying is that I wish you to remain in good health and to be able to continue with your regular life. I say to Ra, I appreciate your concern. I agree that we would go forth today and see what occurs. Yet, in truth, my life is not a regular life. I live with the Holy Being Grayson in a temple on a land that continues to bring to its surface small and large quartz crystals. It is a holy life. Ra laughs and says, You are correct in those words. Yet I still wish for you to be certain that you can continue and still maintain the life that you are living incarnate. I know you will remain incarnate, but you have other channelings to do. I want you to be able to replenish your being. I thank Ra and say, I will agree with whatever you suggest as long as I do continue to receive the Sacred Text.

THIRD LAYER OF THE SACRED TEXT

Ra says, ok! We are in agreement. Then let's go forth! I smile and say that I am grateful for him. Ra says, As I am of you. Now let us continue with our journey together. I nod yes.

Ra stands as do I and he looks to the white curtain of frequencies. I nod ok and he moves toward the white and waves his arm. A pathway appears and he says, this is a little different, a little more gentle to allow you to assimilate the expanded frequencies a little more gradually. I nod thank you. Then we begin to flow upon the pathway.

It is quite beautiful surrounded by nature. We are flowing along on a brown earth pathway. As we continue, there is a light blue coming into view. Ra says that is where we are going. In we go. We flow forth toward the blue which appears as a light blue wall before us, a wall of color and essence. Ra says, We will go through there now. I will take your hand because this will increase the frequencies considerably. I nod ok.

We flow through the blue essence. It is a long flowing through and even though I know there is not speed, it feels as if we are increasing speed as we move through the blue. Ra smiles to me and says it is ok to describe. We are now moving very fast. So fast that our image is barely present as we are essence within the essence. I can hear Ra say that we are all right. All is well.

We continue in this manner for a while. Now there is swirling a presence of nature and the mountains covered in green trees. Ra says that is a deliberate projection because there is a portal we will discover and enter. I nod ok.

221

The frequencies are increasing as we approach the side of the mountain. There is a swirling portal, as if the green is liquid and swirling. Ra says that is our entrance. I nod ok. We flow toward the entrance and it opens like an eye of a camera, turning open. There is a being standing on the other side and he is motioning for us to enter. Ra says it is correct for us to enter. I nod ok. We enter.

The being is the Light Being who brings the Sacred Text Globe to me. He says, I am very glad to see you again. You are brave and I hope that you will be all right to receive again so close to the previous time. I say that I am ready and we will see how everything goes. The Light Beings says that everything will go perfectly, it is that I wish for your comfort during and after. I say that is not my concern but thank him. He smiles and says, You truly are The One. I nod yes.

The Light Being motions and says we must then go forth without hesitation today. We follow the Light Being and we are now flowing down a passageway. As we flow down the passageway, there is a shifting in frequencies, as if we are passing through different chambers, yet there is no presence of any chamber. Ra says I am correct and that it is energy chambers to adjust us to what we will do in this receiving. I nod that I understand.

We continue following the Light Being who is now quite ahead of us. He seems to be at the end of the passageway and is standing, waiting for us to arrive where he is. We are getting closer, yet the closer we get, the slower we are moving. Ra says, That is the intensity of the chamber we will enter. We are given the time to adjust. I nod ok.

THIRD LAYER OF THE SACRED TEXT

We are now before the Light Being. He says, good. You are doing very well. Then let us enter this chamber. He waves his arm and there appears an entryway and it is opening. He steps through and motions for us to follow. We do.

The chamber is very large. It is as if we are inside the mountain and a huge cavern has been made manifest. The Light Being says, This was created long long ago, before the keeping of time. It is so large that I cannot see the top. The being says, as he smiles, That is because there is no top. This is the entryway to the frequencies that will deliver to you the next part of the Sacred Text. You and Ra will flow upward and out of the opening. When you are out of the opening, there will be another being like me who will give to you the next part of the Sacred Text. I wish you well in this receiving. I nod thank you.

Ra takes my hand and motions that we will begin. I nod ok and together we flow upward and upward and upward. As we flow upward, on the sides of the cavern there are lights that radiate outward and when we pass then, they stop. We continue upward. The top is still not in sight. Ra sends a thought to me that we are all right and we will arrive soon. I send the thought, ok.

We are still flowing upward and I can feel my essence shifting and changing, releasing personality presentations. Ra says this is good. The closer we are to the top, the less that I am, but I still am. Ra says good.

We are approaching the top and above the opening I can see blue and white. Ra says that is my projection and I must not do that. I say ok.

We arrive at the top and there is nothing. Just emptiness. Ra says we wait.

I am holding my consciousness clear. Ra says good.

There is a forming before us. A swirling. We wait. I am practicing allowing and not reaching forth to see something be made manifest. Ra says this is necessary. Good.

Now there is a clearing and there is a seeming floor, grey in color. The rest is all white. A being comes forth from the white, which is like an essence. The being is wearing a robe that is dark in color, but no color. Ra says good. The being is moving toward us. He is holding a globe in his hands. It is a white globe and as he comes closer the globe lights brighter. This causes the being to smile.

The being comes to me and smiles and says, You must be the One. This globe recognizes you. I nod yes. The Being says, Now do I place this globe of the Sacred Text within your being. Do you receive it? I say, I am honored to receive this Sacred Text into my being that it might be delivered into the words that are now being received. The being says, There is more than words that are received but I see that you already recognize this to be true. I nod yes. Then receive this globe. He allows the globe to flow forth and it flows into the heart area of my being. It is the largest globe thus far. The Being says that it is large because there are greater frequencies that will accompany the words. I close my eyes and allow the merging of the globe within my being.

The being watches and when the globe is fully aligned with my being, says then that he will depart and return when it is time to receive the globe again. I nod that I understand.

THIRD LAYER OF THE SACRED TEXT

The being departs, but my eyes are closed. I just feel his departure.

Ra takes my hand again and says, then are you ready? I nod that I am. I am waiting for the words to flow forth.

These are the words of the Sacred Text as they flow forth now.

Until the end of time there will be those ones who come forth to receive the words of this Sacred Text. Only the One can receive these words. Many have tried to bring themselves to this location. The Sacred Text would not allow them entry. The Sacred Text is a living entity that holds the Secrets of the Pyramid at Chichén Itzá. The reason that these Secrets are held within this Text is the deliberate placing of Truth within the Text. The Truth and the Histories are given now to One who receives them. It is the time, then, upon earth when the receiving of these words, Secret, are needed to shift what is occurring upon earth. It is time simply because the Text is being received.

There have been many times upon the earth when there was a decreasing of the numbers of beings residing upon the earth. This decreasing has been a deliberate action by those who wish to rule earth. This is the history of earth. If the words are being received now, then it is evident that there are those ones upon the earth who are again attempting to rule and to cause the beings upon earth to be as slaves bid to do the bidding of those in control. *This is a very serious condition, for by doing this, there is a depleting of the life force within all beings who reside upon earth as human.*

Then this text will shift those frequencies and flow forth those patterns and encodings that will activate within the humans residing upon earth those frequencies that will augment their residing and protect the life force within their being. The receiving of this Text, this Sacred Text of Secrets, will bring to earth those ones who will protect the humans, innocent in their residing, and clear the way for a better residing in a more advanced frequency. This advanced frequency will begin to dissolve the control and illusion that those ones determined to own earth for themselves. The dissolving of that which they have and are creating with their distorted purposes will push them into a different frequency where they will be taken to different locations to assist them to release the destructive manners. There are Holy Ones who will proceed with this healing of those ones.

This healing has occurred in the past and those ones were healing only to return to their purposes once again. At the receiving of this Sacred Text and the Secrets, there is a radiating outward to alert those Holy Ones that this now is occurring upon earth with this receiving. There is a different plan for those who have been trying to control earth. The description of the plan rests with the Holy Ones, for they are adept at assisting the spirits within those ones to be made whole. This will be the last attempt by the Holy Ones to transform these ones. They will not be able to be freed until they are transformed. The transformation is a freedom, which they might recognize as the transformation continues. Yet this is of the Holy Ones and not for this revealing.

Now as this Text is received and the Secrets are revealed, then the radiating of this alert occurs. Do not be fearful for the results of this receiving. All is intended for the good of All. *This has been decided that this will be the end of the destruction, the hatred, and the distortion that has covered the earth.* That is the purpose of this receiving. It is the freedom of earth and her human beings. There are many Light Beings upon earth. It is to them that these frequencies flow forth, for the restoration of their beingness. Then the receiving can begin.

I feel my consciousness expanding. I can hear a different language being spoke by many. It is a holy speaking. I can see a circle of beings who are wearing robes and who are speaking together. There is a great rectangular stone before them and as they speak the language, it is being carved as symbols into the stone, which is very tall, rising way above the beings, perhaps six or seven of their height, maybe more. It continues to rise upward as they continue to speak. They have dedicated themselves to this speaking. They are in the number of eight, one standing apart from the seven.

The one that is standing apart in this vision steps forth to me and says, Now you will receive this speaking. This is the Secret of this location. This is the Sacred Text that has been held since this time and before this time that you are viewing. When we are complete with speaking these words, we will dissolve and return to the Source. We will continue to speak as you receive the words. I bow my head to the being who does the same to me. He departs and returns to his station outside of the circle of seven.

These are the words that are given. Still they are in a different language. I wait. Ra say good. He is still holding my hand, which feels comforting.

Naktah Sontoh Freenan. The Secrets are revealed.

Within the creating of the structures upon the earth, there resides certain truths that are presented in frequencies. When the receiving of this Sacred Text is complete, there will be the activating of those structures. Each structure will reveal its Secrets. Yet these Secrets are the activating of all structures, which must occur before the releasing of each structure's secrets.

The secrets that are revealed then will be the building of a new earth. The calling forth of those structures upon earth that celebrate the totality of earth and the fulfilling of the purpose of any and all structures upon the earth. The purpose of all structures created within these purposes hold the creating of an atmosphere, and essence, that will flow forth and nourish the humans residing, for they have become depleted of the true nourishment. This essence will flow downward toward the humans residing upon the surface of the earth. The humans will then shed their persona-established presence and emerge to be who they truly are. This will not be fearful or challenging to them. It will be as a birthing and a great gift of freedom, for many have taken to themselves the illusion of who they might be. This illusion has been in many many turnings of the eras a detriment to the beings, yet it has been believed by those humans that this was a saving grace. This will be dispelled.

Now we speak the words.

Until there resides humans freed to be that which they truly are, the spirit of the holy ones incarnate, then there will be the flowing forth of the frequencies to dispel that which prohibits this residing.

The water will rise upward and there will be some lands that will reside beneath the waters. This is all part of the reforming of the earth. No humans will perish. No creatures will perish. *This transformation of the surface of the earth holds within it the true nature of the earth.*

The earth will be replenished and golden light will emanate from the earth. The golden light will be as food for the humans and the creatures. The golden light cannot be used but resides emanating for the purpose of being received by humans and creatures.

This is one of the secrets. The golden light is the gold that has been referred to in many histories. Yet it is the golden light of the earth. It is a light essence that will not be made manifest into physicality. In the past, such manifesting occurred at the hands of those ones who came from distant galaxies and who were interested in taking with them the manifested gold, for it would then feed the beings of their homes. Yet the gold would not leave earth even as they attempted to accumulate it. Earth would not allow.

Earth is the Mother Being. Earth holds the histories and more of all that has occurred since the first breathing forth from the spark of creation. These are the secrets that are now being revealed.

There have been great beings who came to earth to establish the structures in the many locations upon the earth. There are three hundred and eight structures. All else has been built later and is not part of this frequency. The great ones who came were known as giants, yet they were simply great beings who resided in order to anchor the frequencies within each structure.

THIRD LAYER OF THE SACRED TEXT

The frequencies that have been placed within each structure hold within them the speakings of the giants who placed them incarnate. The giants have breathed forth the histories of other realms and many formings within the universes. There are many different gatherings of beings who are residing incarnate and have freed themselves of the illusion. The giants are among those beings.

The planets that reside outside of this universe are very large and many in number. They are larger than your present largest planet. Your universe and this galaxy has been protected by those large ones. They are as if the parents of this galaxy. The large planets breathed forth a part of themselves and within the part there developed a force that called forth creation. The creation then increased until there formed the planets of your galaxy. Your galaxy is held in love yet the holding is not love but is a caring of a mother. The mother of your galaxy is the gathering of those large planets.

The earth now holds the frequencies of its origin. The histories that are present within all of the structures are beyond the believed years of histories that reside upon earth. This revealing will change the nature of understanding creation itself and the vastness of All That Is.

Now the vastness is being revealed within these frequencies. These words are but words. They are most powerful because they hold and carry forth the frequencies that represent these histories. The frequencies flow forth to continue to create the planets that reside within your galaxy.

None recognize that the planets in your galaxy are continually being created. That is the true nature of creation and the life force that flows forth from creation itself. The large planets are breathing forth even now the continued creation of the planets in this galaxy. Earth is continually being breathed forth. *This breathing forth resides in eternity.*

The many geometric discoveries and interpretations of those geometric presentations are currently limited, though many still cannot comprehend the manners of the formings. The missing ingredients for such understanding reside within these frequencies. When fully received, then even a child will be able to understand the nature of geometric structures for they will be able to know, to know beyond seeing, as will all beings, the full nature of the structuring of all universes within and about each other. For this earth belongs to many universes, as universes overlay each other. It is the nature of the All.

Now these words are written.

Upon the nose of the earth there resides three structures. The structures are of stone but the stone will begin to dissolve and there will be a creation that will begin to appear. The structure will be of crystalline essence and *many who come near the structure will discover that they are healing of all physical maladies. This is a gift of the secrets.*

There resides then the speaking of the All for there is one speaking. This is the one speaking.

Within the All there is embraced totality. There is unity with the All. All else that surmises separation is dead, depleted of life force. This is the decree of the All. The All holds the totality of truth and the expressions of truth. All else is no more. The All holds within it all creations, all universes, all galaxies, all patterns and encodings. The All holds totality in perfect synchronization. All else is no more. The All is.

All that makes itself appear to be separate from the All is but dust in the dissolving of the untruth.

All that has been created from the dust of the illusion holds within it those frequencies that declare them to be no more.

All that has been created by the dust of the illusion is separate from the All because the All holds within it truth and totality of being. Untruth is of dust of no more.

Those who declare truth within the illusion are no more.

Those who declare truth within truth are eternal.

Those who hold the embracing of all beings within their being are of eternity.

Those who created from the nothing are nothing and are not being. Those who create from the nothing, believing that they are of power, are of the nothing and are no more.

Those who are no more are not being.

Those who continue to reside in the untruth and create from the nothingness are held within the nothingness, waiting to be called forth to be created. They are nothing until they are created within truth. Such beings have suffered the releasing of their concepts of power.

Those who have suffered the releasing of their believed power continue to suffer until they are made whole by their own releasing of their seeming individual beingness. Until there is the releasing of that seeming individual beingness and the power of that being there will be suffering. This is the declaration of the All. The All holds truth alone.

Those who suffer for fear of not residing in truth yet choose truth, will always reside in truth and their consciousness will awaken to truth of who they are, the one of the All. Many hold the illusion of separateness yet desire wholeness. Those ones will be made whole. Their suffering will be dissolved and they will be embraced by the All as the children of the All.

This truth is not law. It is truth. Truth holds no untruth. The All is truth. The All is one. The All is the embracing of all that is created within the truth of one.

THIRD LAYER OF THE SACRED TEXT

Some creating occurs of the One and then is held in separate frequencies for the purpose of allowing the All to flow forth in all manners of being. Yet this is not separateness. It is the All expressing itself in numerous manners, unlimited manners, yet still those manners are the All and the substance of the All.

Then the separate frequencies are but an expression of the breath of creation itself. The breath of creation itself flows forth to become the All. Such breath gives the illusion of being separate from the All, but is the All breathing itself forth.

Those who recognize truth will always be.

Those who yearn for truth will always be.

Those who yearn for truth and reside in truth, even in the face of the distortion, will always be.

All beings who reside upon the earth and hold truth within their frequencies will remain upon earth during the great resurgence of truth and the manifesting of truth incarnate. The golden essence will feed the many and they will thrive once again upon the earth. This is spoken long ago and is held until released into physicality. The releasing of the spoken words into physicality brings forth the healing of earth and the warm embracing of the humans who reside upon earth. All beings who reside upon earth are considered humans, for all beings are of one.

No fear. All transformations are of wholeness and are expressed and experienced within the moment and are of one frequency, the frequency of the One, the frequency of the All, the frequency of the creation of All of itself.

Truth is and is made known upon the earth. Now is truth. Now is restoration. Now is the emergence of that which is. Now is the dissolving of that which is not.

Hold to your beingness and watch. Observe. For you will be given the visions of truth and the visions will dedicate themselves to your restoration and beingness. Reside in truth. See not separation from any. Those who dissolve before your eyes are the nothing that has formed itself and is no more.

Hold your heart to totality. Hold your knowing to peace. Hold your thinking mind to the knowing that all is well. Remember truth. The dissolving of the untruth will cause you to wonder, to fear. Fear not, for you are of the wholeness of being. All else that dissolves is nothing. It has been created with the dust of the nothing. Remember this. Allow yourselves to be of the Great Ones, that which you are.

Beings of earth! Now you become that which you truly are. Great Ones birthed of Great Ones. Questioning is of human nature. Truth is of the essence of that which you are.

Then the speaking of these words for this releasing is complete.

Go forth only when you are called to go forth.

Reside in truth.

Then this globe is complete with its releasing.

So be it.

I see the gathering of beings stop speaking and they are facing me. They are speaking a language to me. I can know that it is blessings. They are sending me blessings from the way long ago past. They are becoming white light. They are dissolving, just as they said they would. I breathe my breath into the vision and thank them for all that they have given. I say, I am the One and I have received the words that you have spoken. Oh Holy Ones, I give great gratitude to you. So be it.

Now I am releasing the vision and the Light Being has entered the chamber and is presenting himself before me. He is holding out his hands and the globe begins to release itself from my being. Within the globe is the image of the beings who spoke the words and the very tall pillar of stone. It is swirling and soon disappears from being seen. The Light Being holds the globe and bows his head to me and then turns quickly to flow over to the location where the globe will reside.

Ra motions that it is time for us to depart. I nod that I understand. I am ok, I say. Ra says, We will see how you do after you leave this frequency. I nod that I understand.

We begin departing but a Light Being comes before us and motions that we would depart thought a different chamber. The Light Being says that the chamber will assist to align and synchronize the frequencies that we have been experiencing. He looks to me and says, You have done very well. It is surprising to us how well you have done.

Then he motions us toward a chamber and we flow forth into it. It is of blue light, light blue. Ra says this is correct. We are held within the light and then are flowing upward, even as we are not efforting to do so. We are being carried upward and out of the blue light. We are now then emerging and are in the white. Ra says good. Now we will depart and flow toward my realm. I nod ok.

We are now flowing toward Ra's realm. He is pulling me along as I do not seem to have a will to make a choice. Ra says that is ok. It is part of the frequencies that I received. He pulls me into his realm and we are approaching the two chairs where he teaches me. Ra says, We will go now to the large chairs. I nod that I understand and allow him to continue to pull me along.

I am not depleted, but I believe I am still taking form. Ra says this is true.

We are now both sitting in the large chairs. The seats. Ra is looking to me and is breathing a breath toward me. It feels to be light yellow or light golden essence. Ra says it is the essence of life. I am breathing it in. I know that I am all right. Ra says yes, that I am simply returning and releasing the frequencies that were in the globe at the completion of the receiving. I allow.

THIRD LAYER OF THE SACRED TEXT

I can feel my physicality and the consciousness that resides there is quite expanded. Ra says that is ok. He says to wait a little longer before trying to return. I nod ok. I wait.

I believe I could return now. Ra says to give it a try, but if I find that I am having difficulty maintaining consciousness, then to return to his realm. He will hold the portal open for that possibility. I nod yes and thank Ra. Ra says no words are necessary. I nod ok.

I begin to flow toward my vortex. Alannah is there, blessed Alannah. She smiles when she sees me. She puts her hands on my shoulders and says that I must wait there with her for a short time. I nod ok. This is bringing me back to a frequency that can return to be incarnate. I understand now. Alannah begins to sing and the music fills me and brings peace. I am letting go of trying to return and just being. Alannah whispers good. I would like to return now. She says to wait a little longer. I am agreeable.

I wait. I am breathing deeply in my body-physical. Yet I can feel my consciousness is very expanded still. I wait. I continue to breathe deeply hoping that will help my returning. Alannah laughs and says that is my human nature wanting its spirit to return. It is all right, she says. It is natural.

She looks into my being and says that it looks like I can return now. I am grateful and thank her for her help. She smiles to me and I can feel her love radiating into me. I thank her again and turn toward my vortex.

I am entering the vortex and flowing downward into my body-physical. I feel I am ok. I send the message to Ra that

I am successfully returning. I can hear the portal closing to his realm.

I am all right. I have returned.

So be it.

SIXTEENTH TRANSMISSION
Eleventh Speaking

We have been traveling for a day away from home and I am presenting myself now because of the words that entreated me to continue as often as I can. I am bringing myself to an expanded consciousness and will journey to Ra's realm.

The frequencies are building to such a degree that I am feeling that I would vomit, but I do not and breathe deeply to synchronize what is occurring. I have been told that I am the Living Sacred Text. This astonishes me and once again I am humbled by the honor to participate. I am told I needed to know this fact before I journey to Ra's realm. I nod that I understand. I ask if I projected these messages and the answer is that it is not possible within these frequencies, that now they will shift and I will journey to Ra's realm. I nod thank you.

Now I am shifting once again and feel the frequencies that are carrying me to Ra. I am approaching the portal to Ra's realm and in the next moment all is white, as if I am already in his realm. I can hear him calling me to come forth to the area where we sit in two seats to speak together. I wait to be certain this is correct.

I flow forth to that area in the white and Ra greets me. He says, Come, we will not hesitate for there is much to be released in this journey. He continues, Do not be concerned for repeating everything that I say, for it is the words of the Sacred Text that are the most important. I nod that understand. Ra says, Good, now let us depart from this frequency.

Ra takes my hand and that is a signal to me...a very loud bang has happened upon my home. I am pausing to allow that to dissipate. I do not know what it was. I am breathing deeply and letting go. I don't know if it was an attempt to interfere with this transmission. Ra says to come along and do not allow the sound to become important. I nod that I agree. Grayson came into the room and said that he was standing right where the sound was made but he didn't know what it was either. I will continue with Ra now.

Again I feel the frequencies increasing and again I feel as if I would vomit they are so intense. Now I am with Ra and he is looking to me to be sure that I want to continue. I says that I do. Ra says good and motions toward the white. As if a white curtain, the whiteness flows aside and there is an opening. Ra says, It will look as if we have journeyed through that opening, but we will go a different route, just in case there was an attempt to disrupt your ability in your surroundings to continue. I nod that I understand.

Ra takes my hand and we actually turn toward the opposite direction and Ra speaks some words that I do not understand and then there is a portal, a large vortex that opens before us. Ra says good and then takes my hand and

THIRD LAYER OF THE SACRED TEXT

we flow into the vortex. It is initially dark and Ra says that is so that none will recognize this is a portal. I nod that I understand. My heart area is already activating and feels in physicality to be heavy. Ra says, That is because we will arrive quickly. I nod that I understand.

I ask Ra to help me to remain focused. He turns to me and places his finger upon my third eye area and speaks some words. A white electric force flows into me. I am present. Ra continues to send the frequency into my being. He says, This is needed now. You are entering into a new frequency of the Sacred Text. It will become more intense but you will be able to do just what you have been doing. You are most capable. I nod that I understand. Ra removes his finger from my forehead and looks to me. His face disappears and there is essence, golden essence. Then he says, Come. Do not be alarmed at my appearance. We are together much more than we know. I nod that I understand. Still he takes my hand and pulls me along. We will travel quickly now, he says. And that is what we do.

We are flowing over mountains, we are flowing over lands, we are approaching a mountain and then flow around it quickly to the other side of the mountain. Ra says, Now we will enter, for this is the pyramid where we will receive the next releasing of the Sacred Text which resides within you. I nod that I understand. We wait. We wait for the invitation to enter. Ra says that is correct.

There is an opening that seems to slide into the mountain and we still wait. A Light Being is appearing. The Light Being says that there have been many attempts to stop the continuing of this releasing of the Sacred Text. He says, Enter quickly. We do not hesitate and enter and the opening closes quickly behind us.

Ra and I are standing before the Light Being. The Light Being says that it is not important to speak of the attempted interference. It is better that we continue now with the reason that we are present there. Both Ra and I nod that we understand. The Light Being says, Good. Follow me.

The Light Being is moving quickly and we are flowing behind, and as previously, the Light Being is faster than are we. Yet we are flowing quickly. Ra says, The Light Being is clearing the way for us and needs to go before us. I nod that I understand.

Now the Light Being stands and waits for us. He is radiating great white light. We are entering the light. It is peaceful.

The Light Being looks to me and says, I am pleased at your dedication. It is truly necessary. We must continue. I nod yes. All right now, he says, let us go forth. He motions his arm and we are not entering anything but are transported into the chamber where I have previously received the frequencies of the Sacred Text in the form of different globes. Ra says I am correct.

There are small doors in the side of the wall and that is where the Light Being has accessed a globe previously. The Light Being says that will not occur this time. He motions toward a platform and motions for me to stand. Ra holds my hand and we both go to the platform. It is smooth and is made of a black stone. I look to Ra to see if he is real and this is all real. I continue to receive messages that this is hoax. Ra says this is real. Do not pay attention to the messages.

The Light Being comes to me and says, This platform will rise upward and we will all enter a different frequency. I have created this to assure that you will not be disturbed. I nod that I understand. The Light Being stands also upon the platform and it begins to rise upward, as if floating. We are leaving the chamber and are emerging in another that is filled with green light. The being waves his arm and the green light is cleared. He says, The green frequency has been holding the pristine nature of this chamber. Now we will continue. I nod ok.

The being stands and begins to speak ancient words. There come from behind him several other Light Beings. They are also speaking the same words. Ra and I are still on the platform. Waiting. The beings flow forth and surround Ra and me. They are bringing great white light. We are surrounded by the light and their words. The platform begins to rise up again. Now I can see that we are raising up and into the capstone. Ra says that is true. The platform stops moving and we are inside the capstone of this pyramid that projected itself as a mountain. Ra says yes.

From the very top triangle of the capstone there forms a globe and it flows downward and the Light Being receives it. It is actually a box that is in the shape of a temple. The Light Being comes toward me and as he does, the side of the box opens and there flows forth a golden globe. It remains in front of me. The Light Being says, Do you receive this Globe of the Sacred Text into your being? I say, With gratitude and honor do I receive this Globe of the Sacred Text. The Light Being speaks words and as he does, the globe flows toward me and pauses before my heart area. It is now the color of green. The Light Being says good. This is correct now. He speaks further words and the globe, which is golden within and green on the outside, flows into my heart area. I feel the frequencies of the globe radiate through my entire being. Ra is still holding my hand and says that soon the words will begin to be given. Remain calm. I nod ok.

The Light Being says that he will depart and return when the releasing of the Text is complete. He departs. Ra says, Breathe deeply and then allow. The Text is waiting. I nod ok.

I breathe deeply and the breath that comes out of my nose is golden. Ra says good. Now it will begin.

> **These are the words that come forth.**
>
> The receiving of the words of this Sacred Text bring forth those frequencies that call to the hidden chambers within the earth, call to them to open and to release the elixir of golden essence that the beings upon earth might be nourished. The flowing forth of this elixir does not enter the illusion and distortion, for if it were to enter, there would be the dissolving of that distortion and illusionary presence. The golden elixir flows forth within the truth incarnate upon earth.
>
> The truth incarnate upon earth is presented within the presentation of nature and within the presentation of creatures. There are those in human

form who are capable of receiving the golden elixir. The ability to receive the golden elixir has nothing to do with good or bad, correct or incorrect. Those humans who can receive the golden elixir are residing in a way that refrains from judgment or forms of the frequencies of separation from the whole. For it is known that upon earth there is a great temptation to reside in a separation from the totality simply because the distortion and those who reside within it give the impression that they are separate as well. Yet it is knowing within truth that all beings hold within themselves the spark of creation and the truth that resides within that spark.

Then the golden elixir will flow forth and nourish all humans who dedicate themselves to refusing to judge others, but to allow others to be as they are. This means then that all beings have the right to be who they are presenting themselves to be. This is the All flowing forth to fulfill its purposes of presenting the avenue for creation itself to form itself in all manners. All manners does include those who are dedicating themselves to the distortion of separation from the whole. It is called forth: *judge not any, for all are flowing forth to fulfill prophecies of long ago.*

The prophecies of long ago present the time upon earth when there are many who are residing within the illusion, within the distortion, and there are those ones who have dedicated themselves to refusing to judge any as right or wrong, and those ones hold within them the golden elixir of nourishment of being. The golden elixir flows forth to those one who are dedicated to distortion and as it flows within, there is a pause in the dedication of untruth and a seeming forgetting. *This is the Great Forgetting.*

The Great Forgetting upon earth, as prophesized, is the beginning of the completion of the distortion and the also beginning of the emerging of the truth which holds the All incarnate. The truth that holds the All incarnate is a gradual emerging for it continues to invite all beings to cease from judging and to allow all beings to be as they are and to continue in a journey that is laid before them long long ago. *Those who continue to refuse to judge and to allow the truth to be made manifest about them, are then the holders and the carriers of the Golden Elixir of Nourishment of Being.*

During the Time of Forgetting, it is necessary that the golden elixir be present within those who are of truth. It is also recognized that those who are of truth are also of the human being incarnate which is imperfect. Such imperfection is allowed and not refused the golden elixir. All humans have an inner desire to receive the golden elixir because it is the essence of the life force that forms in physicality. The golden elixir or life force also forms separately from physicality, yet that is another speaking from the Sacred Text.

THIRD LAYER OF THE SACRED TEXT

During the Time of Forgetting, there will be those ones who will come forth to assist those who have forgotten their created purpose in the distortion. There will be those in leadership positions who will no longer be capable of fulfilling their created purposes within the distortion. They are not right or wrong, good or bad. They are simply those ones who functioned according to the pathway that they have been residing upon for many many turnings of the life force within them. During the Time of Forgetting, there is then the releasing of false purposes so that those ones, those leaders, can be assisted in a better synchronization with truth and with the healing of their consciousness.

Across the earth the leaders will find that they can no longer lead, even those ones who are young in human age will not be able to continue in their purposes. This will seem to cause a great chaos, but it is the turning of the frequencies and the releasing of what has been waiting for a very long time to be released so that the earth and those who reside upon her can begin to feel the natural rhythm of earth's gifts.

Those who have banded together to gather power to themselves will discover that the power is illusionary and that there is no such thing as power within the distortion as it is dissolving. Some of those beings will attempt to gather strength to be a major controller or power-monger. Yet this will not be able to occur as that power pattern and symbol that has held the power and patterns of that residing within the distortion and illusion of separation from the whole will no longer be activated. *The symbol for such power is deactivated then and returned to the histories as presented in the carved histories within the walls of great structures.* The walls of these structures will one day be revealed, but this will not occur until there is a synchronization of all upon the earth. The synchronization of the All upon the earth, of all beings who reside upon the earth with earth herself and the nature and creatures will flow forth gradually so that all can have the opportunity to become whole once again within physicality. This process is projected to require several hundred flowings of the keeping of time.

Yet the manner of keeping of time will change, for the previous residing and the intent of the distortion and illusion have slowed time and caused it to pause in a manner that would hold the integrity of earth. As the synchronization occurs, then the frequencies upon earth will begin to unite and that will cause the keeping of time to dissolve. For, it is a natural manner that All is residing in the one moment, wherein there is peace, joy and fulfillment of being. Within the peace, joy and fulfillment of being, because it is incarnate, there will seem to be a continuation of time. The reason for this seeming continuation of time is the fulfilling of the purpose that incarnate, beings will experience the return to the paradise they have always been intended to reside within. Thus, the seeming cause and effect will demonstrate such fulfillment.

Yet there are those who will be of a consciousness that will allow them to dance between the simulated fulfillment within the cause and effect and between the non-physical of paradise in spirit form. *This is called the Dance of Divine Fulfillment Incarnate.* This Dance has been present in the beginning of beings incarnating. Now it will be present at the end of the same journey. Yet none would be fearful of the ending, for such Dance will continue for thousands of the keeping of time in the histories. This is the residing within paradise incarnate and simultaneously holding the consciousness of creation itself. *Conscious holding of creation itself is the beginning spark of creation.*

The beginning spark of creation held in consciousness is creation conscious of creation. *This then is the creation of consciousness.* This is the final creation within the All. The final creation within the All then resides within that called eternity. Eternity is the releasing of time. The releasing of time is the fulfillment of the All.

Then this is the completing of this releasing of the Sacred Text.

The Sacred Text speaks to the One who receives its frequencies in this manner: You have received this Sacred Text many times, yet this is the first time that you have been able to continue. The golden elixir fills your being and assists you to continue. For it is prophesied that this releasing of the Sacred Text will be able to be completed. You are the One. You have always been the One. Even when you have taken form as a seeming different being to fulfill other purposes, you were then and always the One. This is the frequency of the Sacred Text residing within your being. You are the Living Sacred Text. The globes that flow forth are the calling forth of the next speaking from the Sacred Text that resides within and as you, the One.

Now we are complete.

I feel the frequencies within my being and there is a feeling of the returned presence of the Light Being. The Light Being says, You are doing very well. As he says those words, the globe flows from my heart area and into his waiting hands. The Light Being raises his arms upward and the globe returns to the very top of the pyramid capstone. It disappears in those frequencies. The Light Being says, You must depart now.

Ra and I nod yes. Ra again is pulling me along. I am capable, but I am also in a most expanded frequency. Ra says that is all right. I am bringing you out of this area. The Light Being is showing Ra and me the way and we are seeming to enter a chamber that is more formed. The Light Being says that this chamber will assist me to be more formed. He says,

THIRD LAYER OF THE SACRED TEXT

you have been essence and now you are forming that which you are, the One. I nod that I understand, but I cannot open my eyes in spirit form. I do not have a physical vision of this chamber. Ra says that is all right.

The Light Being says that it is time for us to depart. He says to me, You will be all right. Ra will see that you are all right. I nod ok. The Light being waves his arm, though I only know this as I cannot see it. Ra flows forth through an opening in the frequencies, pulling me long. We are flowing back to Ra's realm, which is a comforting feeling.

We are entering Ra's realm and are in the area of white. Ra speaks ancient words and I am returning to a consciousness residing within his realm. Ra says good. Now I am looking to Ra and the essence of his being returns to a form that I recognize as Ra's face. Kind of. Ra laughs at my words. His laughter is a balm. Good, he says, you are ready to return to your home. Go now to your vortex, for it is necessary to reside within that body-physical so that it will not be vulnerable. I nod ok.

I flow forth toward my vortex. I am not going through portals to do this, I am simply flowing toward the vortex. I do not see Alannah, but that is all right. I am ok to return. I flow down the vortex and into my body-physical. I am returning. I can open my eyes. I have returned. I say the words: so be it.

I am honored to participate in this way.
So be it.

FOURTH LAYER OF THE SACRED TEXT

SEVENTEENTH TRANSMISSION
First Speaking

I have been feeling something at the top of my head, which means the crown energy center. Regardless of what I think I need to be doing, this priority of the Sacred Text brings me to this opening today. I am expanding my consciousness further now.

I am already approaching Ra's realm and not the portal, but a similar experience, where Ra is waiting, as if hovering over his realm. I will pause to be sure this is true or if I am remembering and projecting, which I do not want to do. I wait. Thoughts of yesterday come to me, as if disturbing this experience. I am ignoring them and their invitation to participate as if they are occurring right now. In the timelessness, perhaps they are, yet it is the frequencies of this journey that call me to them and that is where I am placing my attention. I hear Ra say come, and still I am waiting.

Still memories come. I will go forth to the portal to Ra's realm. I see the portal. I can hear Alannah's words but can't make them out. She is saying, Continue. Enter now. I bring my consciousness to the portal and breathe it forth. I wait. I can also hear Ra saying, Come. I request entry and the portal opens. This is a different experience but I go with it and enter. There is Alannah and she is saying, Good that you have come. I nod to her and she motions me toward Ra.

Ra is sitting in the large seat and I flow toward him and bring my consciousness to a more expanded state. Ra says, Good. Come here to your seat. I flow upward and am sitting in the large seat next to Ra.

Ra says, We will go forth. Yet I wish to speak with you. I nod ok. Let us go into the next chamber. He takes my hand and we flow into the chamber where we usually sit together and he speaks to me. We are now sitting beside each other. He is still holding my hand, which tells me we are entering a frequency within which he will continue to reside in this manner with me.

Ra waits. The frequencies are blue, light blue. He says Good. Now he waves his arm and there is before us a place or screen and he is waving again to project, perhaps, on to this screen what he would like me to see. I see an archaeological site of sorts. It looks like part of what I have seen as Chichén Itzá. Ra says, That is correct. Then he waves his arm again and I am viewing beneath the location where there are tall pillars, beneath, where I have been before. Ra says Good.

There is a chamber beneath that location and Ra says, You have been here before. I say that it seems to be familiar, perhaps when I traveled with Alannah? Ra says it is similar but not the same location. I nod that I understand. Ra says, I am showing you this because there are others who have entered this chamber. They are exploring and have no desire to cause harm or destruction. Yet it is imperative that we hold the Sacred Text a Secret. I nod that I understand.

Ra says, There is an entryway in this chamber that can lead explorers to the portal to the Sacred Text. I nod ok. Ra says, we will journey to the Sacred Text as we usually do, yet we will have to be very careful to not open to any outside thoughts because it is the outside thoughts that attract the curious who are adventuring. I nod that I understand. Ra continues, This means that you truly must hold your attention to the present moment. I nod ok. Ra says, To be certain, I am asking your permission to place about you a shield which will hold your consciousness clear. I will continue to hold your hand because this shield will deliver to you a freedom from the physicality that you have been residing within. I wish for you to choose to remain incarnate. I say that is always my choice. Ra says, Yes, however, you have not made that choice in this frequency. I nod that I understand and say that I give permission. Ra says Good. Now we will journey into another chamber, one that you have not yet entered. I nod ok. The screen is no longer present.

I am entering what I believe is the chamber Ra referred to. He has released my hand and is standing before me. It seems I am entering the chamber and I am simultaneously standing before Ra. Ra says, *The chamber is a rotating of the illusion of time while holding the present moment as sacred.* The frequencies are very intense. Ra breathes forth a strong frequency and it flows from his mouth toward me. I stand firm. The frequencies are white essence and flow about me.

They are light-filled and bring a golden feeling to my being. Ra says that is the golden elixir. I am placing it around you. It will shield you from external influences. Later when we return, I will assist you to incorporate this shield into your being, for it is needed now. You have been depleted of frequencies through no fault of your own. That is to be expected, however I wish to assist you in your incarnate journey in this way. I wish to say Thank you, but I cannot speak. I project the thought and Ra smiles and says Good.

I am being transformed. Ra says this is the frequency of the shield and asks me if I will be able to go forth with him as I reside within this frequency. I say that I believe I can. Good, he says and takes my hand. Then we will depart from this chamber. I nod ok. My consciousness is very expanded. Ra says that is what will hold me within the present moment. I nod that I understand.

We are now flowing forth from this chamber and Ra is pulling me along. It is not that I am not flowing along but Ra is pulling me because we are journeying very fast and we are as if a blur to the consciousness. Ra says that is correct but to remain in the present more. I nod ok.

We are flowing toward a familiar mountain and Ra says that is correct. The portal to the mountain opens and we flow within and the portal closes quickly behind us. There stands the Light Being, the Keeper of the Sacred Text. He nods to both of us and says come quickly into another chamber and then we will speak. He flows forth and Ra and I flow behind him. My thoughts go to another being and the Light Being stops and turns to me and says, That is a possibility but I ask you to not consider anything yet. I nod ok. We continue following the Light being and are coming closer to where he is standing. We arrive and the being says Good. Now we will enter this chamber.

He waves his arm and we are flowing into a chamber but I discern nothing. The Being says good. He waves his arm and it seems that the chamber walls appear and are rotating, turning round and round. The turning increases in speed and we are lifted, as if in an elevator, upward. The Being laughs at my words. He says, It is now all right to speak of anything, for we are within the frequencies of the Sacred Text. We are actually flowing upward within them. I nod that I understand. I say, The perception of what is Text changes within this experience. The Being says, That is deliberate. It will shift any perceptions that might allow any others to be curious. There will be no manner of available attachment for any, even for us. He smiles and I am gifted with a wave of love and caring.

The Being says, Do not be concerned for anything. I am taking care of everything and Ra is holding your hand which means that you are incarnate and wishing to remain so. I respect that, of course. Yet you must know that you are so very much more than your incarnate beingness. Your beingness presents to you an imperfection that you do not like, yet it is that exact imperfection that allows you to remain incarnate. If you were to present the fullness of that which you are while incarnate, you would perhaps not be able to remain for long. Your perfection is not quite a match to physicality. Physicality holds within it deep distortion and because of your previous purposes with assisting humanity, then that density of distortion holds for you a portal through which you could traverse as your perfection and you would assist the many once again. However, that is not your purpose now, as you know. I simply speak these words in the hopes that you will cease from self-criticism of your form in physicality and whatever you do or not do. Remember always that you are residing in so many dimensions simultaneously because you are the One. The only frequency that you do not incarnate while you journey within your lifely incarnate journey are the frequencies of this Sacred Text. Yes, you are bringing everything into physicality, yet the totality all at once would be too much. That is why we call you forth instead of delivering to you the entire Text. Each receiving is your ability to allow the flowing to its highest degree while you remain incarnate. This is your ability. It is why you are the One. I nod that I understand. The Being says Good.

The Being continues, I also wish you to know that there are many even here in this frequency who honor who you are. It would be to your benefit to every once in a while sit quietly and receive that honoring for it will nourish your spirit in ways that will serve you as you reside incarnate. I nod OK.

The Being looks to me and says nothing but continues to look. We are ceasing from moving within the chamber and the chamber is ceasing from turning around and around. It was as if we were inside a Tibetan prayer wheel. The Being smiles and says, Exactly. That surprises me. The Being laughs

FOURTH LAYER OF THE SACRED TEXT

and says, To surprise you is an ability that I do not take lightly. I smile and nod ok.

The Being says, now we will enter. Ra and I nod ok. The entire area changes as we stand there. We are in the Chamber of the Sacred Text. Then he says, All right now, let us continue. The Being begins moving even as the pillar rises upward. Atop the pillar…I am waiting to see what forms there. The Being looks to me and says Good.

As the Being approaches the pillar it turns into a round form and begins to turn around and around. The being waits. When the turning stops, the pillar is very tall. The Being flows upward to the top of the pillar. Ra and I are still standing at its base, a little away from it. Ra says, That is necessary for us. I nod that I understand.

The Being flows downward and he is holding…I wait to see…He approaches me and he is holding a golden essence that really does not have a form. The Being says, *This is the next phase of the Sacred Text. It is called the Fourth Layer.* This will be your first receiving of this layer. You are capable. I nod ok. The Being moves his hands with the golden essence toward my being and says, Do you now receive this Sacred Text into your being? I say, It is my honor and yes I do receive the Sacred Text into my being. Even at the very last second that I speak those words, the golden essence begins to flow into my being. My entire consciousness is golden essence. I hear the Being say, I will depart now and return when the receiving is complete. Ra is still holding my hand.

I feel the Being is departed and Ra says, Now you can begin. I nod ok.

These are the words of the Fourth Layer of the Sacred Text.

Symbols, floating, symbols within my consciousness. Ra says they will form as words soon.

These are those words.

The creating of the All flows forth always. There is no beginning nor is there an end. There is only the flowing of creation which forms itself as the All in order to know that it is creation. This is the consciousness of creation. *The All serves the purpose of holding creation's conscious knowing of that which it is always.*

Within the forming of the All, the particles of the All flowed forth and because the All is the forming of the consciousness of creation itself, then within each particle there resides the same, creation forming for the knowing of itself. Within each particle, then, there is a continued flowing forth of the All within the patterns of the All that is created by Creation itself.

Within the particles, then, there is a replication again and again of creation knowing creation. This is called consciousness. Consciousness resides within all that is created. *There is nothing that is created without this consciousness.*

All is created in the moment of totality. Consciousness begins to give the illusion of separation from the totality simply because creation becomes conscious of itself. There is not separation, yet there is the journey of flowing forth and then knowing, which is *the creation of time*. Yet time resides within totality and is of the whole and the whole holds all within it.

Within the whole there resides all that has ever been created and will be created. Because the whole then holds time as well as timelessness, there is an expanding manner of the expression of creation knowing creation. The expression of creation knowing creation magnetizes particles together within likeness, within likeness of the manner of expression of creation knowing creation.

Such gathering forms a frequency that resonates always. This is the beginning of forming in a manner that, within the whole, there is a seeming separation from formings that are not magnetized to other formings. Similarity in frequencies automatically unite within the whole. The whole resides within totality. Totality holds the whole within it as totality is.

The receiving pauses and asks me if I can continue to receive. I say yes. Then it continues.

Within the forming of time there begins what is called a journey of creation within itself to further explore the manner of itself within time. *This is called the consciousness within time.* The consciousness within time further magnetizes within time those expressions that are not yet formed but are of the All being called forth by creation itself within Time. *This is called potential forming* within the journey of creation exploring knowing itself as creation within time. The potential is then a pattern that resides within the All yet is called forth by creation's flowing forth within the journey within time.

Within the potential there resides totality. Even as Totality is All and contains all, the potential holds to itself totality. Creation then calls forth the fulfilling of all potential to form within the journey within time. This forming then begins to create within Time that called like frequencies taking form, for Time calls forth taking form. Because Time calls forth taking form, then there is a seeming placement of one creation before or after another. Yet all occurs in the moment, always. Within the exploration of creation with Time, there then is the forming of similar frequencies which continue to gather to itself that which is same frequencies. This causes a type of density for the continued gathering of like frequencies pulls to the center of such forming as the movement to continue to form pulls those frequencies to it. *This then is the forming of physicality*, which forms itself within the journey of time.

The density forms and becomes physicality within Time. *This then is the understanding of the beginning of physicality with totality.*

FOURTH LAYER OF THE SACRED TEXT

Within this Fourth Layer of this Sacred Text, there flows forth this truth. All beings who receive these frequencies are beyond that called the journey of time. Beyond the frequency of time means that there is eternity present within the consciousness of those who receive this Text. The frequency of eternity also resides within the moment of the spark of creation, the moment in that breath that breathes forth the spark of creation. This means that eternity resides before the spark of creation. And this cannot be received or understood within the forming of Time simply because there is the concept of *before*. Yet those who receive these words are residing, even as they receive these words, in that moment, in the breath that breathes forth the spark of creation.

Within the moment of the breath, there is the eternal beingness. The eternal beingness has no purpose. The eternal beingness is. Within the eternal beingness there resides all possibilities, yet there is no calling forth for the fulfillment of those possibilities. Within one possibility there resides the spark of creation. And it is that possibility that causes the breath to flow forth. And it is within that breath that the spark of creation, one of the possibilities within eternity, creates.

Because of the flowing forth of that one possibility within the spark of creation, then there forms within eternity, a pattern. The pattern is the flowing forth of a possibility to reside within an action. An action within eternity rests upon the flowing forth of the spark of creation. *Because all action resides upon the flowing forth of the spark of creation then all possibilities can become.* All possibilities then would flow through the patterns of the spark of creation flowing forth to become itself. All possibilities are simply frequencies that reside within eternity.

There are those magnetizing frequencies within the journey of creation within the flowing forth of the journey and within Time that call forth from eternity those possibilities that are a companion frequency to that which is formed and called physical. This magnetizing then calls forth the fulfillment of that possibility. Such magnetizing and the flowing forth to be created upon the spark of creation's frequencies and actions, then does flow forth to be explored within the journey that contains time. It is formed within the journey which contains time so that the merging of such frequencies with its same already incarnate can occur as a process which is determined to be, so that creation can experience such merging of totality with itself incarnate.

Creation resides within Totality yet is of Eternity. In the flowing of time, then it can be known and only be known within the flowing forth of time, that eternity resides before the spark of creation and thus before the wholeness of totality. This may never be interpreted as separation from the wholeness of being. Eternity is unable to be held within such knowing if the knowing is held within time. Yet it is within time that there is a knowing of these truths.

To know of eternity is to be no more. This is not a completion of a journey. It is the nature of eternity. Within totality there resides all nourishment of being in all manners. Within totality there is the potential of calling forth from all possibilities those matching frequencies. Yet the frequencies that would be called forth must be matching, else there is no reason for the possibilities to head the call. There must be a magnetism within that which is calling forth to that which is called forth. That which is calling forth must become that which is being called forth. Then there is a flowing forth of what could be called in time, fulfillment of being.

Those who receive the frequencies of this Sacred Text are able to reside within this manner, as many have in the histories of the flowing forth within time. *This has been the nature of the manner of creation of great structures within the forming of the many gatherings of physicality.* As within the near-physicality, there have been those formings of fulfillment.

Now the Sacred Text flows forth within the histories of the many formings to deliver to those who receive these frequencies a truth of being. This truth of being delivers the truth of being which holds within it the manner of forming and being. The manner of forming and being refers to all beings who hold within themselves a consciousness that has the possibility of expressing creation known to creation, while incarnate within a beingness. This possibility and the fulfillment of the possibility then creates. Within this creation, creation itself explores itself as a beingness and then as a beingness within the journey of time. Within the journey of time and the knowing of beingness, there comes forth those abilities expressed within the consciousness of creation. Those who bring their consciousness to be a match to the creation of the All, then can reside in totality incarnate.

The residing within totality incarnate lifts the beingness from the journey of time and places the beingness beyond time. *When a being is residing beyond time, there is the fulfillment of all manners of being, as then the totality forms itself according to the beingness...in the moment.*

These beings then are known to be Holy Beings by those who reside in time. Holy Beings are the same as those who reside in time, yet the experience of the journey within time gives the appearance of difference. The Holy Beings are magnetized to those who reside in time because of the similarity of frequencies at the core of that which is creation within each and all. The Holy Ones then are dedicated to bringing the truth of being to those who are residing in time, as then the Holy Ones are uniting with themselves, just as creation celebrates the union of itself with itself. This then is a possibility that resides within eternity.

Then this is the flowing forth of this frequency of the Sacred Text. Many will not be able to incorporate these frequencies within their incarnate consciousness. Yet the frequencies are merging even when the beings believe they cannot understand what is given. This is the nature of the Sacred Text which fulfills itself, just as creation fulfills itself. One in the same.

Then this flowing forth is complete. The receiver of these frequencies and then words is most capable.

There is the releasing of the intensity within my being and I am becoming aware that Ra is still holding my hand. The Being returns and flows to me and holds his hands open to receive the frequencies of the Text that has just been given. It flows forth from my being and as it is received into his hands, the Being flows upward to place the frequencies upon the top of the pillar. As he does then the pillar begins to dissolve. The Being flows down to Ra and me and says, You are doing very well. I nod thank you. The Being says, Then you must depart now. He doesn't need to explain because I understand that the frequencies I am residing within are most expanded and I wish to remain incarnate. The Being smiles and nods yes.

The Being leads Ra and me to a portal and we are surprisingly flowed quickly from the chamber and are now flowing on our own as we begin to return to Ra's realm. Ra is pulling me and we are traveling very fast. We are again a blur.

As we flow forth, Ra says to me, When we enter his realm he will adjust the frequencies of the shield about me and it will incorporate more of what is needed for the journey upon earth incarnate, so that I will have an easier time with everything and that, he continues, will flow forth to include Grayson. I nod yes.

We are entering Ra's realm and he is already motioning about my being and I come to stand before him. He says, This receiving of the Sacred Text is the most expanded yet. He continues, You will have to place your consciousness in an expanded state to correct the words as you usually do, so that nothing is mis-stated. I nod that I understand. Ra says good.

Now go forth and return to your physicality, for I wish you to remain formed and to not dissolve. No concerns, just I wish you to be most comfortable in your residing. I will watch over you, of course, and there is Teacher as well who resides at your side always. I nod yes.

I look into Ra's eyes and feel myself dissolving into him. He says, That is for another time, now you must return. I hadn't planned on that, but now I know that when I look into his eyes there might be another journey at another time. Ra laughs and says, This journey with the Sacred Text IS the journey. I smile and nod yes.

FOURTH LAYER OF THE SACRED TEXT

Then I am flowing toward the portal and Alannah nods as she motions for me to exit. I do without hesitation and I am immediately flowing into my vortex to return to physicality. It is a comfortable flowing into my body-physical. I am returned.

All is a great gift, more than the word gift can say.

So be it.

EIGHTEENTH TRANSMISSION
Second Speaking

We are traveling and are in Georgia. Yesterday I saw the Light Being Keeper of the Text appear as if waiting for me. I said that I would receive the next transmission as soon as I could. It is 7:30 am and we are in a hotel room. I will open now and see what transpires.

I am expanding my consciousness and I can see the Light Being waiting. I will have to expand further to be able to journey to Ra's realm first. I am now approaching Ra's realm…I am not having a easy time with expanding my consciousness but I can see the portal to his realm. I am bothered by thoughts and will have to expand up several levels. Maybe because I am in a location away from home. I feel the presence of Ra. I am now in his realm. I am where the very large chairs are. I am becoming more present there. I hear Ra say, Good, now come to the other chamber. I am entering the chamber where Ra usually speaks with me.

He says, My dear, you are dedicated to the Sacred Text and that is admirable, most definitely. Are you certain? I say yes, I am. Ra says, All right now, then we shall depart. I am pausing so that I don't project. Ra says good. Ra surrounds me with frequencies and says, now we will depart. He is standing in his robes and I am beside him. He takes my hand and we are moving, flowing.

Now we are moving through the inside of what seems to be a vortex. Ra says to be very present now. I nod ok. I can see the mountain, all green, and we are approaching the side where there is a portal. Ra says, They have been waiting for us. I nod that I know that to be true. Ra smiles to me and says that it is good that I have come in this day. I am glad to hear that from Ra as I was wondering about receiving the text in a hotel room. Ra says, But you are not in a hotel room, your body is. I laugh which feels freeing.

Now we are near the portal and it is already opening and a small circular platform slides out and Ra says we will stand on it. We do and the platform moves us to another frequency where there is no portal or even mountain. We are simply in another frequency. Ra says this is the layer of the Sacred Text that we are receiving now. I nod that I understand.

The Light Being…I am pausing to be sure…We are now in a chamber of sorts, which pulses in form and then out of form. Ra says good. The being and several others are in white robes and are speaking ancient words which I do not understand. There is the sound of…I don't know what is making the sound. I thought a gong but I am not sure. Ra says it isn't important to discern that. I nod ok. The beings come forth and are silent now with heads bowed. The primary Light Being comes to us. He says, You are correct. I have been calling you. I recognize that you are incarnate, yet the Text has been pulsating and I have not experienced that before. In fact, he smiles at me, I haven't experienced any of this before. Yet I thought that you might come because it is pulsating. I say, I am grateful that you called me. I will always come when I can. Physicality might cause me to not be able to come immediately, but I will come. The Light Being says, That is good. He sends a different feeling than good, but I don't know the word for it. He is smiling and says, That is because what I have sent you is a frequency. I smile as he is also.

Then he says, We will begin. I nod ok. Ra takes my hand and the Light Being bows his head to Ra and says, It is an honor to be with you. Ra says, It is the same for all of us. The Light Being nods yes.

The Light Being then motions toward my right and says, This way is the way for the next transmission. We begin flowing, though there is nothing to discern. The other light beings remain. We are now being under a great light that is beaming from above, it is golden but is now blue. It is flowing downward to where we are, downward from a very high place. The Light Being is standing and is as if staid. Ra whispers, Yes he is preparing to receive the next portion of the text. I nod ok.

The Light Being is now showered in white light and a vortex flows about him. There is a gathering of essence in his open hands. The vortex stops and the Light Being comes to me and offers the essence in his hands. I nod yes. In the next moment, the essence is golden and is formed as a long snake-like cylinder. It is waving itself and then is going to enter my heart area. I nod ok. As soon as I nod ok, the golden takes a different form. It changes from a golden plate to a golden cup, to a golden essence and then flows into my being. I am now receiving the next part of the Sacred Text.

I can hear a high sound, a high tone. The text seems to be riding on that tone to my consciousness. I wait.

These are the words given.

In the beginning of the third era in the forming of the many realms and the beings who would reside within the realms, there came to be an awareness that those who formed where unable to bring their consciousness to an awakened state of being. In the overseers, there was great concern for it was believed that beings who resided in the realms must be conscious and be able to not only discern communications but also to understand the nature of the communications. Those overseers consulted and decided to recall the beings in the third era. Those beings were united with the All and rested in the gentle releasing of any experiences within the third era.

The overseers then determined that there would be a different species to flow forth within the third era. There was not yet the forming of any planets or galaxies. There was simply a realm. The eras of the realms are different than the eras of physicality and those formings within physicality, especially within galaxies.

There then came forth an Ancient Being from the outreaches of the All forming as a frequency that held within it those patterns and encodings that would assist in the calling forth of the consciousness that would remain awake to truth and to the nature of creation itself.

The Ancient Being came before the overseers and offered the patterns and encodings to the overseers for their examination. The overseers received that which was given and upon examination they were pleased that the possibility of formings would be beneficial to the eras of realms. The Ancient Beings then did breathe forth the patterns and encodings into the third era of the realms being created in the moment, as all is always created in the moment.

From the patterns there formed beings who held within them the consciousness of truth and more so, truth within warm embracing, for that was and continues to be the nature of the Ancient Ones.

The ones that formed have been called or named by others who were observers. They were called the *Giants of the Third Era*. They were, then, very large beings and while they resided within the third era, because they were awake within truth and warm embracing, created a manner within the realm that gave to them an experience. One of the experiences was to reside within a type of physicality. Yet the physicality of the giants was one of taking form and releasing form, and the physicality did not give to them a type of experience that they could reside within and place their consciousness of truth in order to experience truth in physicality. The giants then decided to gather encodings and breathe their life force into those encodings in order to create a physicality that would remain as they were remaining. A physicality similar to their very own beingness.

They created vortexes, and *then different forms that became the sacred geometry.* They found great pleasure in moving within the sacred geometry and discovered that when they called all forms to them, the formings of geometry, as it is called, created something greater. Combined then, there were forms that became more, that when combined, the square, then the cube, then the triangle and then the pyramid, then the circle and then the vortex. They discovered that the formings together then held different frequencies, each able to be called forth to create yet another experience within their manner of experiencing physicality. The giants then continued creating. And *their creating resonated as the third era within dimensions and realms.* The physicality of such creating was still frequencies yet there was a leaning toward a more dense forming and the giants called forth the more dense forming in order to explore their own ability to create and to then reside within their creations. This creating impacted the All.

The All radiated outward, yet when it radiated within the third era of the realms and dimensions, the All carried with it into the flowing forth, all that had been created and all that had been taking form in all manners. This then expanded the dimensions and realms of the third era. The giants then rejoiced and allowed, for it was within their awareness that such creating that they had been participating within, was also forming as the All flowed forth in all manners and it was perhaps not exactly their creating but, they thought, was the directing of that which was already created within the All. This brought a question in the awareness of the Giants.

The giants wondered further about the All and the manner of what resided within the All, as it was already created. The observers were most happy and excited about the questioning of the giants. The observers journeyed to the giants and embraced them with the full knowing of the observers. *The giants became.* That is, the giants came to be as the observers and held within themselves the consciousness of the creating within the All. Then all that had been created within the third era came to be the forming of the third era of dimensions and realms.

Within each dimension and realm, there was held the frequencies of the giants including their search for the nature of creation within that called sacred geometry. *Sacred geometry resided.*

The giants then requested to journey into other eras of dimensions and realms. The observers believed that there was not a challenge or a gift to the giants in the form that they requested. Yet there was the fourth era of physicality upon earth. The observers offered such residing to the giants who considered the offer and then requested a manner of residing temporarily so that they could determine if the fourth era upon a physical planet called earth would be to their benefit and enjoyment. The observers agreed.

The giants then did reside upon earth for four hundred years. During that time they did form in physicality those same sacred geometrical formings. The formings began as essence and then, because of the physical nature of earthly residing and all that was already formed upon earth, then the formings came to be physical. The cube came to be physical. And the pyramid came to be physical. Yet there was a yearning within the giants to merge the formings of the sacred geometry in physicality as they did as essence. Their formings did then come to be called tetrahedrons and the frequencies that resided within such formings radiated outward and *the surface of the earth's physicality changed.* The frequencies increased and all that was formed upon the surface of the earth began to be held in a geometric perfection. There then resided upon earth those tones and frequencies that called forth that forming of many many different species who entered earth's essence through the portals that were formed by the sacred geometrical creations.

The portals were a celebration of truth and the further knowing of creation itself, as *the patterns of creation itself flowed forth to be revealed within the sacred geometry*. All beings of all species came forth to celebrate the gifting of the knowing of creation formed and held within the sacred geometrical structures.

Some species came to reside within the structures and to call forth the frequencies of their previous residing. This meant that the structures held within themselves the encodings of the species and within the encodings of the species, there came forth a forming, beings who were of the species yet were of the sacred geometry within which they birthed as taking form from frequencies. This began, then, an abundant population upon the surface of the earth.

Earth became abundant with beings who were aware of creation itself, who were aware that they were formed within the sacred creations and were of essence of being. *These beings were the first Light Beings to reside upon the earth.* Their steppings created upon earth locations where creation formed from the magnetic pull of essence residing incarnate and also of creation itself within the moment. Physicality upon earth shifted and changed.

Those who resided upon earth radiated outward the frequencies of truth and that called delight in taking form. Many many beings felt the radiating outward and came forth to see what was causing such radiating. Many advanced beings came forth to examine what was occurring upon earth. Those ones examining then did begin to reside upon earth's surface as well, for the frequencies embraced them and the consciousness that resided within the geometrical structures uplifted the consciousness of all who came forth. *This then was the forming of the fourth era upon earth wherein all beings were awake and held within themselves the joy of forming.* There was not yet that called birthing. There was only the forming from essence of being, from creation's essence of being.

This then was the first calling forth of essence of being to take form as the many in order to reside incarnate so that the frequencies of the geometrical structures would enhance the consciousness and the ability to hold creation itself in the moment. Such holding created further and further and the All then did flow forth in many manners to mirror all that was being created. *This creating within the All formed what could be called galaxies and universes.* Physicality was uplifting within its forming and the consciousness of creation itself was held within all that was created in this manner. The All then celebrated consciousness of itself and the creation of those structures that held within them the many different manners of creation, essence and physicality.

The entirety of creation then did be held within the frequencies of the All. Then there was formed that which is called Invitation to Know. *Invitation to Know was and has been and continues to be the manner of residing within the frequencies that were formed upon earth during the fourth era.*

This then is the speaking of the Sacred Text.
So be it.

The frequencies flow from me into the hands of the Light Being and he is radiating them upward to be released. He comes to Ra and me and says, You must leave now, for the frequencies are most expanded and this one still resides incarnate.

Ra says yes and I nod to the Light Being. Ra takes my hand and pulls me along. We are leaving the chamber and even the mountain and the greenery. Ra says we will go directly to his realm. I am glad. I say to Ra, That receiving was most advanced. I hope that I received it correctly. Ra looked to me as if surprised and said, My dear, it cannot be received in any other way but perfectly. I nod I understand and am relieved.

Ra brings me to his realm and then motions that I must return to physicality . I understand and bow to Ra and flow forth to my vortex to return. I enter the vortex. I have thoughts of Alannah, but do not see her.

I am now entering my body. Returning. I am in a hotel room. I find that nearly humorous. I am grateful.

So be it.

NINETEENTH TRANSMISSION
Third Speaking

I have returned home and after having an in-depth talk with Grayson about the possibilities of our future residing, I am getting ready to expand my consciousness and go forth to Ra's and possibly to the Text. I have seen the Keeper of the Text look over his shoulder to me, and that means perhaps that it is getting closer to the time to receive the next transmission. I have felt my consciousness expanding and will now engage in that expanding.

I am moving through the realms of possibilities and am lifting up out of that frequency. I can now perceive the portal to Ra's realm and am now in front of it. I hear the words "enter now" and will see if the portal opens and those are actually Ra's message. It has been a rather long time since I have been here, while we were on vacation. I hear the words that there is no such thing as vacation, that the journey is continuous and the manner in which we interpret the journey determines the manner in which our consciousness participates with the frequencies.

The message continues, This means that during a journey there are always possibilities that present themselves…according to the nature of our consciousness. When we determine ahead of time what will appear, then we are limiting the frequencies made manifest. This is neither right nor wrong, but it is something that we must continue to be aware of. The more that we let go of our plans, the more that the true plan can become evident, which will fill us with joy.

I am wondering about this teaching coming through now, when I am at the portal to Ra's realm. The answer comes, you have been wanting guidance, you and Grayson, and it will come when you are expanding your consciousness, regardless of what other purpose you reside within. Now you will go forth into Ra's realm. I ask, who is this guidance coming from? The answer is: the All.

I let go of thinking about what was delivered and focus on the portal to Ra's realm. I hear his voice saying, Come. He appears as if above the portal and motions for me to come with him. I am happy about this and flow upward toward Ra. He says, It is good that you came now. I bring my full attention to Ra and he takes my hand and pulls me toward .. I will see. Ra laughs and says good. Ra says, You have filled yourself with much input lately. I say yes. Ra says, Now you will let go of all of that and come with me. I say yes. Ra says good.

We are moving toward the chamber where Ra talks with me. But he pulls me past that chamber and we are flowing upward, which to me means that we are entering a more expanded consciousness. Ra says good. Ra says, We will go now to the mountain.

FOURTH LAYER OF THE SACRED TEXT

We are moving very fast, as if through time. All else is blended together and is a stream. Ra says *that is the substance that physicality is comprised of and waits direction for forming.* I ask, How does the direction work? Ra says we will have that conversation another time. We must continue to the mountain. I say, Yes, of course. Ra smiles and says, You are a most curious being. I smile and say, I suppose I am. Ra says, Now we will approach the mountain.

It is green with trees and Ra says, This is a mountain that exists only in this realm. I nod that I understand. We flow toward the side of the mountain and there is a swirling, a round swirling. Ra says, The mountain is adjusting to our frequencies. Focus now, most intently, he says. I nod ok. I bring my focus to the present moment with Ra.

I hear the keeper say, Good! You are here! The swirling…I am projecting. I will wait. Ra says good. We wait. Ra says the mountain and the portal are adjusting to us. We will be entering a higher frequency this time. I nod I understand. I am not trying, I am allowing. I know this is right.

[I tell Grayson that this frequency will affect him. It was given to tell him that.]

I feel that frequencies radiating outward from my being, even my being in physicality. Ra says, Good, that is true, but to remain focused here with him. I nod ok.

Now the Keeper is on the round platform as it slides outward toward us. The Keeper is radiant and happy. The Keeper says, Now is the most important transferring of frequencies from the Text. I feel an expanding in my heart area. The Keeper says, Come now. It is time.

We flow forth to the platform and then it slides into the mountain. It seems to be taking some time to do this. The Keeper says there is an adjusting occurring while we flow forth on the disc. There are now patterns forming beneath our feet, upon the disc. The Keeper says, That is the beginning of the Text as it greets us. He seems to be most pleased about this. He nods to me yes, and smiles widely. I feel the excitement from him.

The disc slides into the mountain now, all the way, and we are being. I am being with Ra holding my hand. The Keeper says that we should follow him and motions his arm forward. There is a flowing forth and we follow him without effort. There is great light coming forth, so great that I actually open my eyes to be sure it is not the sun shining on me in physicality. Ra laughs and says that there is indeed great light. The Keeper looks over his shoulder, still smiling, and we continue to flow forth.

We are now in a chamber and the Keeper reaches into the wall of the chamber…with both hands…and when his hands emerge they are filled with great golden light, essence of being. Ra says, We must remain still now. I nod ok.

The Keeper then brings the light toward me and he asks if I am ready. He is still smiling. I nod that I am. Good, he says, and then the golden essence flows toward me and into my being. My entire being becomes golden essence. I am no more. I am the golden essence. Ra whispers, Good. The Keeper says he will depart now and return when the transmitting is complete. I nod ok.

FOURTH LAYER OF THE SACRED TEXT

The golden essence begins to swirl inside my being. I am becoming a being. Ra says I am becoming a being who can receive this transmission, more expanded. Waves of frequencies flow from my beingness. Very powerful. If on earth, the waves would dissolve everything. Ra says, That is all right as we are now in the protection of the mountain.

The symbols begin to form inside of my beingness and then they are becoming words. I say, thank you.

> **These are the words.**
> In the creating of beings there came forth some who were most advanced with regard to flowing forth successfully within different frequencies while maintaining the sense of beingness and also the sense of totality. These then were considered the next teachers who would assist to adjust the frequencies of all that was being made manifest in all manners in the All. Even though the All continued much creating of the many who were unaware of not only who or what they were, but also how they came to be, there was the flowing forth of the assistance of the most advanced beings. *The purpose of this flowing forth was to assist all in the All to become conscious of truth itself being made manifest.*
>
> There were those within the All who received the frequencies and became aware of truth made manifest as themselves. There was further a flowing forth of the truth that all was the All and the All was everything made manifest. The All turned upon itself,

291

rolling itself around as if a vortex in order to adjust the frequencies of that which was being made manifest so that all would contain the knowing of truth made manifest. This action within the All was not created by any being or purpose. It was the nature of the All to flow forth within itself to emanate truth in a manner that would allow the All to continue to flow forth within that truth and not within the distortion that had begun because of the nature of the unawake.

The All continued in this manner for many cycles of flowing forth, through many cycles of the taking of form and releasing of form. When the All ceased from swirling within its vortex, there was then situated within the All the patterns of truth made manifest. Truth is a frequency. It is not words. Then, *within all that was being made manifest within the All, there was continued the frequency or pattern of truth made manifest. This was then and is now and ever more, the nature of the All.*

Through many realms and then within the realms, the eras within the realms, there flowed forth such truth made manifest. Even within physicality as it came to be formed, there was held the frequencies of the Knowing of Truth made manifest, truth that all was the All and the All was the all.

Now there is a shifting in my being and there are more frequencies that are radiating outward. There is also an adjusting of the symbols again and then the forming of words. I say thank you.

These are those words.

Within the conscious knowing of the Truth made manifest, there came to form gatherings of the different manners of understanding such truth. *Understanding means that the truth itself was entering into a consciousness that unknowingly held the illusion of separation from the whole.* Such gatherings then called forth beings to reside within them and there formed different species within the forms of truth made manifest within understanding. The forming of species resulted in further separation, as each forming became aware of the others. Because the awareness was interpreted as *the others* then there was a further building of the illusion of separation from the whole. The species of each gathering then began to create and form. The creations came to be more dense and there then formed, through the consciousness of truth made manifest, what has been called planets and galaxies.

The species within each forming began to reside in ways that urged them to create. None of this creation was right or wrong. It was simply creating. Creations formed upon the foundation of Truth made manifest according to understanding became held within the physicality that was formed. Creations then did not form and unform, but remain staid within that creation. This produced further distortion within the nature of the planets, and within the species there came to be a dependence upon the staidness of their creations.

There is a shifting of frequencies again and I am allowing.

These are the next words of the Sacred Text.
The frequencies that flowed forth from each gathering, each species, each planet and each galaxy began to meet and to form together. Yet because there existed then those formings of untruths, because truth made manifest formed through understanding, there came to be what is called *the illusion of non-union*. All is the All and is always all. Yet this forming, this meeting of the many different frequencies caused what is called *the first battle*.

The first battle was an automatic occurrence as it was the result of the illusionary creations trying to maintain themselves when the merging, the Truth of One, came forth to unite all within the All. There was a refusal. Within the All everything was always and continues to be one. Yet within the illusion within the understanding of truth made manifest, there was the illusion of beingness separate from the whole, as it was made manifest in more dense formings without the truth of taking form and releasing form. *This battle to maintain the seeming individualness of the frequencies began a darkness within the All. The darkness was neither good nor evil. It was. The darkness continues to hold the battles to maintain separate creations.* Such maintaining caused what is called a heaviness within the All. The heaviness was actually the holding of such illusionary untruth, while it resided within the Truth of One.

This is the foundation for all that is made manifest within physicality when there is a desire to create something definite. There is not a law for such forming, yet there is within the consciousness of those who create in this manner, a participating within that illusion and that first battle. Creation must take form within the All, must be allowed to take form. The consciousness of all beings residing incarnate in all manners, in all species, in all planets and galaxies, in order to allow creation to flow forth in its highest fulfillment, *must hold the Truth of One primary. This is the Sacred Teaching of this Text.*

The Sacred Teaching of this Text says that all beings are one being. All creations are the All flowing forth to take form for the fulfillment of flowing forth. All beings holding truth within their consciousness would then allow the flowing forth of the All to form itself as their fulfillment. When all beings are residing in this manner, then there will be the dissolving of the darkness, of the heaviness, as *there would then be a releasing of the seeming separate understanding of Truth made manifest.* When this does occur, then the entirety of all that has been created within the All becomes holy, becomes truth itself and there is then the Oneness of Being consciously filling the All. This is a Return to One. This is the unforming, the Return to One, and then the breathing outward once again of wholeness of being as the All continues to form itself.

The releasing of dedicated creation for the fulfillment of physicality is primary. It is the Secret within this Text. This Secret has been revealed many many times. Most beings cannot or will not let go in this manner. There is a magnetic pull to create. That is a natural manner of participating with the All. Yet the individualization of such creating holds the consciousness of beings incarnate and further deepens the heaviness within which they reside. An uplifting of the spirit and the consciousness is waiting to occur. It has been waiting for a very long time. *This Secret is now revealed once again.*

Residing in the moment of One, holding Truth to be the All flowing forth to be all. Knowing that each moment is a holy moment of creation according to the All, which manifests in all manners of fulfillment...this is the consciousness that brings to all creation, even physicality's frequencies, the Truth of One, the Truth made manifest.

The Secret is now revealed once again. There will be the flowing forth of more of the Secret so that the All can embrace its own Truth made manifest. This embracing is the fulfillment of the All and the flowing forth of the All within that fulfillment. This then is the creating of the next era within which Truth resides as fulfillment once again, as it did in the beginning.

FOURTH LAYER OF THE SACRED TEXT

Then each moment is filled with the truth and frequencies of fulfillment of being.

There is no interpretation to fulfillment of being. There are no words to take the concept further. There is only fulfillment of being. Then it is for all within the All to embrace fulfillment. Each moment holy. Each breath holy. Each participation with the fulfillment as it is made manifest, holy. This holy is the nourishment of all that is created, even in physicality.

Those Great Ones who observe and then assist, then are once again returned to their own fulfillment, for they have been keeping watch over the All. There are no answers to the question, how can this be? There is only the beingness.

Each pulse beat of the All in this manner is golden. Golden is the essence of creation itself. Creation itself is and is not. There are no further words about this being creation, simply because no words can ever form such an expanded truth.

Yet this Text will continue to reveal more Secrets, for it is the time, the moment, the breath within which such fulfillment can occur. The alignment of the All with its All Created, is the golden of creation itself. Then there is the forming and unforming of the All.

There are many secrets within such truth. This Text is created for the revealing of those secrets. There is a flowing forth of the frequencies to take form in manners that can be revealed through words. Words are inadequate for such revealing, yet the frequencies of the Sacred Text have been adjusted to take form as words for the betterment of the All.

These Secrets are revealed as Truth. Truth that has been held within the highest frequencies flowing forth to be made manifest. Because of the heaviness, such Secrets have been held. Now it is the time for the dissolving of the heaviness which has become dark with little light. Dark with little light is the epitome of the illusion of separation, the untruth. Now the Secrets of this Text flowing forth to not only challenge the untruth, but to dissolve the foundations of such untruth, that the fulfillment of the All can be expressed in all manners.

This then is the First Volume of the Sacred Text. The next revealing will begin the Second Volume within which the Secrets will be revealed in a more expanded manner. This vessel is capable of receiving this flowing forth. We are the Keepers of the Text. This is a holy moment. *Holy means the uplifting of all that is created to its fullest capacity of One.*

Then upon the next meeting, there will be the further transmitting of the Second Volume.

It is with great celebration that this flowing forth continues.

Then this transmitting is compete.

I pray that this is correct, that all that is written is correct. I say to Ra that sometimes it feels like I am writing this. Ra laughs and says, That is because you become the Sacred Text expressing itself. I nod that I understand. Ra says, We will wait now for the Keeper to appear.

The Keeper and the others all appear. The one Keeper approaches me and receives the flowing forth of the golden essence. The Keeper says to me, Do not be concerned for any about you who are not holding the holiness while you receive the Text. That is of another frequency within physicality. I nod that I understand. The Keeper continues to receive the golden essence. It is emptying out of me. Ra holds my hand and says, I am maintaining your integrity of being. I nod ok.

The Keeper is surrounded by the others and the golden essence is flowing upward. It is as if the entire chamber is flowing upward. I hear the Keeper say to me, You must leave now in order to remain incarnate. I say thank you.

Ra pulls me along and we are exiting the mountain. He is pulling me quickly through the vortex and we are, I think, returning to his realm. Ra says yes. We arrive in the first chamber of Ra's realm, where are the large seats. Ra says that I cannot sit on the seat now for it will dissolve my beingness. He says I must return to physicality now. I nod ok. He still holds my hand and actually comes with me past his portal and to my vortex. This is usually what Alannah does, but Ra is with me.

Ra says, This is most important what you have received in this transmitting. He looks into my eyes. He says the Text resides within you now. When you return for further transmitting, the golden essence will appear and augment what resides within you so that it can be transmitting into words, into the Second Volume. I nod that I understand. Ra says, I am most proud of you, my dear. He places his first two fingers on my third eye and repeats, I am most proud of you. I can feel white light entering my being. It is helping to align my frequencies.

Ra says, Now you can return. Rest in this day. I nod ok. I say, Thank you Ra for all that you continue to give to me. I am most blessed by your presence in my journey. Ra smiles and says, There is much more to all of this than you know, and that is as it must be. You are a most advanced being, even if you doubt the truth of those words. I laugh and Ra says that because I could laugh, then I am ready to return. I nod to him not as a yes, but as an honor to him. Ra lets go of my hand and motions for me to flow down into my vortex. I enjoy his presence so, but I release it and begin to flow down my vortex. I feel the presence of Ra following my return. Then he says, good. And the vortex is closed. I am returning to my physicality.

I am adjusting my frequencies, my consciousness.

I am returned. I hope that Grayson has experienced the frequencies.

So be it.

VOLUME TWO

This was received at the completion of the First Volume:

This then is the First Volume of the Sacred Text. The next revealing will begin the Second Volume within which the Secrets will be revealed in a more expanded manner. This vessel is capable of receiving this flowing forth. We are the Keepers of the Text. This is a holy moment. Holy means the uplifting of all that is created to its fullest capacity of One.

Then upon the next meeting, there will be the further transmitting of the Second Volume.

It is with great celebration that this flowing forth continues.

TWENTIETH TRANSMISSION
First Speaking

I am excited to receive the beginning of the Second Volume. I can see the Keeper smiling and also very happy. Although I usually rest after a transmission the previous day, I can feel my crown energy center expanding and I am going to journey to Ra's realm and see if he is in agreement.

I am expanding my consciousness and am flowing forth to Ra's realm. I can hear Ra and he is saying, Just flow over the top and come in. I am doing that and by-passing the portal. I am entering Ra's realm. Alannah is present and she is motioning me to go forth to the chamber, the second chamber. I nod to her and flow forth into that chamber. Ra is sitting in his seat and even though I think he will motion for me to sit in my seat, he stands and says, Good that you have come. Let us to go forth to the mountain, for it seems that it is possible that the second volume will be transmitted within that location. I nod ok.

Ra takes my hand and says, This will be a bit different, for the frequencies are and will be most expanded for the Secrets to be able to flow forth. I am at your side always and will tend to your beingness. If you feel as though you are being asked to do too much, just motion with your hand and I will make further adjustments. I nod that I understand. Good, Says Ra, then let us depart.

We begin flowing once again very quickly and we are a blur, through the possibilities of forming. Ra says good. We are continuing to flow. This flowing is more intense that previous journeys. Ra says Yes.

We are approaching the green mountain, covered with trees. Ra says we will wait here as we have come closer. We are waiting. There is an image of the Keeper above the mountain and he is motioning us to come above the mountain. We flow forth to where he is.

The Keeper says, We will enter the chamber through the top of the mountain this time. The peak is the capstone, always, and it is there that we will begin the receiving or transmitting of the Second Volume. Both Ra and I nod ok. The Keeper waves his arm and we see the top of the mountain open and we are flowing into the area.

It seems to be very small and then it is very large. The Keeper smiles and says, That is the nature of this area. It is larger because the frequencies are more expanded, as you have experienced previously. I nod that I understand.

I wait. We all wait. We are still.

There forms around us a white translucent globe. We are inside. The globe begins to turn around and around, yet we are continuing to remain still. As it turns, there are different colors flowing, subtle colors. There is a pyramid that forms in the hands of the Keeper. It is a golden pyramid. The Keeper steps toward me and asks if I will receive the Second Volume of the Sacred Text. I say it is my honor to receive. The Keeper

FOURTH LAYER OF THE SACRED TEXT

holds his hands, palms upward upon which rests the golden pyramid, reaching it toward me. He motions for me to hold my hands. I look to Ra who nods and lets go of my hand but puts his hand on my elbow to maintain contact. I nod gratitude.

I reach my hands forward with my palms upward and the pyramid radiates light and the Keeper says to me, You must say the words. You will know which words. I nod ok.

I speak the words, I am the One. I am the One who receives the frequencies of the Sacred Text. I now do open to receive the beginning of the Second Volume of holiness of being. Let my receiving be clear and accurate, let my heart remain pure, and let my purposes be fulfilled within this receiving. So be it.

The pyramid changes color. It changes to many different colors, one after the other. The Keeper says, The Text is aligning to your being. I nod that I understand. The Keeper says to me, Do not fear, you are most capable of receiving these frequencies, else you would not be here. I nod ok.

The pyramid changes to golden essence and begins to flow toward my being. It situates itself in my open hands and then flows to cover my entire being. Ra still holds my elbow and for that I am grateful. I am becoming golden essence. I can sense that also Ra is becoming golden essence by his connection with me. We are both radiating great golden light. The Keeper has covered his eyes with his hands. He says, I am not allowed to see this, but I must remain present for a little longer. I send the message back, thank you.

We are held within the golden essence and we are not able to move. I am at peace. There is the beginning of symbols forming or the coming forth of the words. The Keeper says that he must leave now and will return when the transmission is complete. I nod ok.

The words begin to form, even as Ra and I are staid within the golden essence as it has become and we are it. Ra sends the thought that all is well.

These are the words that flow forth.

We, the Keepers of the Second Volume of the Sacred Text, come forth now to deliver to you the secrets contained. You are the One. Then we release to you the beginning of this Text and all of its Secrets. Do not be concerned for accuracy. Nothing can change one word of this Text. It is not possible. I nod that I understand.

We, the Keepers, are about you to assure that you receive what is given with ease, for there is great respect for you, the One, and for what you are participating within. I nod yes.

Then you may begin, the one Keeper says. I nod ok.

These words flow forth.

They are forming...symbols forming into words.

In the great expanse of the All there reside several golden globes placed there by the Holy Ones for the specific purpose of releasing the ingredients to One who would come forth during the times of darkness

FOURTH LAYER OF THE SACRED TEXT

formed within the All. The contents of each globe contain the frequencies that will assist in the releasing of the unintentional and intentional embracing of the darkness and densities. They are called forth to the awareness of the One so that the One can receive the frequencies and begin the freeing of the heaviness from the All and the releasing of those who have been held captive, unknowingly, by the density.

The first globe flows forth for the One to receive.

The globe is beautiful and I am observing it flowing toward me. I can see across the All and there are several golden globes. I wait to see if one will actually flow forth to me. Then in the next moment a golden globe is right in front of me. It has a joyful frequency and a portal, like a doorway, opens and there flows forth a pathway to walk upon. I look to Ra and he nods to me. He is holding my hand again and we both flow forth into the globe. It appears to be a library with many many volumes. From the top of the many shelves, a volume flows downward and comes to reside in front of me. It is now an open volume. The symbols flow forth to enter me. They enter all of my energy centers. I feel that I am like a light bulb. Ra smiles to me.

In the next moment I can feel a voice flow forth through me. It is a deep voice with much vibration.

It says.

I am the speaking of the Second Volume of the Sacred Text. This speaking will begin the changing of the formed residencies of the many who reside in the density and darkness of the unknown to Truth of One.

A shifting occurs and I can feel the words forming in my being, as they have previously. I believe we will continue in this way.

The Secrets Revealed now flow forth.

Each flowing forth challenges the density and darkness which holds the untruth. The suffering within physicality has grown to such a degree that the light of truth is barely present. This speaking and frequencies will begin to shift and change that darkness.

Long ago the observers of the All saw that there were many within the formings within the All who were suffering and reaching forth for some kind of salvation. They created many ways to participate with in order to find that salvation, which continued to allude them. The suffering continued.

There came within the flowing forth of the All those frequencies that began to contain the suffering, to end the suffering by returning all within the containment to the dissolving into nothing that it be created once again in a pristine nature. Yet when this process was attempted, the All itself refused to allow such dissolving. This was a first within the All and from the All. The observers released their plan and remained as observers.

The All turned itself around and around once again, forming and unforming and when it was complete with such turning, there were several contained areas that held the density and the darkness and the depth of suffering. The All allowed such residing to remain.

Within the densities, there came forth several light beings who journeyed within the darkness and density to reach out to those who were beseeching relief. Many began to be relieved of such suffering. Yet when the light beings released their participation, there were others within the density who used their power to magnetize those nearly awakened ones to return to their suffering. This continued for many many turnings of the All.

Now there came forth those ones from the All who were created to be Holy Ones. The Holy Ones were created as a response to the powerful magnetization within the density and suffering as a balance of frequencies within the All. The Holy Ones then did gather the contents of the densities and formed one very large globe, within which was contained the suffering, the beseeching, those who were nearly awake, and those who maintained the power over the continued suffering.

This darkness formed as a globe began to journey within the All. There were no other frequencies that would embrace the darkness, the globe of all that it contained. It journeyed throughout the All for a very long turning of the All. Still the All allowed such to be.

The Holy Ones began to breathe a breath into the globe of darkness. They breathed forth in this manner and **this is the First Secret Revealed.**

From the golden essence of creation itself, which resides within all beings, the Holy Ones did breathe deeply and then held the breath on the tongue of their being until it formed a golden globe. Then they did take the globe from their tongue with the first two fingers of their left hand and they did then place the breathed golden essence of creation as a globe into the darkness and density of the dark globe. Each Holy One breathed forth this golden globe of creation itself and placed it within the darkens. Each Holy One proceeded in this manner for seventeen times, exactly seventeen times.

Then the Holy Ones breathed a strong breathing from the heart of their being, calling forth the wholeness of their union with One and breathing it forth upon the darkness, breathing exactly sixteen breaths each.

Then the Holy Ones gathered their hands, uniting until they surrounded the globe of darkness and they began to turn themselves, united, in a clockwise direction. They continued until they were moving quickly and as if a blur. They continued in this manner for many turnings of the All.

When there appeared one radiating light within the darkness, the Holy Ones ceased from this turning. They remained still and held to themselves the truth of that which they were and are: totality incarnate in the form of Holy Beings.

With the receiving of these frequencies, then, *the Holy Ones are now in the moment participating in this manner around the globe that has been called Earth,* for there resides within and upon Earth great darkness, density and the power to control the suffering. To control suffering resides against the totality of the All and the All not only allows such actions, but contains those frequencies that enable such participating by the Holy Ones. This is the path to wholeness of being, the path to consciously knowing of Truth, the path to residing within the moment of creation, which is all moments.

This manner of being can be participated within by all who receive these words, for there is the ability of many through their consciousness, to place themselves as Holy beings about the earth. Many will participate. This is the purpose of this globe and the releasing of this manner of being. *You who receive these words are the next Holy Ones and are Light Beings who have the ability to enter into your expanded consciousness and to participate in this manner given.*

The All parts the seas of the illusion so that you can go forth in this manner. This has been participated within for many many turnings of the All. Yet now there are those who are most capable of participating in this manner, many Holy Ones, Holy Light Beings. It is to you that the releasing of the density and darkness rests upon. *You are the next Giants, taking the Holy Earth within your hands and breathing your breath upon Earth, placing your golden globes within Earth, and encircling Earth with the intensity of all that you are.*

Now the Secret of this globe has been released into the holiness of this text.

We are the Keepers of this globe and we are the Keepers of the All.

Now we will release this globe from the revealing of this manner of participating, for there will be those who will embrace the revealing and feel the urging to participate. It is with you that we place the welfare of that which has become Earth, though Earth of long ago was most different. Still this Earth upon which you reside holds the holiness that is waiting to be revealed, that it might dissolve the power over the suffering. *The time is now. The moment is now. The breath is now.*

Then we, the Keepers, have completed the releasing of the contents of this globe. Other globes will release more. This is the beginning.

FOURTH LAYER OF THE SACRED TEXT

Then we call forth the essence from this Holy One who allows the transmission through her being. For she has been the One over and over again. And we bow to the one who holds her to himself, Ra, that he might know that we recognize his greatness and holiness.
So be it.

The flowing forth of the golden essence begins to leave my being and flows into the globe. I can feel that we are exiting the globe and are beginning to be outside of the globe. There is one being who presents itself and says to me, I have known you since the first time that you participated with us. Now all is most powerful and you are most capable, once again. Go forth and return, for the globes await their revealing and releasing of secret participations for the betterment of all formings within the All, for there are more than the Earth that require releasing. Earth is the first. It is the most in need.

I nod to the being and then the being is gone. And Ra and I are outside the Globe. Ra says, We will wait. The Keeper of the Text begins to flow forth toward us and he is still covering his eyes with his hands. He says, You are both glowing so boldly with golden light that I am not capable of looking at you. I am calling forth the others to speak the words that you will return to your natural forming so that you can return this One to being incarnate. I nod thank you.

The Keeper speaks words that I do not know and the others begin to appear behind the Keeper. They all begin to speak the words together and there is the sound of a bell that continues to ring, a sound that continues to surround both Ra and me. I can feel my essence beginning to form once again. Ra squeezes my hand to let me know that I am correct.

The Keeper removes his hands from in front of his face and says that we are now ready to leave this frequency. He looks to me and says, You have done very well with this new frequency. I nod yes. He says, What you are doing will change the contents of the All, the contents that have been waiting for a very long time to be changed. That is all that I can say at this time. I now thank you.

The Keeper says we must depart now and motions for us to flow forth to an opening. We flow forth and are once again in a vortex of very fast flowing. Ra says that this is the way to return to his realm. I send the message that I understand. We are moving very fast.

We are in a blue light and are approaching Ra's realm as I recognize the frequencies. It is as if we are spit out of the vortex. Ra laughs at my description. He says that he is proud of me and that I must return now. I nod that I agree and thank him. We are both standing above my vortex and Ra nods to me and I enter the vortex to return to my physicality. I look into Ra's eyes as I flow downward and then the vortex closes and I no longer see him, but I hear his words, Good, very good.

I am now returning to my body physical. I am very expanded in consciousness.

I am returned.

So be it.

TWENTY-FIRST TRANSMISSION
Second Speaking

I have seen the Keeper of the Sacred Text atop the mountain, waiting for us to appear. I said that I would but needed to rest first. I journeyed to the Holy One, which always brings me joy. There, the Holy One invited me to enter the Paradise that the Holy One created. I said that I wanted to open to the Sacred Text but that I was depleted of energies. The Holy One accompanied me into the Paradise. I haven't yet had any recall of that experience, but now I am greatly restored in energies and grateful for it.

Now I will journey to Ra's realm and see if it is indeed time to return to the Sacred Text. I am expanding my consciousness…I realize that when I feel as though I have a headache it is really my crown chakra letting me know that it is time for the Sacred Text, that the chakra is expanding. Now I know how to interpret that feeling.

I am moving toward Ra's realm and I wish to speak with him about something that was said to me by the Keeper. Ra appears atop the portal and motions for me to enter from above, as I did last time.

Ra smiles and says that he is glad that I have decided to come. He says, I know you have a question. Yes, I say, the Keeper said that I needed to maintain my body size in order to remain incarnate while receiving the transmissions of the Text. And, I am very unhappy about the extra weight that I am carrying in physicality. Is there something that can be done?

Ra motions me to follow into the chamber where we usually have teachings. He motions for me to sit and I do and he is in the seat beside me. He takes my hand and says, We will begin to speak of your answer, but if we are called to the Text, we will have to abandon that speaking and go. I nod that I understand.

Ra looks to me and says, You have not yet learned the basics of physicality according to your desires. This does not mean that you make manifest anything. It simply means that you can decide.

I say, decide about what and how?

Ra says, Physicality is illusive. It takes form and releases form always. You are holding that distaste for your current body size and that means that when physicality takes form it will follow your choice, even if it is something that you do not like. Do you see? Wherever you place your focus and interpretation of physicality, then it will form to fill that choice.

Now, how you can change the nature of your body weight is different. Again it is a choice, but you must focus on that choice. Now the choice isn't to lose weight. It is to choose to be the weight that you want. And then, to continue to place your awareness there. This is not manipulation of physicality. More so, it is an awareness of the taking of form and the choice that you, as the divine essence, wish to have as your vessel.

I say, I have tried a lot of different avenues and some have lasted for a while, but…

Ra says, I know of your histories. Still, it is time to let go of not liking the nature of your body physical. That is the letting go. Choose your size and then give gratitude for that choice. It sounds very simple, but it is powerful. I will assist you.

Now, he continues, with regard to what the Keeper said, I believe that even if you attain the body weight that you would like, you will still have enough mass to be able to remain incarnate while participating with the transmissions of the Sacred Text. But that is something that can be decided during your transformation of your body though choice.

I say, ok. Thank you. I appreciate your counsel and assistance.

Ra says, It is now time for us to depart and to journey toward the mountain. Are you ready? Yes I say. Ra says, Then let us depart.

Ra stands as do I and he takes my hand and we begin to move, once again, through the fast moving journey through all possibilities. Ra smiles and increases our speed. He says, One day I will teach you about this, but for now we must arrive at the mountain. I nod that I understand.

We emerge from the possibilities and are in the greenery of the land where resides the mountain. I see the Keeper at the top of the mountain and he is very happy to see us. He is still in a distance.

I feel my consciousness expanding. We are closer to the Keeper. Once there, the Keeper is in white robes and they are flowing as if wind is blowing upon him. The Keeper says indeed the wind is blowing upon me, for I have been holding the opening of the mountain for your arrival. I am happy that you have arrived. I nod to him as does Ra. Come, the Keeper says.

The top of the mountain opens and we are moving through a spiral tunnel, we are flowing directly downward, but around us is a spiral, blue in color. The Keeper turns and says to me, You are becoming more accurate with your discernment. I nod thank you.

We flow into the capstone of the mountain and wait. We are waiting for everything to synchronize and appear. The Keeper stands in front of me and says, This will be a more advanced frequency. Ra will be with you as he usually is and I will stand guard outside this chamber once you begin. I will assure that you will remain incarnate during this receiving. I say thank you. He looks deep into my eyes and I stand still to wait for his discernment. He says, You have been to the Holy One. I nod yes. He says, Then you are ready. Yes, I say.

We then stand and wait. The chamber begins to turn around and around, as we stand still it flows around us. It is like the traveling that Ra and I do to arrive at the mountain, only this is inside and the flowing about us is a blur. We are not, but the flowing is. This says to me all possibilities. Ra whispers to me to remain clear. I nod that I understand.

FOURTH LAYER OF THE SACRED TEXT

The Keeper holds up his right arm and the flowing slows and then stops. We are surrounded by a great expanse yet we are still in the chamber. The Keeper says, This is an image. I wish to prepare you for the next transmission. This image holds frequencies. Now we will invite the image to be with us more and you will be able to align your frequencies. I nod ok. Ra holds my hand and we are still.

The expanse comes close and it is as if we are standing on it. The blue light flows upward from my feet and into my being. I am being adjusted. The Keeper says, This will only take a brief time, but I believe it is necessary. I nod ok.

The blue essence or frequency flows upward and is actually flowing out of my eyes, my nose, and my mouth, and then from my heart energy center. The Keeper says, Good. Then he waves his arm and the entire image dissipates.

The Keeper says, Now we will begin. He speaks words in a language that I do not know. The Keeper says, This time there will be a volume. It is not yet time for another globe from the All. I nod I understand.

There comes forth the library as I remember it. At the very top shelf there is a volume that is floating downward. The Keeper holds his hands outward and the volume flows down and on to his hands. The volume is open to a page. From the page there appears a white light and a being, something like a whirling dervish, is swirling around in the white light. The Keeper breathes a breath upon the white and it stops moving. From the volume where was the white light there comes forth symbols. And then letters of the alphabet that I know. This continues but none are words. The Keeper says, This is a manner of allowing the translation to occur so that you will be able to receive the Text in words that you can transcribe, as you have been doing. I nod ok.

This continues for a while…and then…the Keeper closes the volume. He says, there is another volume that is more appropriate for this receiving. Nothing is wrong, it is just that you both are presenting a very strong frequency together and there is a better volume to match that frequency.

The volume in his hand raises upward and returns to the position on the upper shelf. The Keeper stands firm and speaks some words that turn into a chant. It is beautiful and his voice is beautiful. From the place where we are standing there comes a podium. It is rising upward and is in front of the Keeper. The Keeper says, Ah. Much better. He continues to speak the language I do not know and then there forms atop the podium a white globe. The Keeper takes the white globe and brings it to be in front of me. He says, Now I ask you to receive this next transmission of the Sacred Text. I say that I am honored to receive it.

At the finish of my words, the globe flows toward me and flows right inside of my heart area. It is white essence and fills my being. Ra whispers, All is good. I nod ok.

The essence fills my being and there is a force or energy that is building and coming to the surface. I wait.

This is the speaking.
These are the words of the Sacred Text as they flow forth for the knowing of the many and the knowing of those who receive the sacredness.

FOURTH LAYER OF THE SACRED TEXT

I wait.

These words flow forth.

When the number of one hundred have received the frequencies of the Sacred Text, there will be great transformational upon the planet where those ones reside. This is true for all planets and beings who reside upon them. This first allowing is to occur upon planet Earth for it holds the most dense darkness of all of the planets. This is not a judgment against Earth. It is occurring and that is what is determined. The being who receives this transmission is pure of heart and able to receive. The Text is given in this manner.

I am hearing a different language. But I wait. It seems to be saying Allah Akbar. I still wait.

These words flow forth...

On the evening of every full moon there comes forth those frequencies that can purify the manners of incarnating truth and wholeness.

I am told *this is not the Text*. I wait. I have never had this happen before. But I wait.

I can feel the Keepers breath upon my being.

The white essence within my being changes to blue. And I wait. Now it changes to golden essence. I hear the Keeper be glad.

Ra whispers to me, Do not be concerned. *This is a way to bar interference.* I nod that I understand.

The Keeper speaks some words and the frequencies change. The Keeper appears and says,

We will now journey to the capstone and the frequencies held there. I look to Ra and he says, It is time. The Keeper nods yes. I do not know what they are referring to. Ra says all is well.

We are dissolving our beingness and then forming in the capstone. It is a golden pyramid. The Keeper says, *I apologize for not informing you of this procedure. It was not given to speak of it to you lest those who wish to cease this receiving learn of our plans.* You are now in the capstone and through the previous experience, you will not be disturbed. I nod ok.

Ra holds my hand and the Keeper says, Now I call forth the Sacred Text to be received by this one who is the One.

I feel a bit overwhelmed by the frequencies. I feel my physicality breathing quickly. Ra says that will pass. I nod ok.

I am given the image...no, says Ra, do not allow it. I nod ok. Ra says, Remain here. Do not allow thinking to enter. I nod ok. The Keeper says, This is the next level of the Sacred Text. It is given now because you have received the Secret from the first globe. I nod ok.

The Keeper raises both arms outward and upward. He is transformed into a golden pillar. The pillar has many symbols written upon it. The pillar begins to turn around and around. The symbols flow off of the pillar and form a globe before me. The pillar stops and the Keeper appears. He steps to me and says, Now you have the Sacred Text. I must leave now and return when you are complete. I nod ok and bow my head in honor of the Keeper. Ra does the same. The Keeper turns and leaves the area.

The globe is before me and is lighted golden. There is a flowing into my heart area and then to my mouth. And then to my knowing.

These then are the words.

When the All formed itself as the many, there came forth from the many those ones who called to the All, asking to be given the permission to journey into the All. The All embraced the asking of the many. This was their permission. The many then did flow forth into the All and began their journey into the full knowing of the All.

These ones have been called the Great Ones for they have held the knowing of the All, even when the All has continued to flow itself forth in all manners possible. The Great Ones became the lovers of the All. The Great Ones asked the All if they could remain as if separate from the All in order to observe all that occurred within the All's flowing forth. The All shifted its frequencies and this gave those Great Ones permission to remain as if separate from the All's flowing forth that they might observe all that flowed forth within the All. *This then caused them to become what has been known as The Observers.*

The Observers thought of themselves as the caretakers of the All. Yet the All did not require caretaking. Still those ones loved the All and embraced their own purpose of observing the All's flowing forth.

Within the flowing forth there appeared great darkness and the Observers began to question the great darkness within the All. They not only observed, but began to make a judgment, a judgment that the darkness might be harmful to the totality of the All. Still they were as if separate from the totality of the All.

There came forth Three Giant Beings who requested speaking with the Observers. The Observers agreed and the Giant Beings breathed their breath upon the Observers. The Observers became as one with the Giants and there was a flowing of understanding and knowing between them. The All felt the merging of the Observers and the Giants and *there formed within the All, Great Joy.*

The Great Joy flowed forth and when it came to the darkness did then surround the darkness and within the core of the darkness there came forth a being. The being was unknown to any of the All, but known to the All itself. The Great Being said to the All, do not allow this to occur, for I am the core of the darkness and it is I who hold the integrity of the Darkness. The All considered the demand.

Still the Giants and the Observers remained united and the Joy continued to flow forth within the All. The All did not respond to the demand from the being of the Core of Darkness and that one did return to the core and breathe forth fire into the darkness. The fire then did glow bright and became. The All adjusted itself to accommodate the ball of fire. Within the core of the ball of fire there was a small center of darkness and it was there that the being remained. The being became the keeper of the ball of fire. Those ones who were the Giants and the Observers released their union and observed the ball of fire. It was their agreement that such a ball of fire was most beautiful. Their determining of beauty to describe the ball of fire then did radiate throughout the All and the All was pleased at the determining. *The Ball of fire was then loved by the All and those who observed its creation.*

This then was the creation of what has been called by those who reside upon Earth as the Sun. Within the ball of fire, within the sun of earth there resides a being who is the keeper of the ball of fire. Within the All, there is acceptance of the ball of fire and its continued spewing of itself from itself. Within the All there are several balls of fire, created in the same manner.

There came the moment when the request from another keeper of the darkness requested to be allowed to remain as darkness that the All declared that it would allow the darkness to reside. This caused a rejoicing in the being who resided in the core of darkness and also a rejoicing in the core of all of the balls of fire, including the sun of the Earth.

There was then a radiating of the frequencies of totality and a celebration of allowing of the All of itself to continue to form in all manners possible. For it was known that *nothing can change the All from being the All and that it continued to flow forth itself to explore and experience and express all manners possible.*

All manners possible became then, for nothing was denied. The Observers found all manners possible to be called *Freedom to Be*. Freedom to Be resided within the All through the Eras of the beginning of the forming of what is now called physicality.

There came then within the All and within the forming of physicality those beings who found that they were free to form themselves in any manner possible because that was the essence of the All taking form and releasing form. Those ones became *the Ancient Ones* and resided within the All within the Freedom to Be.

When there came to be formed the many galaxies and within them the many planets and stars and creations of light, the Ancient Ones then did discover the many who had formed themselves upon several planets. The many held within them the knowing of the totality of the All, yet they did not hold the knowing of the Observers and the Giants. The Ancient Ones flowed forth to guide the many, for their knowing of physicality's grasp was limited. The Ancient Ones wondered about the limited consciousness of the many. How did it come to be?

The many did speak with the Ancient Ones and declare that they had the Freedom to Be residing in an unknown wherein there was the discovery of being. They wished to maintain the unknown within their being so that they would be able to continue to discover the more of the All as it made itself manifest even in physicality. The Ancient Ones stepped back from assisting the many, for they had declared their right to Freedom to Be.

Within the All there resides many declarations to be, some of freedom, some of simply the gathering of like formings that declared their forming to be. Within such formings, the All turned around and around, assisting the formings to continue to reside within the All as the All. This has been the manner of the All as it did absorb totality of itself and in so doing did become as if a declaration of its own beingness. *This came to be called the All's awakening to the All as it resided in all manners of being.* Awakening within the All to its own knowing did then flow forth and unite with all that had been and continued to be made manifest within the journey of the All.

From the Core of Creation there flowed forth a spark which created light within the All. The Spark of Creation held within it the one moment of being and not being. This then radiated through the All and within the All's knowing of itself. There then formed the All in a manner of taking form and releasing form, the pulse beat of creation itself. The All then was transformed within the spark. All declarations were dissolved, for in the releasing of form all declarations are no more, only the creation itself resides. Then the taking of form resides in purity of being and declarations are no longer held. This releasing of the declarations changed the All so that it was a pure frequency. Within the pure frequency the All held the spark and the spark held the All. *This was the beginning of totality within creation itself.* This meant that the All was creation itself and creation itself breathed forth the All as itself. *This then began a new era in the totality of being.*

The new era held purity of being and that which was the All mirrored itself toward the new era, yet was not received by the new era because the purity of being held a frequency that declared totality. Yet the declaration itself flowed forth within the All and the purity of being and this declaration by its very intent allowed the past histories of previous eras to be as a mirror to the All, yet not an image of the All. The All held perfection of being and the previous eras held the Freedom to Be. This caused the possibility of the merging of the two eras. This has not yet occurred in the flowing forth of the All.

What was the past era and what is the present era are possibilities that flow forth to be. The present era is turning itself round and round in order to dispel the urgency of the forming from the past era of all that appeared to be in physicality. The present era holds truth and creation. Nothing more. This era will be called Paradise, if it is able to remain of itself. The All within this era flowed forth the automatic freedom of the All to determine if it will flow forth to take form in all manners. *This determining has not yet occurred. The All is residing in peace and celebration of its union with Creation.*

This then is the current forming of this new era. The Giants and the Observers and the Ancient Ones are observing from the previous era. There resides within those ones what is called great hope for the maintaining of this era to be.

In the histories of creation, there resides numerous frequencies that have gathered themselves to be. These gatherings have been called eras yet there is more to know about the gatherings of creation. The patterns of creation form in a manner that calls forth a mirror of the same creation. This causes the totality to present to itself a manner of...

[...The frequencies are increasing and causing my body to breathe fast. Ra whispers to me, All is well. I know this to be true and am allowing the increasing of frequencies...]

The mirror images of that which is created has caused the totality to become of itself an inability to be solitary. *This is called then the Truth of One.* Within the Truth of One there is no separation, only union. *Union is caused by the reflection of all creation to mirror to itself the truth of its own beingness.*

There are those who have determined that they could change the totality in a way that would allow them to examine the nature of this union, this mirror imaging and perhaps even the essence of creation itself. *Yet those ones have separated themselves from the union and thusly from the full knowing of that which they seek.* These ones have resided in many civilizations upon many planets within many galaxies. Still there will be no answer for their seeking because creation itself has and is always one spark.

The spark of creation is, even when it is mirrored and becomes of itself another, still the totality of the spark will not allow separation from the whole. It is only in the consciousness of those ones in the different gatherings of being that can hold the possibility of the concept of separation from the whole and such holding has caused many gatherings to become distorted. *It is the distortion that becomes the globe of darkness and within the globe of darkness there is also a mirror image of itself.* This is creation as it forms itself over and over again in the moment, in the one breath.

Many who have flowed forth from galaxies to explore the possibilities of separation from the whole have only discovered the mirror images of themselves, for there is always union and separation, even in exploration, cannot occur. All is one. All is the All. All of the All is residing within the Spark of Creation itself which forms as the All and Creation as One. *This is the Truth of this Sacred Text as it flows forth for the possibility of the many to once again hold within the conscious knowing.* Such conscious knowing then is mirrored throughout the totality, for as one is, then all is.

This is the declaration of this Sacred Text.

This is the complete flowing forth of this portion of the Sacred Text.

We release this receiver of these frequencies.

I can feel the intensity of the frequencies as they flow forth from my being through my third eye. I am being relieved of the intensities. Ra is still holding my hand for that I am grateful. We are both releasing the frequencies.

The Keeper is waiting for the releasing to complete. We also are waiting.

The swirling of the images of the galaxies, the creations, the planets…all that has been spoke of…are now presenting themselves and then dissolving. We wait. It is a most magnificent presenting and then releasing. Ra whispers, Yes, it is.

There is a swirling within my being as if the flowing of…the flowing of the DNA and such flowing is situating itself into my being, as it is meant to be. Ra is holding my consciousness for I am a bit overwhelmed by the frequencies. Ra says, You are doing ok. Just remain present. I nod ok.

Now the Keeper begins to make his presence. He is approaching slowly and with his approaching there is a further relief of the intensity of the frequencies. My body is breathing regularly now. Ra says this is good. The Keeper approaches me and says, You have done very well. You are loved and honored. Now I am present to receive the frequencies of the Text from your being. Just allow them to flow forth to me. I nod ok.

I believe that the Text is flowing from me. I do not feel anything. I am in a type of stasis while all of this is going on. The Keeper is speaking a language I do not know. This might be the calling forth of the frequencies of the Text. I do not know. Ra whispers to remain still and to remain at peace. I send the message that I am all right. Good, he says.

I am still waiting for the Text to be released. I decide that I will speak the words: I, the One, now do release the frequencies of this portion of the Sacred Text, in gratitude and celebration of the completion of this transmitting. So be it.

FOURTH LAYER OF THE SACRED TEXT

The Keeper says, Good!

I am still waiting. Ra begins speaking a different language and there is a shivering of the frequencies about my being, as if the blue is shimmering from his words. Then there is a falling away of the blue essence within and about me. I can now see the Keeper who is looking at me with concern. I smile and nod that I am ok. The Keeper looks to Ra and they both are smiling as in relief. I am in relief also.

The Keeper says, I will return to replace this frequency within the Sacred Text. Now you both must depart. I will not accompany you for I will be holding this frequency while you depart. Be well, he says, and return when you hear my call or when you can. I nod ok.

Ra pulls me along and we are exiting the capstone of the pyramid. Now we are flowing quickly through the blur of the possibilities. I am glad to be returning and glad that Ra is holding my hand tightly as he pulls me along. That is the best that I can do. Ra laughs at my words.

We are now approaching his chamber, his realm, and I am glad for seeing it appear before us. Ra stands before me and says, This was the most powerful yet and you have done very well. Do not reflect upon this experience for a couple of days. Allow it to settle. I nod ok.

Now, he says, I will accompany you to the vortex to your physicality. Come. He is still pulling me along and we are moving through the beatify of the green grasses and the pathway that I traveled long ago with Alannah.

Ra now stands above my vortex and says, Return now for it is time. I nod to him and thank him for the honor to participate with him. He laughs and says, No, it is I who thank you for the honor of participating with you. We both laugh. It feels good to laugh with Ra.

Now return, he says. I nod ok and then flow into the vortex. I know that Ra is watching but I am focusing on returning to my body physical. I am returning now. Breathing. Allowing myself to settle within the physical.

Breathing deeply.

I have returned. I am most grateful for this experience. Most grateful.

My crown is very expanded....

So be it.

TWENTY-SECOND TRANSMISSION
Third Speaking

I have been without much energy all day and have been in back and hip pain. The Keeper has helped me. When he appeared to me I said that I had to rest because of the lack of energy and pain. But, much to my delight and surprise, the Keeper was appearing to assist me, holding out white light to flow toward me. I rested and the light helped with my pain. Yet I am still, even in this evening, feeling the same. I am wondering if journeying to the Text and receiving it is what is being called for me to do. I will journey to Ra and see what he thinks.

I am expanding my consciousness. I see the Holy One smiling at me. Holy One always brings a real smile to my face. But I am going to Ra now. I bow my respect to Holy One and continue to Ra's realm.

I am approaching the consciousness to be able to go to Ra. I feel exhausted, but I now wonder about that feeling as an interpretation of consciousness. I am at the portal to Ra's realm and I am going over the top as he has called me to do in the recent past. I am very depleted of energy. I hope Ra can help me understand.

I can feel the presence of Ra and I am flowing over the top above the portal to his realm. I can feel that he is in the chamber where we usually speak together. I bow to the seat, Ra's large seat, and then continue to the chamber. Ra is sitting there and he says, Ah! You have come. Good. Come and sit here. He motions to the seat I usually sit in when we are talking.

Ra says, It is time for us to visit the Text, yet I wonder at your condition. I say, Yes, I am confused by it and am feeling quite depleted. Ra says, You are re-assimilating yourself after your long journey and then the integrating of frequencies with the Second Volume of the Sacred Text. The Second Volume is asking more from you. I nod ok. Ra continues, we can journey to the Keeper and ask for his advice. He is more in charge of the frequencies of the Text and how they flow forth. I tell Ra that the Keeper helped me today. Yes, says Ra, I am aware of that, but still there must be something that can be done to help you not only with your energies but also with your pain. I say, that would be wonderful. Ra says, Good, then let us go to see the Keeper.

Ra stands and motions for us to flow forth. The vortex appears and we are once again flowing through the frequencies of possibilities. Ra takes my hand and says, All will be well. Fear not. I nod ok.

We continue to flow through the frequencies that are a blur. I feel as if I cannot hold consciousness and I tell Ra this. He says to continue with him and see if the Keeper can help. I nod ok, that I am so very tired. Ra says that he has a good feeling that the Keeper will help. I nod ok again.

FOURTH LAYER OF THE SACRED TEXT

We are flowing forth and emerge at the beauty of the green land and mountain. Ra motions that we will go directly to the top of the mountain. This happens quickly and we are waiting at the top of the mountain, waiting for the Keeper.

The portal opens and there slides outward as if disc and we step on to it and it slides back into the mountain. There are several of those who are in white robes and sometimes participate with the Keeper. They part and the Keeper steps forward to us.

It is good that you have come, the Keeper says. All is well. You are simply feeling the frequencies of this next releasing, the next transferring of the Text into your words. I nod ok. The Keeper says, I apologize that this might continue to be experienced in this manner. I will see what I can do to help you, to alleviate the fatigue and pain. I say, thank you. I appreciate your efforts. The Keeper nods.

He motions to the middle where he came forth, the middle of the line of the others in white robes. We follow him. I nod to those ones, even if they are not looking at me, I know they feel the honor I am radiating forth to them. I am honored that they are present.

The Keeper motions to a portal shaped like a tall door and it opens like the eye of a camera. Ra smiles at my description. The Keeper motions that we should not hesitate to follow and he continues at a rather fast pace. Ra and I follow.

We are now entering a chamber and there is a familiar very tall area filled with volumes. There is the pedestal already raised. And then there is a small round pool of water, light blue in color. The Keeper motions that I should stand in the water, but that Ra should stand on the outside, that he can still hold my hand, keeping contact, but that he should not go into the water. We both nod. I flow forth and am now standing in the water. It is cool. There is a swirling about me, as the water swirls in a clockwise motion, round and round. It is as if my being is filled with the blue water, inside my being. The Keeper says that all is well, to just allow. I nod ok.

The Keeper says that there is a portion of the Second Volume that would like to come forth to be given to me, would I accept it? I say that I will and ask if I will remain in the water during the receiving. The Keeper says, No, you will come out of the water, but I will give to you a seat and Ra a seat, so that you are more relaxed during the receiving. I believe this will assist you greatly. It is a very special seat. I say thank you. I ask, why is the seat special? The Keeper smiles and says that he knew that I would ask that question. Then he sighs and says the seat has been used by many advanced beings. *It holds the frequencies of maintaining the integrity of being while expanding consciousness to accommodate the expanding frequencies of the Sacred Text and other frequencies.* This is the first time, the Keeper says, that you have been sitting in this seat during this receiving. You sat here many times in other eras. I nod that I understand. Good, says the Keeper.

He motions and invites me to flow upward from the water. Both Ra and I are flowing forth to follow the Keeper. We are flowing toward two seats similar to those in Ra's

FOURTH LAYER OF THE SACRED TEXT

chamber, which are situated just beneath the tall, very tall collection of volumes. We situate ourselves and the Keeper looks to us and then says, Good. I am relaxing into the seat. There is on each arm of the seat a molded form where my hands and arms fit exactly. Ra's is the same and we are both nodding that it is ok that he is not holding my hand at the moment.

When I put both my arms and hands in the form, it lights up and radiates warmth. It feels like peace. Yet still, this all feels to be quite a lot to experience. Ra whispers, All is well. This is just different. Your being will begin to adjust and everything will flow forth easily. I nod ok.

The Keeper kneels before me so that his hands are across from my heart. He is holding a volume that is open and is radiating light. He asks if I will receive this Text. I say I am honored to receive the Text. He nods to me and then, without further speaking, the light flows forth and into my heart area. It is golden and fills my being.

I can hear the Keeper say, I will leave now and return when the receiving is complete. I nod ok.

My consciousness is very expanded. I feel that I could actually fall asleep. Ra whispers that everything is all right, to continue to remain open to receive the Text. I nod ok.

The frequencies synchronize and I can feel the flowing forth of the words of the Text.

The words flow forth in this manner. I clear my thoughts and wait.

There is an image of a very tall ebony man or being. Very tall, with ceremonial feathers or collar upon his chest and shoulders. He has a headdress of one large piece that covers is third eye and flows upward. He is statuesque. I wait.

He says, This is the releasing of the Sacred Text which has been held beyond the counting of time. I come forth to open the gateways that the Text can flow forth to you who are the One, who are the receiver. He says to me, Are you capable of receiving this Sacred Text?

I say, It is my honor to be considered and yes, I will do my very best to receive completely and with holiness, the Sacred Text.

The being nods yes and then turns from me. We are now transported upon the land of the Pyramid of Chichén Itzá. The being enters a passageway into the land and then returns with a tablet in his hands. It looks to be very heavy, but he is carrying it with ease. He stops in front of me. He says, This is the Holy Text, the Sacred Text. When I place this into your hands, it will transform and become compatible to your receiving. There will be a moment while it is transforming that you will be tested. It is the nature of the Sacred Text. Do not fear, for you are the One and it is yours to receive. I nod ok.

The being places the Tablet on the lap of my being, for I am still in the chair that has the molded portions for my hands and forearms. The Tablet becomes a golden light and it feels that it would burn my being but I am not afraid for as the being said, I am the One and it is for me to receive this text. I wait. I hold my focus on the Text. I hear Ra whisper, Good.

FOURTH LAYER OF THE SACRED TEXT

There is a churning of the frequencies and then there is a singing of many beings coming from the light, from the Tablet that is now light. The singing is powerful and it brings me to another location. I am sitting at the top of the pyramid with many steps. I am in the chamber at the top of the pyramid. There are columns about me but I am in the center of that space.

There is a blue swirling about me but I still wait. All is occurring as I wait. The frequencies are so intense that I feel that I might vomit. Ra says all is well. I know it is, yet the frequencies are powerful and surround my being. Ra says they are surrounding me to protect me. I nod ok.

Then everything is ceased and peaceful. The being stands before me and says, Now you will receive the Sacred Text into your being. You are free now to receive and to place the frequencies into the words of your being, your familiar words, for that is what you have been doing and that is what you participated within long long ago. I nod that I understand.

>
> **These are those words.**
>
> I hear a foreign language, deep sounding. That shifts and changes and I am now beginning to receive the words of the Sacred Text.
>
> As the time approaches for the earth to be transformed, there are many beings who are refusing to allow such transforming. This was expected by those who agreed to come forth to assist in the transformation, the releasing of the darkness,

that the earth would once again reside in light and truth and peace. There are those factors that believe that their power is unimpeachable. Yet their power is nothing but illusion. All is One. That is not illusion.

There comes forth upon the earth the histories of all that has resided upon the earth during the many times, the unfolding of time, the many eras and formings...to reside co-habitably, to be as one residing. In peace. The many species that have resided upon earth release their human projected image and stand firm in the truth of their form of species. There are many different forms. Yet there are those who look to each other and find peace and celebration that the truth is being revealed to the totality of that which incarnates upon the earth.

This is the fourth era. It is forming and has the possibility of remaining formed, for there are those who have come from great distances to assist in this transformation. There are many caverns in the earth that hold truths and histories and more so, Tablets of Sacred Teachings. These caverns begin to open and the encodings and formings of teachings in encodings flow forth to cover the earth. Those who demand to remain separate and in the illusion of separation from the whole are dancing as if the flowing forth of the encodings are as if hot coals and they are not able to stand upon them. This is the refusal of truth and the embracing of the distortion.

FOURTH LAYER OF THE SACRED TEXT

These beings will dissolve of forms and their spirit will be released to return to creation itself, for they are distorted as well and know not of truth as they have been residing in their own created illusion for many many turnings of the year.

This is occurring now, as we speak of this history, for that of which we speak is history and much has occurred after this time upon earth. We speak of the histories so that the beings of earth can know that there is hope-fulfilled for peace and the residing together as one. This transformation and adjusting to the many facets of species and their formings and manners of being occurs during several hundreds of the keeping of years' time. *It is after seven hundred of years that there is then residing upon the earth great peace. Yet even before this completion there is the beginning of peace in the forms that allow the inhabitants of earth to begin to adjust, for even those who know of totality have held within themselves a type of separation from the whole that is resting upon the physicality within which they have been residing.*

The transforming then begins to dissolve the physicality of illusion and begins the expanding of truth as it forms itself incarnate. This is what the inhabitants upon earth, including humans, have been adjusting to in order to remain and to celebrate truth incarnate. They are most dedicated to this fulfillment of purpose. Many species are enjoying the transformation, yet it is the humans who are determined to participate in a way that supports and enhances the expression of truth incarnate. It has been their spirit-purpose for a very long time, into many lifetimes as the cycles are called.

There are many species or beings who have removed themselves from earth's frequencies during their own histories and who are preparing to return to reside within their own lands and manners of being. Even those ones will find it difficult or perhaps different in adjusting to the changes, for none who return will find the earth as they believed it would be. Nothing is maintained in the illusion. Nature herself reforms and participates in the cleansing of the illusion and destruction that has occurred within the separation from the whole as those in seeming power did wreak their destruction upon earth and within nature.

Yet be it known that nature is peaceful and will always be, for it is the closest to the fulfillment of truth incarnate. *Nature holds within it those patterns and frequencies that can and will re-establish wholeness of being incarnate in all beings.* This has been called healing by some, but in truth, it is nature being as it always has been.

Now this speaking of the histories flows forth for the many to know of what is called the future and the past. Be it known, however, that both the past and the future are residing in one moment called the spark of creation. Many do not understand this truth and that is acceptable while residing incarnate in physicality. Yet there does come that time when all beings are asked to let go of concepts that they have held to themselves, believed that those concepts help them to understand the great truths. Yet it is those concepts that prohibit them from allowing the great truth to fill their consciousness and their beingness. This is expected and also it is expected by those who observe, that there will be those ones brave enough to let go and allow. These brave ones then begin the journey in physicality of the expression of truth incarnate.

The evidence of truth incarnate appears as a great light that emanates from the earth and it is such emanating that causes the many who are observers and Ancient Ones to celebrate and to come closer that the evidence is confirmed.

Hear these words. Once the earth is transformed, then there is a radiating outward of those frequencies toward those other realms and galaxies that are waiting for the advanced frequencies to flow forth for their own beginning of transformation. For it is known that *if the earth, the planet of darkness, can transform then all can transform*. If the earth cannot transform, then it is futile for others to attempt this transformation for all is lost. That is the importance of the transformation of earth.

Those who reside upon earth, holding their truth, holding the ability to expand consciousness to such a degree that they can embrace truth as it flows forth to be incarnate, are those ones who are called the saviors of all that is incarnate. Though those ones would never call this of themselves, all of creation does.

This speaking is of the past and of the future, yet all resides in this present moment and it is this present moment that holds the possibilities of such transformation, for All is One and One is All.

Then this speaking of the Sacred Text and the histories of the earth and its residing though the many eras is complete. Yet there will be more, for this is but the beginning of this speaking. Much must be learned, much must be prepared for the transformation and the Sacred Text holds that which is given for the assistance of such transformation from the darkness to the light.

Then this is the completion of this section of the Sacred Text, the Histories and the admonishments, the guidance and the frequencies of truth that they are now held within this incarnate manner. The One proceeds in honor and that honor and proceeding is greatly appreciated and celebrated. This is not the first time that this being has been seated at the top of this pyramid. This is the last receiving of the Sacred Text in this manner. This One will receive all there is to receive of the Sacred Text and then it will have been given. *There is no future receiving. This is the final receiving, for this has been occurring for a very long time.* This One is most capable. We know this One well.

Then the flowing forth of this Sacred Text is complete for this receiving.

I am still sitting atop the pyramid and I can feel the frequencies of all that has been given. I have a slight memory of sitting here previously in other histories. Now I will bring my consciousness back to the seat beside Ra and allow all that has been given to rest in peace.

I am letting go of the pyramid and its beautiful surroundings. I am now returning to my seat beside Ra in the chamber at the top of the pyramid of the mountain.

The Keeper appears as if in a hurry and says to me, You have done well. That was most powerful. You must leave this chamber now so that you can remain incarnate. Ra says to the Keeper, All is well.

Both Ra and I stand and I turn and bow to the seat that is releasing its glowing. Then Ra takes my hand and we follow the Keeper. He is flowing quickly and we are following. We are now outside of the mountain and the Keeper says, It is my sincere wish that all is well with you. I thank him. He continues, Be at peace. Go to nature, it will replenish you. You know this. I nod yes.

The Keeper looks to Ra, I bow my being to you, Oh Great One. Ra nods thank you and bows his head to the Keeper. Then the Keeper says, I leave you to return to your abiding.

He all but disappears and we are now flowing quickly through the possibilities and all is a blur. Ra says to me, All is well. I nod yes.

We are bypassing Ra's realm and journeying directly to my vortex. We are standing at the top of the vortex. Ra says to me, This releasing of the Sacred Text is most powerful. You have done very well. Do not diminish all that you are doing, my dear. We will continue, for you are most capable.

Remember, he continues, when you are feeling depleted, it might be time for the Text. I am not certain of that fact, but it appears that it might be true. I say, I believe you might be correct.

Ra motions for me to return to my physicality and I look to him and bow to him and thank him for all that he is doing for me and with me. He laughs his great laugh which feels wonderful in my heart. Then, he says, return now.

I am flowing downward into my vortex and into my body-physical. I am glad that receiving is complete. When there is such diverse speaking and words of the Text, it is a demand to be ever present and focused. I have done this. Now I will rest.

I am returning to my body. Breathing deeply. I am returned.

So be it.

So be it.

TWENTY-THIRD TRANSMISSION
Fourth Speaking

I am replenished after yesterday's visit to the lake. I am looking forward to what will be received today and am opening my consciousness now, expanding and prepare to journey to Ra's realm.

Different memories of groups held with Pretty Flower come before me. And now I am expanding further, to a higher frequency, which Teacher has taught me to do. I am now approaching Ra's realm and I am flowing over the top of the portal area and into his realm, adjusting my frequencies there.

I wait. I do not want to project anything. I wait. Ra flows to me, already in his robes and motions for us to proceed. No words are spoken or thought-sent. We flow together into the blur of possibilities, Ra takes my hand and we are moving very fast. I do not know where we will end.

I discern two locations, one is with the Keeper of the Sacred Text in the mountain and the second is on the land of the Pyramid of Chichén Itzá. I allow each to reside. It is not my choice to decide. Ra whispers, Good.

I am now being pulled to the mountain and the Keeper. Ra again says, Good. The being, the Ebony Being is standing, waiting. I say to Ra, what will we do? Ra says, We wait. It is not up to us to decide. It is the Text that decides. I nod ok.

I think to myself, I open to the next receiving of the Sacred Text as it flows forth to me to be received by the many. Ra again says, Good. He has heard my thoughts.

The Ebony Being turns and returns to the portal. He has excused his releasing. It seems the choice has been made and we are flowing toward the mountain and the Keeper. Yet I feel the frequencies of the Ebony Being to be most powerful. Ra says, It will always feel powerful. That is the nature of that which is given there. I nod that I understand. Ra says, Do not feel responsible for any of this. You are the receiver of what is given, not the decider. I say that I am relieved to be just that. Ra laughs.

We are at the green mountain and wait. The Keeper appears and motions for us to follow. We are flowing quickly. It appears there is another mountain top. The Keeper looks over his shoulder and nods yes. We are following. A opening appears in the second mountain, which is covered with greenery. The Keeper stands at the entryway and motions for us to enter, as he will hold the portal open until we have entered. We flow forth into the mountain.

Once inside, we are now in a very large chamber filled with light. A blue swirling comes about us and the Keeper stands within it and says, You are now entering the phase of receiving more of the Secrets. This flowing about us fulfills two purposes. The first is to place about you a frequency that cannot be viewed past. The second is the adjust your frequencies so that you can easily receive the next transmitting of the Sacred Text. I have created this blue essence especially for you so that you can receive with greater ease. I say, Thank you. The Keeper nods to me and then to Ra. He says, soon the blue will dissipate and we will begin.

Just as he says those words, the blue begins to dissipate and we are standing on a large platform which rises into a great white light. The Keeper says, Now we will be able to receive the volume that waits for you. I nod ok.

I see across the great expanse of the All and see the golden globes spread out in different locations. The Keeper says, We will now wait to see if one of the globes will come forth. If not, then we will open to receive a volume. We all wait, the Keeper, Ra and me. Ra is holding my hand, which is always reassuring.

A globe in the distance begins to turn around and around and while turning does move toward us. As it approaches, it is very very large. The Keeper turns and faces the globe. He says, We are honored by your presence. The globe radiates a golden light as if responding to the Keepers words. The Keeper motions for me to come next to him. Both Ra and I move beside the Keeper.

The Keeper says, This is the One. The globe radiates golden light again. I am prepared to receive if that is what is to occur. I bring my consciousness to its most expanded state. When I do, there opens in the globe a portal in a rectangular shape. I wait.

From the Globe there flows forth three beings. The being in the middle of the three is holding a small globe, golden globe. The three stand before us.

The two beings not holding the globe come on either side of me. Ra is still reaching within the standing to hold my hand. *He is holding me so that I will continue to remain incarnate.* I send the thought, thank you.

With the two beings, one on each side of me, there is a shifting of the frequencies. They are moving closer and closer to me until they are touching my frequencies with theirs. We are merging. I can feel a swirling of frequencies within my being. Ra speaks some words that I do not know. Again there is a shifting.

I have to bring my focus back to this moment with them. Ra says, That is ok because the shifting of the frequencies was intended to include the fact that I am incarnate and that is why my focus went to something in my physicality. I nod ok, that I understand.

The Keeper steps forth and adds his frequencies to what is occurring. This prompts the being with the globe to move toward me. He turns to the Keeper and says, Now you will give this Secret to the One, for I am too high a frequency to deliver it into her being. You are the one to do this. The Keeper nods and then holds his hands outward and the being places the golden globe into his hands. The globe turns around and around in his hands and adjusts to the Keeper's receiving. The Keeper breathes his breath upon the globe and the golden essence turns to white essence. The being nods and says, This is now perfect. The Keeper nods yes.

FOURTH LAYER OF THE SACRED TEXT

The being says that the three will remain until I have received the essence of the Secret and then they will depart, as will the Keeper, until I have received what is to be given. Then they will return and receive the globe once again. The Keeper nods as do I and Ra.

The Keeper approaches me and asks if I will receive the essence within the globe. I say, I am the One and I gratefully receive the essence of this globe. I am honored. The being nods yes, that is correct to say. I nod to him as well. It is a transferring of the honor of the essence of the globe, both the giant globe and this small one being presented to me.

The Keeper extends his hands toward my being and the two beings beside me step apart from me. The essence swirls into a vortex and flows forth to enter my being. I am accustomed to the essence entering my heart area, but this time it flows forth and enters my third eye area. I am filled with very fast moving visions and then they are also a blur. I am filled with white light. I hear Ra whisper, All is well.

I feel the words flowing forth. The two beings beside me join the third and they are receding into the giant globe. The Keeper says, I will depart now and return when the receiving is complete. I nod ok.

Now I wait.

These are the words that flow forth.

It is a different language and I wait for the shifting to occur. The ancient language has a rhythm to it, almost as if a chant. Now the words begin to change and the frequencies have increased once again.

There is a movement, a shaking of where we are and Ra says that is simply the adjusting of the frequencies to reside within me and to bring the releasing to a language that can be received. I nod ok.

There is a large opening in the area around us, as if a crack has occurred and the energies part, revealing a blue as blue as the sky upon earth. Ra says not to mention physicality. I nod that I understand. The blue enters where we are flowing forth as a river of essence of blue. It surrounds us. We are being transported it seems. Ra says this might be true but to not project. I nod ok. We are as if suspended in the blue.

It feels as if a being is coming. Ra says he sense that also. It is the Ebony Being. He is smiling and says that it is good that we are meeting in this frequency. He bows his head to me and then to Ra. We both bow our head to him. He motions in a direction and invites us to flow forth with him. Another shift in frequencies. We are entering the .. Ra says not to project. I nod ok.

The Ebony Being motions the blue aside and we are once again on the land at the Pyramid at Chichén Itzá. The Ebony Being says good. You have arrived. I nod yes. His smile is covering his entire face. He is very happy. He says, now you will receive the next part of the Sacred Text, for this has been held in secret until now. I nod that I understand.

There are several beings, all dressed in ceremonial ways, with feathers, painted faces and bodies and they are dancing, shaking globes that are filled with seeds, it seems. They are chanting and surrounding Ra and me. My solar plexus is pulsating. I can feel my body-physical breathing fast. Ra says

FOURTH LAYER OF THE SACRED TEXT

to not focus on it, that he is taking care of the physicality. I nod ok.

The Ebony Being steps in front of me and says, Now you will receive the next revealing. I want to nod ok, but I cannot. He looks into my eyes and I feel that there is a flowing forth of words from his eyes. I am frozen, not able to move. He speaks some words that I do not know and then claps his hands loudly. The others stop moving. We are all as if staid. There is a tall stone, a rectangular stone. The symbols come alive and move into…move into one symbol. The symbol is released from the stone and comes to the area between the Ebony Being and me. The symbol turns around and becomes a disc. It is a living disc. It moves and places itself against my heart area. I am overflowing with frequencies. The Ebony Being speaks some words and then motions for the others to leave. They do, as if in a line, one behind the other. The Ebony Being says, Now is the releasing of that which you have come for. I am able to nod yes.

He steps back and says he will return once the receiving is complete. He departs and it is Ra and me standing upon the land. The land is very alive. Ra says yes.

The flowing begins. I send the thought, help me to receive this in the best way possible. Ra says, so be it.

These are the words:

Upon the earth there came gatherings of beings. The gatherings were in different locations upon the earth. There came the time of the near full moon in the month of the sky people and it was then that those in the gatherings began their ceremonies. The ceremonies were held in the honor of the sky people. Gathering in many layered circles each gathering in their own location upon earth, the beings began to drum. The rhythm of the drumming began slow and steady and when there was a synchronization of all of the gatherings upon the earth, then there came forth one being in each gathering, one being who held a flute. When the playing of the flute began, then the drumming increased until both the flute playing and the drumming were in the same frequency, a high toned frequency. This drumming and flute playing continued through the night.

In the moment before dawn, there came from the sky several ships that hovered above the gathering and a being came forth from each ship and stood in the center of the gathering, beside the flute player. The flute player handed the flute to the being from the ship and the being then pointed first to the land and then to the ship. There formed a golden beam of light. All the beings in the circle, each in their own location, stood and began to move into the golden beam of light. Each one stood within the beam of golden light and then stepped out while the next being entered the beam of light.

Within the beam of light there resided the Truths of the All. The Truths of the All held the knowing of all creation in all forms. The beings received these truths and when the last had entered the golden light, then the light dissipated. The being from the ship handed the flute back to the player of the flute. He looked to all of the beings who had entered the golden beam of light and then turned and returned to the ship which then departed.

The first being who had stood in the golden light stood in the center of the circle and said:

These truths flowed forth from the All:

In the creation of the universes there came forth those that resided nearer and nearer to each other. One after the other the formings in the universes made way for each other's ingredients so that the two universes became one very large universe, which accommodated all of each of the two. This became the largest universe in the All.

Within the largest universe of the All there flowed forth from the center, a spark of creation. This spark of creation was the mirror image of the spark of creation from which the All flowed forth long ago. Within the Universe, then, there flowed forth a consciousness. *The consciousness was called the Second All.*

The Second All radiated its consciousness outward until it included all of the Universe and then stretched itself beyond the universe and into the frequencies of the First All. The Second All honored the First All and its consciousness and then returned to the galaxy to reside in what was its own domain.

The two Alls did then reside. The Second within the galaxy resided within the domain of the first, for the First All was the All, even was it all that was created within it. The Second All that resided within the galaxy was then residing within the entirety of the First All.

The Two resided for what could be called eons. From the Second All there flowed forth a consciousness that became encased within a gathering of beings. The gathering of beings ventured forth to explore the contents of the galaxy. Within their exploring they formed within the essence of the galaxy certain globes. The globes spun of themselves and arranged themselves to accommodate each other. The beings were pleased at their creating. Within the globes that were created, there were several that began to hold a consciousness. The beings were pleased at the developing of consciousness upon several of the globes.

Because of the consciousness upon several of the globes, there formed then beings, as a mirror image to those who created the globes. The beings began to explore their own residing location, upon the globe. The beings who created the globes became the observers because they were most fascinated by the developing nature of those who resided upon the globes.

The beings who resided upon the several different globes did then determine that they would go forth and explore what other globes held beings. This began a manner of journeying between the globes. Some were discovered to have no inhabitants while others were discovered to have inhabitants similar to those who were exploring. When the frequencies were able to be merged, the beings, the explorers met upon the globes and began to share what was discovered. They learned that each globe held certain truths and what combined the truths became as one truth. The beings were most thrilled at this discovery and determined that they would continue to journey to each other's globe, gathering the truth that was made manifest.

When the beings had gathered together and then held between them a one uniting truth that spread itself across the galaxy as if tying the globes together with the frequency of truth, there came forth a power between the globes. It was the power of the truth that forged as one truth, as if pulling the frequency called the globes to come together. There formed a dance of the globes wherein there was held a consciousness of the One Truth. The observers remained observing and allowed without interfering, for they were most amazed at what was occurring and most amazed at the power of the One Truth. They did not know what was contained within the One Truth, only that it had developed and was calling all of the inhabited globes to move closer to each other.

As the globes turned of themselves and also moved their orbits closer to each other, there came forth a great sound through the universe. It was the sound of the planets gathering together within the One Truth, the Truth of One. There came forth within the sound an embracing of all of the planets moving closer and closer to each other. As the sound increased in vibration, the planets moved together and merged together, all at the same moment. There were eight globes merging together as one. Merging together within the Truth of One.

Though this merging was beyond time, it was many many turnings of what would be time before there was a complete merging. What did form then was one large globe which resided in the center of all of the other globes that did not hold beings or a consciousness of beings. Once the large globe was situated within its location in the universe, the frequencies of the one large globe flowed outward and in its flowing outward caused the other globes to arrange themselves around the globe, the large globe. *It was the first forming of what came to be called a galaxy.*

The large globe then did send forth a wave of consciousness which flowed forth to many of the globes surrounding it. Even to the furthest did it flow forth this frequency of consciousness. The consciousness resided then within all of the globes. The consciousness did not reside as the same, but resided in a different frequency upon the globes. The frequency upon each of the globes was intended to comprise the Whole of One together, but individually they were a part of the Whole of One. *It was this manner of being that caused the magnetic arranging of all of the globes to accommodate each other as they formed around the one large globe, the parent globe of the consciousness.*

The observers were most pleased with what they saw and discerned. Their pleasure caused them to journey forth and to once again create globes. Their creating resulted in the establishing of many galaxies within the Second All. This then was the creating of all that resided within the Second All. Yet it would be known that all that resided within the Second All, then, also resided as a part of the First All. For the *First All was and continues to be totality.*

This then is the beginning of a history that is revealed for those who have the capability of remaining without falsities, for the Truth of Histories flows forth within truth itself. Those who receive this frequency and the words of this frequency can and will reside as One in the moment. For the All embraces all beings who can and do receive the Truth of One and the Truth of the All as it continues to flow forth in exploration of its own journey within itself.

This then is the first revealing of this history which is also the present.

Then this transmitting is complete.

So be it.

I feel the ending of the transmission and the Ebony Being comes forth to be part of the releasing of the frequencies, for which I am grateful. The being from the globe comes forth to receive that which was given to me, yet that which flows forth from me is not lighted, but is a frequency that is complete. The being receives the frequency as it enters a globe held in his hands. The being nods to me and then to Ra and then to the Ebony Being. He turns and returns to the great globe, the giant globe. The globe spins and then leaves our presence. I can discern that it is returning to its location in the All.

The Ebony Being looks to me and says, You have done well, for this history was not known and now it is. I release you to depart from this land and to return to the chamber of the Keeper, for it is there that you will reform and then be able to continue in your own purposes. I bow to the Ebony Being as does Ra and the Ebony Being turns and returns into the portal.

I want to look around but Ra says we must depart. I nod ok. We are moving now toward what seems to be the area of the Keeper. We emerge into the chamber and the Keeper is standing waiting for us. He says, All is well. I smile at the words as they have been also Ra's words. The Keeper says, you must return now to your realms. We both nod ok and then begin to turn but the Keeper says, *Know this to be true: all that is received changes the nature of physicality and all realms. Yet it is the physicality of earth that is wanting to shift and change and that is and has been part of the purpose of all that is being given and received. I cannot speak further of this truth but I wish you to know that you are both most revered among all beings.* He bows his head to us and we return the same.

Now, he continues, you must certainly depart. He waves his arm and we are no longer in his presence but are flowing through the blur of possibilities. Once again it spits us out and again Ra find this to be humorous wording. Ra accompanies me to my vortex and looks into my eyes. He says, Long ago it was wondered if you would appear again to receive once again. This receiving is beyond any that has occurred long long ago. This is The Receiving. I nod that I understand. He smiles and motions for me to return to my home upon earth. I bow to Ra and then move into my vortex. It is easy to return now.

I am entering my body and there is an automatic adjusting, for which I am grateful. I am fully entering my body physical.

I have returned. I am so very grateful for this participation.

So be it.
So be it.

TWENTY-FOURTH TRANSMISSION
Fifth Speaking

I am ready to go forth to Ra's realm and then to receive the Sacred Text, if this day is in fact the right time to receive. I am expanding my consciousness…and I am flowing over the portal to Ra's realm and arriving at the chamber where are the two very large seats. I have seen no one yet.

Alannah appears and smiles to me and says as she motions to the further chamber, Ra awaits you. You are correct, it is time. I nod to her and flow into the next chamber. There is Ra, waiting for me. He says, This time we will need to be most focused. You must not project. I say I understand. Good, he says, then let us go forth!

In the next moment we are flowing through the tunnel of the blur of possibilities. Again, we are moving very fast. Ra says to remain present and I nod ok. It seems we are in the blur for a very long time. Ra says that we are, that we are journeying to another location. I am surprised but nod ok.

The blur bends downward and we are flowing downward. Ra says we will now soon be where we will be. I nod ok. We seem to be entering the earth or entering a land beneath the surface. Ra says, We are entering the chambers beneath the Pyramid. We are now entering a tunnel carved within the land. Ra takes my hand and is pulling me along, even though I am moving, he is moving faster and pulls me along.

There is a great feeling of wholeness here. It feels as though this tunnel was used by those who held a high consciousness. Ra says, That is correct. Now all of a sudden, we are stopped. We are facing a wall of earth, of land. Ra says to be very still. I nod ok. We are being transported. We are being transported to a ship, a star ship. Ra says, Yes, I am correct. We take form in the star ship and there are several beings to greet us. Their form continues to change until they are forming to match our appearance. Ra says that is to make our communications easy. I nod that I understand.

One being comes forward and says to me, Anaktah! I bow my head and speak the same word back to the being. The being bows to Ra and says to Ra, Now you have come once again. It has been many turnings of the stars that you have stayed away. Ra nods yes. The being says, Now we will proceed for the time is correct. He motions for us to follow.

We are moving through a hallway, past many different rooms, some of which I can see into and others I cannot. Ra says to focus straight ahead. The being looks over his shoulder and says, You have always been a curious one. I realize that the being knows me but I do not as yet have any recall of the being. The being says, This journey is designed that way, to assure that all is in the present and is not colored by the past. I nod that I understand.

FOURTH LAYER OF THE SACRED TEXT

The being stops and says, Now we will enter the inner chambers of the Pyramid. I am surprised by those words. We step upon a platform that moves downward and in the next moment we are in a lighted chamber that appears to be familiar. The being says, The Keeper will tend to you now. It is good to see you again. I nod thank you. The being smiles and says, You are stronger now than ever before. That is good. I nod again. Then the being seems to dissolve.

From the side of the chamber the Keeper comes forth and says that now is the time to receive the Text. I nod ok. I know there is not time for talking about what we have just experienced. The Keeper nods yes.

The Keeper reaches into the pocket of his robe and pulls out a large golden key. He inserts it into the…No, he moves toward me and offers the key to me. I open my hands face-upward and receive the key. The Keeper says, This is the next speaking of the Sacred Text. You will know what to do. I nod ok.

I have the key resting upon my palms and then Ra says it is important that he hold my hand. I nod ok, so I take the key in one hand while Ra takes my other hand. We are instantly transported outside on the land of the Pyramid of Chichén Itzá. The Ebony Being comes forth and says, you have taken a round-about way to arrive here. That is admirable, for none will follow you in this way. I nod yes. The Ebony Being points to the tall rectangular stone with the symbols upon it. I see that there is a place that will receive the key and I move toward it. I look to the Ebony Being and he nods yes. I place the key into the stone and it lights the keyhole. The Text is flowing into me from the hole that the key is still residing in. I feel the Text within me.

These are the words that flow forth.

Each time that the star people came to bestow upon those who resided upon the land, the truths, there is a change in the nature of the land. The earth becomes more situated in its movements and the movements become slow and graceful. After the full turning of several movements of the stars, the earth is flowing in a manner that the star people find to be compatible with other planets that are flowing in a similar manner. The star people tell the beings that they will not be coming to the earth again. The people begin to weep and to moan. This startles the star people. The leader of the star people steps forth from the star ship and faces the people. The leader sees their sorrow at the news that they will not be coming to see them again. The leader reflects upon what is seen and recognized and then speaks these words to the people.

When the stars are aligned as they are now, gather yourselves together and speak the words that we have taught you. Hold your thoughts to be of holiness and Anaktah. When you do this, we will come to you without our star ship. We will form before you and will speak with you. We will continue to do this until you have absorbed all that we have to give to you. At that time, you will begin to forget who we are.

The beings protested, saying that they will never forget the star people. The leader says, *But you will forget and that is meant to be. Then you will be living in a way that will lead you toward greater discoveries. Perhaps others will also come to speak with you, others from a different system, perhaps from far away.*

The people are quiet and listen to the leader. He continues, *You have much to learn, but this is truth: You are advanced beings who have come here to live and to know how to hold Anaktah while incarnate. You do not know about all of this yet because you are holding innocence. It is your innocence that allows us to come to you. We are united with you in many ways, ways that one day you will recognize. Now you are in the process of birthing yourselves to yourselves. You are learning who you are by your experiences here upon this land.*

The leader continues, *Hear these words, beloved ones. One day you will have forgotten and there will be those who come to you and discover your innocence and they will begin to tell you how to live, how to bow down to them. Listen to them and then go forth and hide in nature. Nature will hold you within it. Do not do what those ones bid you to do. They are holding ill purposes. Do not fear what I am telling you. I had not planned to speak of this yet, but you are more advanced than believed. Remember these words. Speak of them to none others, but remind yourselves to each other that when this day comes, you will run to nature. There will be respite from this storm that flows upon earth within nature.*

The leader speaks, *Now let us sing the songs that we have learned together, for they honor who we are together.* He begins to sing a song in a different language and the beings join in the song. There forms a great white light in the space between the leader and the people. The light is a transportation frequency and the leader steps into it, as do the others, and they are transported to their star ship. The beings continue to sing as the star ship departs.

This is the history of the knowingness of the people upon earth and the source of their knowing. The star people came to earth many different times to bestow truth and all manners of being within the consciousness of the peoples who were ready to receive.

There did come the time when the peoples, the beings, forgot the star people. A few did remember and continued to hold the ceremonies at the arrival of the aligning of the stars, yet even they began to let go of such ceremonies. It wasn't that the beings came to ill practices. It was that the beings began to reside upon their own, with the knowingness residing within them.

And when there came upon them armed great ones who demanded that they follow their ways, in the secret of the night when the moon was dark, they fled to the forest, to nature and hid. On the third night of their hiding, a portal opened in the side of the mountain and the beings fled into the mountain. After the very last one entered, the portal closed. The beings were in darkness, but one said, We are the light. We are the holiness. We hold the knowingness within us. From those words came great light and the beings saw that they were inside a great chamber. The leader of the star ship appeared to them in essence form and directed them to different areas within the mountain. They resided within the mountain for many turnings of the keeping of time.

It is now that those beings are ready to emerge from the mountains, to go forth among the people to assure them that they are holding great light and that there is a way for them to be and to know. The beings from the mountains will be called Holy Ones, but they are truly the first beings who received from the star people.

This pattern has been occurring upon earth over and over again. There have been and continue to be many cycles upon the earth, cycles that hold within them the knowing of truth and then the darkness of forced servitude to untruth. This pattern has now become so great that there is the forced servitude to the untruth that holds within it the forming of great suffering. Those who hold the untruth have little caring for the suffering. They are fearful of the suffering, for it portends to an avenue that they feel arriving for them, within their beingness. One day the star people will come again, many many star ships will hover above the earth. Nothing from the forces will be able to touch the star ships for they reside in a different frequency, one of truth. There will be those who will tell the innocent ones to go to nature, to hide in nature. Then, once again, there will be the salvation of portals within the mountain. Within the mountains, the people will remain safe while the earth changes its surface once again.

When the surface of the earth is replenished in innocence once again, the portals will open and the people will emerge to find paradise before them. Even though fear will continue to reside within their heart, still they will come forth and discover that the earth has made herself new once again. A new beginning will take form. This is the last of the new formings. For the earth has declared she will no longer hold the untruth upon her being.

These words are spoken for the knowing of the many who can hold truth within their being. These histories reside yet there is the knowing that all histories are residing in the one breath of truth, within creation. This knowing becomes deeper as the beings who accept the truth and embrace the

FOURTH LAYER OF THE SACRED TEXT

freedom of the truth, become at peace within their own journey. When beings are at peace within their own journey, within their day, then there is peace upon the land and the frequencies support the manner in which beings can reside within the freedom to be as one. Then is the truth spoken in this day for those who are able to receive this truth. Receiving this truth changes the nature of the consciousness of those who receive, embrace, and reside in peace as they hold truth within their breath of one.

Now this is the speaking of the Sacred Text for this transmitting.
So be it.

The light is dimming and the key is now back in my hand. I give the key to the Ebony Being who smiles and receives it. He bows his head and motions to the tunnel of possibilities. I am surprised to see it here. The Ebony Being says, You have been here for a very long time, though it may not seem that way to you. You must return now. I nod to him, as does Ra.

We enter the tunnel and are moving quickly. As always, everything is a blur. Ra is pulling me along as my consciousness leaves the site where the truths were spoken. Ra says, We will return now to your portal. I nod ok.

Now the peace of the green land comes over me and I see that I am above my portal. Ra says, You are doing very well, my dear. Very well. I say, I am blessed, Ra, to be within this journey. Thank you. He bows his head and then motions for me to return to my physicality. Without hesitation, I flow into the vortex and flow down to my body. I am at peace. My mind wants to think about everything that was spoken, but I know it is best to let go and to reside in peace. After a while, I will return to the words.

I am in my body. Consciousness is very expanded but I am returning.

I have returned. I write this before I am actually returned and smile at that fact.

So be it.

I whisper, I pray that this is all correct. Let it be correct. I hear Ra whispering, It is correct, my dear. Be at peace.

l let go and be at peace.

So be it.

TWENTY-FIFTH TRANSMISSION
Sixth Speaking

I've had a few challenges the past days and, in truth, I'm hoping that the receiving of the Sacred Text will assist me to align myself also. In the past I would decide that I "should" get aligned before I enter this journey, but now I have a different concept. This receiving is for humanity and the histories of humanity and also for those who receive it initially. Those happen to be me and Grayson. I believe we are often challenged in our beliefs, shoulds and should-nots. Sometimes the challenge is freeing. I am choosing that option today.

I am expanding my consciousness and journeying to Ra's realm. What used to be a procedure is now a quick journey to his presence. I am in his presence in his chamber. He says, You have taken to yourself many different scenarios in the cause and effect and they have become a burden to you. I nod yes. He says, Come and sit here with me. Ra points to the large chairs and I nod ok. We are both now flowing upward to sit in the very large seats, which again means that we are or I am expanding my consciousness further. Ra says, Here we will speak for a little and then we will journey forth for the Text. I say, That would be wonderful. Yes, he says, yes it is.

Ra says, Why do you think you are the One? Why do you think that you are participating in this receiving of the Sacred Text?

I think for a moment and say, It seems I have done this before.

Ra says, Why in this lifetime are you the One?

I say, Truthfully I do not know.

Ra says, Good. Now let's surmise that you are the One because you have always been the One, that you birthed long long ago to reside upon the lands of the many planets and your purpose was to be certain that the wholeness of being would reside incarnate upon those planets. He looks to me.

I say, All right I can surmise that, but I do not have proof inside my being that is so.

Ra continues, Then surmise that you were chosen to do the same for the planet earth and that the planet earth could not hold the Wholeness of Truth while there were those who were dedicated to ruling the consciousness of any who came to reside upon earth.

I say, I have two questions. Firstly, who decided that I would be the one to go forth in this manner. Who chose that for me? And second, who was upon earth to rule?

Ah! says Ra. Now we will get to it, won't we. Firstly, there is a council of beings, ancient in their own journey and in the journey of creation itself. When you journeyed forth from the Divine Mother, you were pure. It was then that those Ancient Ones gathered you to them and began to teach you all that they could teach. Your innocence was maintained and they were delighted to teach you. They became your family. In fact, when you were a child you visited them while you sat upon a petrified log in the Arizona desert, and projected your being into the mountain, Superstition Mountain. Those who were there were and are the Ancient Ones who are your family. They are most loving, kind and warm embracing. You must remember this. When there is any issue with your earthly families, remember that your true family resides with those Ancient Ones. This is not to diminish any earthly family at all. But it is to give to you a source for that kindness and love that at times is absent from the relations within humanness. As you have said many times, humans are imperfect and that is part of the journey incarnate. At times you have found this truth to be bothersome, and at other times you have found that truth to be an avenue for your compassion. You were chosen to go forth by your family of Ancient Ones and you were most pleased to have been chosen. Your power of consciousness resided within your innocence of being.

And the second answer is that there were those from other realms who discovered the beauty of earth and her resources, as they have been called. There were those who wanted to harvest earth's ingredients for their own planet. This caused a battle of wills right from the start. And, it continues even now. Yes, there are those who are conscious of the struggles of the humans who reside, yet the purpose of the majority of those present upon earth is to subjugate those ones so that they can continue to harvest from earth. I have seen your heartache at knowing this is occurring. Yet you are now receiving the Holy Text and that will change everything. You must believe this and know this to be true.

I say, I can say that I hope it to be true. I want it to be true. I believe it is possible. Oh Ra, I just don't know if the earth can be saved from all of this. It seems that the chaos is increasing, that the killings are increasing, and that the hatred continues to grow. I do know there are those who hold truth and love. I simply wonder if it is enough.

Ra says, You have always been truthful of your feelings and doubts. That is good. Yet hear my words: You ARE the One. You are here to make sure that earth is not only saved, but that the humanity that resides upon earth is also transformed. The transformation occurs within the frequencies of the Sacred Text. That is your purpose here now. THIS is the truth. Can you receive it?

I say, Yes I can receive it. I also say that as the One, I am still who I am incarnate. To myself, I am simply a being. I mean that with all of my consciousness. I am simply who I am. I continue within this purpose because I can and because I choose to. It is an honor. A very deep honor.

Ra says, Good. Now perhaps we will go forth. I say, yes. Thank you for our conversation. Ra says, I am always here for you. Remember that. Any time that you wish to speak of an issue come to me and we will speak together. I say, Thank you.

Ra says, Then let us go forth! I smile and we both lift from the seats and flow forth toward the tunnel of possibilities. Ra says, Yes we will take that route. It is the most direct. I nod ok.

Ra takes my hand and we are entering the tunnel of blur, as I call it. Ra smiles at my words and then focuses on the flowing forth. We are moving slowly initially and then Ra looks to me and nods and we are entering a higher frequency which moves us along quite quickly. I send the thought, Thank you Ra.

We are journeying through the blurs yet there are some slight forms. Ra says, We are coming close to the other side of creation. I find it interesting that he has said "other side", but Ra says to focus on the present that perhaps we will discuss that at another time. I nod ok.

We are coming upon the Holy One's frequency. The Holy One is there smiling at our arriving presence. The Holy One says, Good. I have requested that you come here first before going to the Sacred Text. Both Ra and I are standing before the Holy One. I can feel the love and caring flowing from that One.

The Holy One looks to me and says, You have entered difficulties. That is part of earth. Now this is nothing new to you. You have expectations of earth that are not possible. You must hold your consciousness above the cause and effect that tends to bury so many in despair. You have entered despair and it has taken much from you. Now I will repair that distortion so that you can continue in the best way. Now, my dear come to me and I will embrace you. I look to Ra who nods yes, and then I flow into the warm embrace of the Holy One. Total Love flows in and around me. I am in white light.

I am white light. Holy One sends some thoughts to me and I nod that I have received them. They are private for me.

The Holy One continues, You are not of the earth. You are the One. You are simply incarnate for this journey. Come here more often and I will assist you, my dear one. I think, Thank you. The Holy One releases the embrace and I am whole once again. I ask that the Holy One help me to remember all that he has said and given to me while I am incarnate. The Holy One says, That is possible always. Bring yourself here. I nod ok.

The Holy One says, Now you and Ra will go forth for the Sacred Text. The Holy One steps back and releases us from his frequencies. We are, it seems, quite far from that frequency. The Holy One waves to us and then removes from our consciousness. Ra looks to me and nods no, and then adds, We can speak of this another time. Let us to forth. I nod ok.

I am bringing my consciousness to focus with Ra. He says, Good. And waves his arm and we are flowing forth toward…I do not know. Ra says Good. We are in the white essence. Ra says, Choose to go forth to receive the Text. I nod ok and speak the words, I am the One and it is my choice to go forth to receive the next transmission of the Holy Text, such receiving is a great honor. So be it. Ra nods ok.

We are now approaching a pyramid. I believe it is the great pyramid in Egypt. Ra nods yes. It appears that the capstone has been removed and we are flowing forth toward a platform at the top of the pyramid. Ra says we will not remain here long. This an adjustment to our frequencies, which has always been the purpose of this pyramid. I allow the frequencies to reside about me. It is most intense. Ra takes my hand and says, this will be for a short time. Do not think of anything else. I nod ok.

Now we are lifted from the platform and are as if on a disc, standing on a disc which is carrying us away from the pyramid. We are soaring and I have the thought come to me that we are going toward the Himalayas. Ra says that is true. We are now close to a temple in the mountain. Ra says, We will enter here for beneath. The temple is the residing of the next part of the Sacred Text. It has been held here for a very long time. I nod ok.

There is a type of platform that reaches outward from the temple and there is a being standing on the platform. He appears to be waiting for us. Ra says, That is true. We come closer, the disc brings us closer and the being nods to us and then raises his arms outward and upward and there comes from the ethers a great golden bird. I look to Ra to be sure I am seeing what I am seeing. Ra laughs and says, Yes, this is our next mode of transportation. We both bow our heads to the bird and in the next moment we are on the back of the bird and the bird is flying or moving away from the being on the platform. The being is smiling.

We are flying down the mountain and there is a frequency that radiates from the mountain and the bird's flapping wings creates an entryway and then the bird, with us upon its back, flies through the entryway and we are entering the frequency…and then we are leaving the bird and standing upon a platform. The bird flies away and I am looking at his departing image, sending thank you to the bird. Then I focus on where we are.

We are simply on a platform, waiting. Our frequencies are adjusting to this new area. Ra is still holding my hand. A very tall being comes forth, even bending its body a little to emerge from the opening before our platform. The being says: You have now come. We are prepared. Come now with me. Ra nods ok as do I. The being radiates forth peace.

It is not that we flow forth following the being. More so, it is that we are *as* the being flowing forth and are in white light. All is very bright. It is as if we are the being.

We are standing now, of ourselves, in front of a table, a stone table, and upon the table is a glowing, golden glowing box, like a small treasure box with the domed top. The being is now standing on the opposite side of the table from us. He has made his size the same as ours, which to me again means that we are all of the same frequencies and consciousness. The being nods yes.

The being picks up the golden box, with golden essence flowing all around it. He opens the lid and the golden essence flows outward and flows directly to me. The being nods yes and I am open to receiving the golden essence. The being says, Now the Ancient Text, the Sacred Text flows forth. I hear bells ringing and feel uplifted by their sound. The being nods yes.

As the golden essence is about me, I am entering a great hall. I have been here before but I keep that previous time out of my consciousness. I am in a great hall and...I am

FOURTH LAYER OF THE SACRED TEXT

being, just being and waiting. I hear the words echo, You have come. Now sit in your place and receive what is to be given to you. I see the seat to the side of the great Buddha. It is in the same position that I sit with Ra in his realm. The voice says, Come now, for it is time. I flow forth to the seat and it is a round seat, as it was long ago. I bow to the place where the Buddha would be, but I cannot perceive a presence, only a frequency. I sit upon the seat and bring myself to stillness. I feel the Sacred Text flowing upward from the seat which is, it seems, like a column that goes deep into the…deep downward. The Text flows upward through the column and is entering my being…But now I am told that is not true. I am sitting upon the seat and the frequencies are arriving from the column. The frequencies are transporting me to another location. It is a location as in an ancient library once again, but there are not books. There are scrolls.

There is a being in the library and comes to me and nods yes. Then he is going toward a scroll that is lighted golden. He takes the scroll with much reverence and then a platform appears before me and the being places the scroll on the platform and opens the scroll before me. I see moving symbols. The being nods yes. Then the being bows to me and departs. The symbols rise up from the scroll and are dancing before me in a vortex. I wait.

The symbols take many different forms, transforming themselves again and again. I wait.

Now the being returns and motions the vortex to return to the scroll and he rolls the scroll back to itself and bring it back to the library. I am observing. He stands back and looks. Further upward there are other scrolls, many thousands. He looks upward and sees another scroll that is radiating golden essence. He flows upward and receives the scroll. He holds it to himself, aligning it horizontally to his beingness. Then he is coming toward me, bringing the scroll.

He stands before me and says, You are more advanced that I initially understood. This now is the scroll that is to be given, to be released into your being. I nod yes and then say, I am honored. The being nods yes and then places the scroll on the platform and rolls it open. Again I see symbols, living symbols. The being says, These now are more compatible to your consciousness and the purposes that have been unfolding within your journey with the Sacred Text. I will depart now and return when your receiving is complete. I nod ok. The being bows his head and then departs.

I am already receiving the symbols into my being. They are filling me. I hear the sounds of bells, gongs, and high-pitched sounds as if the ancient women are making them. The area is cleared and I am standing on a land, a great expanse where I can perceive images of ancient dancing and chanting. The image of a being still in a slight image as if in a cloud, comes toward me. The being is wearing feathers and his face is marked with colors. He looks into me and then shows me his teeth, clenched together. I am not afraid, but his face seems to be taking a fierce look. He then turns and goes back to the gathering.

I am now returned to the great expanse and Ra appears and takes my hand. He nods to me and I nod back. We are now standing together and there appears a vehicle form in the sky. There is a beam of light from the vehicle and from the beam of light there comes forth a being wearing a robe…No, Ra says that is simply the essence around the being. I nod I understand.

The being comes forth and places a white essence disc upon the land and invites both Ra and me to stand upon it. We do. Then there is a column of white light that surrounds us. I say to Ra that this seems to be a very long procedure. Ra says not to think about that but to stay in the moment. I nod ok.

I see the symbols dancing around as a stretched out vortex. The symbols are beautiful. I can hear the words beginning to be translated into the language that I can receive. It is a beautiful sound. I don't see the being but I know that the being is holding the integrity of the column while I receive the Text, the translation of the Text.

>**These are the words that flow forth.**
>
>We are the beings light years from the requiring of the Sacred Text to be released. We come forth to assure that the integrity of the truth within the Text is maintained. We are here to assist you. I nod ok. These then, the words say, are the symbols of the Sacred Text turned around so that they can be received within your receiving, for there is much to flow forth to you and through you. We are here to also protect you. I nod ok. Then we will proceed, the words say. Then we will proceed.

This is the flowing forth.

I bow my head to the receiving and allow.

Within the earth there are several chambers which hold ancient truths designed to maintain the integrity of the earth and also the integrity of the original purity of being as the earth formed again and again. This is the seventh forming of the earth now, according to the records that are maintained within the chambers of the earth.

There is only one remaining forming, the eighth, which forms when the entirety of this Sacred Text is received and then released into the consciousness of those who reside upon the earth. This is the re-establishing of purity of being incarnate. Purity of being incarnate is a frequency that holds within it totality.

Totality within purity of being does not mean that all of physicality's presence must be perfect, for it is known that physicality cannot hold perfection and also remain as physicality. The Sacred Text now received holds those frequencies that allow for such imperfection but also pull to it those frequencies that hold untruth, for it is the untruth that has held the demise of the earth during previous formings.

This Text now holds those patterns that call forth the great distortion. The great distortion can be defined as those frequencies that hold destruction, and the great refusal of truth in oneness of being, hatred. Hatred holds the viciousness of previous formings of earth wherein there were those ones who held little or no honor toward any other forming but their own forming. Again and again this has been the demise of the holiness of the purposes of earth. For earth has always held the purpose and frequencies of paradise. *Paradise is defined as those frequencies which embrace totality in all of its forms yet also hold the truth that all forms are one form.*

Now these frequencies flow forth with these words from the Sacred Text.

These then are the truths to be received within the frequencies of the Sacred Text, held from the very beginning of the first forming of earth, held within the many chambers within the earth designed to hold truth itself. The chambers are fewer now for there has been the releasing of part of the Sacred Text upon previous earth's formings. Now there will be a complete releasing, for this is the last.

The One Light is.

Within the One Light is a Spark.

Within the Spark resides frequencies of all possibilities in all realms and manners of being.

When there is a calling forth, the Spark pulsates to become and then, releasing the pulsating, to return to no forming. This is the pulse beat of creation itself.

Within the pulsating, creation then flows forth according to the calling forth.

The calling forth always comes from the Ancient Ones who have resided within the totality since the first breath breathed forth from the Mother.

The Mother resides.

All that resides in totality flows forth from the Mother, including the Spark of Creation itself.

The spark of Creation Itself resides within the navel of the Mother. There is no other residing.

Within the navel of the Mother exists the multitudes of formings, including the arrangements of galaxies and universes.

It is the breathing forth of the Mother that places such formings into the ethers of the All, which the Mother allows to be.

Within such formings there came to be a gathering of forms that held within their magnetic forces, that called the planets and within the planets there formed one, one that the Mother designed to be the presence within the All of her purity of being, her love, and her holiness. This planet was eventually called earth. In the beginning it was called Yeatah, and then Conchos, and then MeLantah, and then Sanctos, and then Elantah, and then Ekontoh, and then SiNah. When the frequencies upon the planet became a misrepresentation of the original purpose, then the planet was called Earth-1, then Earth-2, until there is now Earth-12. Earth-12 has one purpose and that is to return to the original purpose as breathed forth by the Mother.

Within the caverns within the earth there are those holdings of frequencies that hold within them the breath of the Mother. This breath will be released from each cavern when the consciousness of the beings who reside upon earth has shifted to such a degree that there can be a receiving of truth.

Until there is an ability to receive truth within the physicality of earth's surface, the caverns will continue to hold such frequencies. It is the Mother who will decide when the caverns will be opened to the surface of the earth. Such opening will deliver to the inhabitants of the earth great freedom to be. Such freedom holds and will hold within it a radiating frequency that will not be able to be entered by any who are holding the purpose of destruction and control. For those days are numbered and few in counting.

This has been the histories of the earths and now becomes the present of the current earth. Many are present to assist in the transforming of the consciousness upon the earth. Upon previous earths there has been great chaos which led to further destruction and distortion. This earth's transforming of frequencies within the consciousness of the beings who reside upon earth will hold within it peace and embracing of truth. The many who are present to assist in this have begun to reside close to the ethers of the earth. Some have even incarnated upon the earth in the form of human.

The first signal that the consciousness is turning toward truth and away from the illusion of great distortion will be that called the return of the rivers to their natural manner of being. This means that any diverting of the rivers or waters of the earth will be destroyed so that the waters can return to their most natural forming. Many will be praising the return of the waters to their lands that have been starving for the replenishment that waters bring when united with the contents of the land.

The second signal that the consciousness is returning to shifting to an expanded manner that will contain truth itself will be then the return of the trees that have been taken from the land. This means that those areas where the land has been stripped of trees will begin to return and trees will begin to be formed once again as if they were never removed. There are those who will assist in this forming so that there will be little fear or concern for the humans and other beings who reside or did reside within the forests and the lands with trees. The peoples will be cared for and will find their living accommodations shifted and changed but in a manner that will hold the sacredness of their residing within the land of the trees.

FOURTH LAYER OF THE SACRED TEXT

The third signal of the consciousness returning to truth will be the dissolving of those structures that have been created for the purpose of celebrating the ruling of the peoples of the lands, for those structures have been built upon the blood of the peoples and the sorrow of the mothers of those peoples. This dissolving will take any who reside within them to a different frequency where they will be cared for and assisted to remember truth. This might involve what is called a very long time, yet within those frequencies there is no time. All will be cared for.

The fourth signal will be the returning of the vessels from the stars and the beings from the vessels will come forth to assist beings to begin to assimilate truth in a manner that will allow them to release attachment to taught untruths and the embracing of freedom to be. Those who come from the vehicles from the stars are held in great honor for they have been coming to all of the earths to assist in raising the consciousness and then teaching of the truths and how participation within those truths can assist in the fulfillment of the purpose of any and all beings who reside upon and within earth as she begins to fulfill her own purpose.

The last signal will be the clearing of the airs, the essence upon the earth that enters the bodies as breathing of all beings. For there has been a pollution of the airs, deliberate by those who wish to control. This will be the purification of the airs. Those who rebel to the allowing of this purification will be taken, again, to areas where they can be assisted to gradually return to the truth of one, which they abandoned long long ago. It is not to judge those ones, but to have great compassion as does the Mother for those who journeyed far from her warm embrace and then upon releasing, they were far from her embrace, determined to create such an embrace by their own doing. This, of course, was not able to occur and they were blinded by their own efforts. Now they will be restored and once again be able to reside in the embrace of the Mother. Again this might take a long time, yet within such restoration there is no such frequency as time.

This then will be the signals to those who are aware and awake to this transformation upon the earth. There will be many who will interpret such signals as great destruction. This has occurred in previous transformations upon previous earths. Yet because there are many who are present to assist, there will be less and less interpreting once the beauty is recognized. None will be harmed and many more will be restored. Yet the definition and knowing of restoration will not take the form within the beliefs of the many who have determined what they must have or have not in order to be joyful and free. Those beliefs will be challenged and then

FOURTH LAYER OF THE SACRED TEXT

released. It is and will be a loving process from the Heart of the Mother.

There are those pockets of gatherings upon the earth that have held the truth and the living embrace, yet even those ones will be asked to release their beliefs, for some of the beliefs through living do contain the support of the illusion of separation from the whole. This will be a great transformation for the many and a great light will be restored within those beings. They then will go forth and assist the many, some assisting simply by expanding their beautiful consciousness. Others will go physically forth to assist the many. They will not enter into the dens of untruth, for there are others who will go forth to assure that those ones are removed and then cared for within a different frequency.

This occurring upon this earth has great possibilities. This Sacred Text has been held until this releasing, for there are those who will feel the releasing of the frequencies, not especially the words though they are important, to those who can receive them, and those frequencies will ignite in those ones a great light of fulfillment of purposes now beginning to occur incarnate.

Then this is the speaking of this portion of the Sacred Text, a portion that has been waiting for what could be called a very long time.

We, the beings from the stars, hold true the contents of this Text that it be receive as it has been held. Then we will release this One who receives the Text and then we will depart, for then there is the settling of the frequencies until they are released to the many of humanity who are waiting for relief and for the receiving of these frequencies. For, once all of the parts of the Sacred Text are received and then released to the peoples upon earth, there will be a great sigh of relief of earth herself, for earth awaits the Sacred Text to reside upon the surface of her being and that then those frequencies begin earth's transformation within herself and with the beings who reside upon earth.

Then we are complete with this transferring of the Sacred Text. Let all that is holy be held within this transferring and all else be dissolved from the presence of this being, the One, who receives the Text and then to hold in protection the One who receives from the One...who holds the name of Grayson, an ancient name held within the continued forming of the earth again and again. For this One who holds the name Grayson has resided upon the earth many many times and is known by the Ancient Ones as a comrade or friend, partner and One who is held in high esteem. The Ancient Ones are most pleased that this One is the second to receive the Text, for it has been his purpose long ago and continues to fulfill that purpose now.

Then we are complete for this speaking and this transferring. We, the beings from the stars, release this One and that one who is called Ra. We bow our entire being to those two, for there is great fulfillment occurring.
Then we speak the words so be it and then depart.

There is a great sound as if a thunder in the departure of the ones from the stars. Ra and I are standing upon the great expanse once gain. He looks to me, nods, and then takes my hand and we are flowing forth once again. The releasing of the Sacred Text from my being flows forth into a vortex and I can see that it is flowing forth into and onto the scroll, which feels to be very far from my being. Ra says it is, but to remain still while the flowing or returning occurs. I nod I understand.

The symbols, golden symbols flow from my being. I am relieved of those frequencies. I can discern that the being has taken the scroll and is returning it to the location in the library of scrolls. Ra nods yes. Then the being nods to us, we do the same and then we are freed from the library's essence.

Ra motions to me that it is time to return. I nod ok.

We are flowing forth and then into the tunnel of blurs. We are returning very quickly. Once again, we are spit out of the tunnel which causes Ra to laugh at my description. Yet he does agree. He motions that he will accompany me to my vortex to return to my physicality. He says, This has been a very deep releasing of the Sacred Text. I nod that I understand. Ra says, It is not known how the next releasing will occur, but we will be together and go forth. I nod ok and add a smile. Ra motions for me to return and I bow to him and then to the land around the vortex. Then I flow into the vortex and begin returning to my physicality.

I am flowing into my body. My consciousness is very expanded. I am seating myself and breathe a breath of gratitude and peace. I am returned.

I am so very grateful for this participation that I have been given.

Then I speak the words…

So be it.

So be it.

VOCABULARY

All's Awakening to the All. The All did absorb totality of itself and in so doing did become as if a declaration of its own beingness. This came to be called the All's awakening to the All as it resided in all manners of being.

Anaktah. The word that calls forth truth in a manner that is neither against untruth and is a residing. A residing brings forth great light into the darkness. Not the darkness of evil or the darkness of untruth. This great light is. It is.

Anaktah-Sonotoh. One manner that truth experiences itself is called Anaktah-Sonotoh. Anaktah-Sonotoh holds the frequencies of what could be called vortex, as truth then does flow forth within journey. This is the first journey of truth.

Awakening. Awakening is the moment, the current moment within which creation is in union with the all that it has created within its journey within itself to know itself.

Cycle. A cycle means that physicality, because of the nature of its density, experienced itself as a separate entity and then the merging of that entity back into itself. This was an exploration into what is called **separation from the whole**.

VOCABULARY

Darkness within the All. The battle to maintain the seeming individualness of the frequencies began a darkness within the All. The darkness was neither good nor evil. It was. The darkness continues to hold the battles to maintain separate creations.

Elanto-Grotoh. The rulership of the entire planet by such force that none could refuse but to bow to that force.

Enaktah-Sontoh. The histories are written over and over again of the journey of these beings who played within the illusion of separation from the whole, as they caused the density of physicality to become greater and thus the merging to become more of a challenge, the merging or union being an illusion in itself as nothing is separate. The beings found this to be most curious, or **Enaktah-Sontoh.**

Enaktah-Kolientoh. Enaktah-Sontoh became Enaktah-Kolientoh in that the curiosity was held within illusion and the truth of union hidden. Thus Enaktah-Kolientoh became the nature of the journey within physicality. This nature resides upon this earth and because it resides upon this earth, it is then contained in all earth's journey of itself to itself.

Essence of Being. The essence of being then caused the earth to be as invisible, with the exception of certain frequencies that radiated outward as a warning that there was an absence of forming.

First Battle. The first battle was an automatic occurrence as it was the result of the illusionary creations trying to maintain themselves when the merging, the Truth of One, came forth to unite all within the All. There was a refusal.

Flesancha. A holy consciousness is called Flesancha. Flesancha can be attained by residing in the moment of one. Residing in the moment of one is a most natural manner of residing. It is a holy moment wherein the consciousness simply is in union. There is not a "union with". There is simply union.

Within truth as formed by those who reside upon the planet by choice becomes conscious of such residing, then there is integrity of residing. This then calls forth Flesancha. When Flesancha resides within the consciousness of truth incarnate within and upon the planet, then there is another opening through which truth can explore more of what is created in the moment. This opening now occurs upon earth.

Freedom to Be. All manners possible became then, for nothing was denied. The Observers found all manners possible to be called *Freedom to Be*. Freedom to Be resided within the All through the Eras of the beginning of the forming of what is now called physicality.

Frenatcho. The combination of minerals combined in such a manner that they are liquid in nature, yet more solid than liquid. This covered the earth and earth was still able to maintain her substance incarnate.

Fulfillment of Being. Fulfillment of Being is not the same as being fulfilled by arranging physicality to fit the believed needs. More so, Fulfillment of Being is also a frequency which magnetizes to itself wholeness and it is wholeness that holds within itself the full nature of fulfillment which is the complete cycle of the journey to know more of that which each being is consciously.

VOCABULARY

Great Joy. The All felt the merging of the Observers and the Giants and there formed within the All, Great Joy.

Holacktah. Truth flows forth from the union of the breath and the essence of the life force. Truth is the merging of one force with another and the union or merging produces a vibrational frequency. This vibrational frequency is called Holacktah. Holacktah is truth before it enters the consciousness. Holacktah is formed truth, sacred in the moment of its forming. Truth holds no concept or belief. Truth, Holacktah, stands of itself, yet as it is, then there is the innocence of itself. Within the innocence of Holacktah is the avenue through which can be accessed sacred essence of life force. *This accessing requires a holy consciousness.*

Humuntuk. The name for the combined species that came to reside upon earth and having developed themselves to be different in appearance but basically the same. Found in the Third Layer of the Sacred Text.

Illusion of Non-Union. Because there existed then those formings of untruth, because truth made manifest formed through understanding, there came to be what is called *the illusion of non-union.*

Insanity. Insanity is a manner of residing upon physicality's plane but holds within it the frequencies of distortion to such a degree that the mind and spirit of the being is entangled with concepts that are detrimental to all beings, but especially to those ones.

Invitation to Know. Invitation to Know was and has been and continues to be the manner of residing within the frequencies that were formed upon earth during the fourth era.

Nature of the All. Within all that was being made manifest within the All, there was continued the frequency or pattern of truth made manifest. This was then and is now and ever more, the nature of the All.

Observers. The All shifted its frequencies and this gave those Great Ones permission to remain as if separate from the All's flowing forth that they might observe all that flowed forth within the All. This then caused them to become what has been known as The Observers.

Paradise. Earth has always held the purpose and frequencies of paradise. Paradise is defined as those frequencies which embrace totality in all of its forms yet also hold the truth that all forms are one form.

Peace. There has been developed with the All from the All, that which is called peace. Then we will speak of peace as it refers to humanity's ability to choose awake, to be awake to truth of union, to the truth of creation in the moment. *Peace within humanity is a frequency that embraces union.*

Second All. Within the largest universe of the All there flowed forth from the center, a spark of creation. This spark of creation was the mirror image of the spark of creation from which the All flowed forth long ago. Within the Universe, then, there flowed forth a consciousness. The consciousness was called the Second All.

Secret within This Text. The releasing of dedicated creation for the fulfillment of physicality is primary. It is the Secret within this Text.

Senacktah-Sontoh. This then formed a new planet which was called Senacktah-Sontoh or planet of truth. This is the planet now of earth.

Separation of Self from Self. Because the beings are of creation and hold the truth of union, then there is also an illusion of separation of self from self. This is the frequency of illusion of separation from the whole as it is made manifest within the consciousness of beings incarnate.

Separation from the Whole. Separation from the whole is not existent. It is an interpretation of physicality's journey within itself, within the density of physicality which brought to the experience a projection of physicality and then a merging with that projection. This then developed what is called a **cycle**, as the projection gave the illusion of reality to itself.

Totality of Being. This releasing of the declarations changed the All so that it was a pure frequency. Within the pure frequency the All held the spark and the spark held the All. This was the beginning of totality within creation itself. This meant that the All was creation itself and creation itself breathed forth the All as itself. **This then began a new era in the totality of being.**

Truth of Union. The truth of union is an interpretation of creation itself forming and unforming, as an expression of itself to itself. Thus came the experience of union within creation itself.

VOLUME THREE
Coming Soon

The Keeper says: *Now we will enter into a new phase of the Text. This will be the Third Text, which will be again more intense in frequencies than the previous two. You are now capable of receiving this transferring of Text.* I nod ok.

The Keeper continues: *Within this volume, there will be words and information that will seem strange to you. You are now experienced in receiving whatever is given and that is why we can enter this the Third Volume.* I say that I am honored. The Keeper nods yes.

The Keeper says: *Now we will situate ourselves in three locations simultaneously. The reason for this is that the combination of the three locations and the Text flowing forth from the three locations simultaneously is how the Text has been protected until now. For, each location holds a partial of the Text and when brought together, the entire Text is then transmitted.*

The Keeper continues: *We will remain in this white essence, but it will be as if a capstone and the other three locations will be the three sides of a pyramid, each holding the Text. The fourth side holds the frequencies that are as a protection that was created long long ago, created for this time when the Text will be transmitted* to One. You, of course, are the One. The protection will be activated as soon as the Text begins to flow forth to you. I nod ok.

The Keeper says: *This now is the closest to the core of the Text. Yet there will be a time when the Core will flow forth to you. These receivings are preparing you for that receiving.*

ACKNOWLEDGMENTS

To those of the Spirit Realms, Dimensions and Frequencies:

Teacher and Alannah trained and refined my abilities to travel in non-physical realms and expanded frequencies while remaining incarnate, to prepare for the journey with Ra, without whom there would be no Sacred Text. There are no words to describe the relationship that Ra has gifted to me and to all who participated with us in the receiving of the frequencies of the Sacred Text.

Ebony Being, the guardian of Gobekli Tepe and dimensions beyond the physical, holds secrets yet to be revealed, and who led the many journeys into safe passage. A friend from long long ago.

The Line of Beings is really the Observers who determined they would assist to care for and protect me from those who tried to sabotage the receiving of the Text.

The Keepers, All, are beyond dedication and who held the frequencies sacred and safe for thousands of years until this time to reveal the Text upon Earth.

The Holy One. There are no words to describe the assistance, love and caring that The Holy One gave and continues to give to me.

ACKNOWLEDGMENTS

To those in physicality:

Grayson Howell, my husband and partner in life, is the One who participates with the Sacred Text through his true dedication to fulfilling the necessary purpose of incarnating the Text into physicality. For over a year, Grayson was the only being who knew of and experienced the frequencies of the Sacred Text incarnate. Thank you for your continued participation and support.

Kathy Wirtanen and Nick Lavender kept their word to hold secret my speaking of a "special project" without knowing exactly what it was. Others who later did the same are David Wirtanen, Jessica Serrels, Garrett Serrels, Diane Coleman, Dorthy Carpenter, Jo Boardwine and Beth Bourgoin.

Richard Jennette and Carol Ferrant in special and unusual circumstances gave generously to the publishing of this Volume.

Colleague and friend, Craig Burdett is the magic behind my website design and development, books and programs. It is his artistic creativity that makes everything beautiful, practical and just plain lovely. He is now also known for his new specialty: The 12-second fix…just when I'd given up.

I hold you all, spirit and physical beings, in my heart and am filled with who you are to me and to this work that I am gifted to do.

Miriandra

www.ingramcontent.com/pod-product-compliance
Lightning Source LLC
Chambersburg PA
CBHW050849160426
43194CB00011B/2082